ONE SIZE

does not

FIT ALL

Discover YOUR personal path to a happier life

A practical and engaging approach to creating a happier life, based on your individual personality, values and strengths

Author: Lisa Jansen

BANOVALLUM BOOKS

First published in Great Britain in 2019
by Banovallum
an imprint of Mortons Books Ltd.
Media Centre
Morton Way
Horncastle LN9 6JR
www.mortonsbooks.co.uk

ISBN 978 1 911658 00 9

Printed and bound in Great Britain by CPI.

the Author lived in a Campervan while writing this book.

To New Zealand – My Happy Place
Thank you for letting me make you my home.

&

To My Saltwater Family
You are what took my life from good to great.

*Lasting happiness is a mindset.
How many people R Taking antidepressants
and are still depressed?*

Acknowledgments

I T FEELS surreal to be sitting here writing acknowledgments for a book I wrote that is about to be published. It is a total dream-come-true moment. I feel incredibly proud of what I have achieved, but more than anything, I feel grateful that I have been given this opportunity.

While you can certainly write a book entirely on your own, I think most writers will agree that writing a book is teamwork. You need people who inspire and encourage you to get started, you need people who support you throughout the journey and who push you to keep going when it gets tough, and you need people to help you polish and publish the book. I feel fortunate to have had many amazing people alongside me at every step, and I want to take this opportunity to thank them.

My deepest thanks go to Steven O'Hara, Daniel Sharp and the rest of the team at Mortons Media Group for giving me a shot and believing in this book. It is hard to find publishers that are willing to give first-time authors a chance. It's even harder to find any that are as supportive, transparent and collaborative as the Mortons team has been.

Publishing your first book can be overwhelming. There is a lot of uncertainty and many new situations. I feel very lucky to have a publisher who always answered all my questions, always listened to my opinion and helped me publish a book that I am genuinely proud of and believe in.

Thank you to my editor Pauline Hawkins who helped fine-tune and polish the book. Thank you to Rosie Ward for designing such an awesome cover and thank you to page designer Kelvin Clements for turning my words into a beautiful looking book.

A very special thank you to my beta readers who have provided so much valuable feedback, support and encouragement. Thank you, Alana, for being the first one who read the book from start to finish. Your positive feedback kept me going when I doubted myself and this book. Thank you to Terri for sharing such fantastic suggestions even though we barely knew each other. Thank you to Eve for all the feedback and encouragement and for being the best friend anyone could ask for. Thank you to everyone else who read parts of the book and shared their thoughts and suggestions with me. One Size Does Not Fit All would not be what it is without your input.

This book would not exist if I hadn't turned my life around the way I did. I wouldn't have been able to do that, if it hadn't been for the people who guided, supported and inspired me along the way. The last 13 years since I moved to New Zealand have been such an incredible experience. Sometimes I still can't believe how far I have come. None of that would have been possible without a number of important people.

Thank you to Dr Deb Shepherd from the University of Auckland for introducing me to the concept of personal development and for being an amazing mentor during a very crucial time in my life. Thank you to my Sparkies, especially Sonali, for being my first New Zealand family and for showing me what it feels like to belong somewhere. Thank you to the Banff crew for giving me a home when I needed one and for bringing so much fun into my life. Thank you to Celine for being such a special colleague turned housemate turned life-long friend.

Thank you to my parents and siblings for all your support over the years.

Very special thanks to my saltwater family; Eve & Preston, Andy, Alana & Hugo, Skye & Dave, Jo & Robbie, Adam, Nina & Anton, Sam, Luciana & Graeme, Damiana & Aaron, and all the little ones. I cannot tell you how grateful I am to have you in my life. You are what took my life from good to great, and there is no way this book would exist if it hadn't been for your friendship and support.

Last but by no means least, thank you to you, the readers. I love writing to help and inspire people, and the idea that even just one person will get a lot of value out of this book is what motivated me to write it and what kept me going through the difficult phases. Thank you for reading my book. I hope you like it.

Contents

Introduction

"All who have accomplished great things have had a great aim, have fixed their gaze on a goal which was high, one which sometimes seemed impossible."
ORISON SWETT MARDEN

Is YOUR life as amazing and fulfilling as it could be? Chances are, you don't think it is, otherwise you probably wouldn't have picked up this book. Maybe you feel mostly unhappy and like you're not living up to your potential. Maybe you feel like your life is going pretty well and that you have a lot to be proud of and grateful for, but that there is still room for improvement. No matter where you're at right now, you probably picked up this book because you feel like your life could be better and happier.

You're not alone. Even though most of us have more than ever before, our lives are more comfortable than ever and the fundamental needs of most people are met, true and lasting happiness still seems to be hard to find for many.

I used to be one of those people. Today, I'm extremely happy. My life is fun and meaningful, I have amazing friends, I feel comfortable with who I am and I'm fit and healthy. My life is better than I could have ever imagined. However, that wasn't always the case. Up until about 12 years ago, I was unhappy. My life felt boring, meaningless and like it was going nowhere, and I felt lonely and disconnected. I was severely overweight, unfit and unhealthy, depressed at times and without hope. I had no purpose and no goals and no idea how to change my life for the better. I wanted nothing more than to feel happy and

3

content, to feel like my life was meaningful, enjoyable and worth living. I wanted to be able to look in the mirror and feel a sense of pride and confidence. I wanted to feel like I was living life to the fullest and that I was the best version of myself. Today I do, but it was a long journey.

The more I read and learned about happiness and the more I talked to people about it, the more I realised that many others feel similar to the way I did for so many years. Some are outright unhappy with their lives and themselves, while others are somewhat happy but feel like they could be happier, and others are already pretty happy but worry about maintaining that feeling in the long run or just want more happiness. Regardless of their specific personal reasons, there are millions of people out there who are searching for a happier life. But like me, many don't know how to turn things around and change their life for the better. It comes as no surprise then, that Amazon lists more than 100,000 results when you search for "happiness" in books. Even when you narrow it down to books in the self-help category, you are still presented with more than 20,000 results — and that is just books and doesn't even include the countless articles, courses, podcasts, documentaries and all sorts of other content. There surely is no shortage of insights and wisdom on the topic. So why, you may ask, did I see the need for yet another book about happiness? Great question!

The answer is: because I believe that most of the existing literature and advice around happiness misses a key point. I'm not going to claim that I've come even close to reading all 20,000 self-help books about happiness, but I have read quite a few. Many of them have delivered incredibly valuable insights, lessons and ideas that have helped me on my journey to a happier life. However, the more I read, the more frustrated I became with one specific issue: most of the current advice takes a one-size-fits-all approach to happiness.

Authors present Five Steps to a Happy Life, the Six Principles of Happiness or The Secret to a Happier Life. While their insights and advice undoubtedly have been helpful throughout my journey, they often overlook the fact that we are all unique individuals. Most authors base their insights either on research that reports what works for the average person or the majority, or on spiritual concepts that, while often valuable, simply don't resonate with everyone.

Authors of books on happiness often only put very little, if any, emphasis on the fact that their advice might not be applicable to all readers. Only a very few encourage readers to consider the advice given in the context of who they are. In short, they don't seem to pay much attention to the fact that a life that is fulfilling and happy for one person might not be so for someone else and the way to finding happiness is different for different people, simply because they have unique personalities, values, strengths and weaknesses.

A lot of the existing literature on happiness can be beneficial if the reader can analyse and interpret the information in the context of their own personality, values and beliefs. However, that is often challenging to do, even for the most self-aware people, and basically impossible for anyone who does not have a clear picture of who they are, what motivates and drives them and what ultimately will lead them to a happier life. Therefore, any suggestions, methods, techniques and advice around happiness should take individualism and uniqueness into account — which is what this book aims to do.

People have often asked me what it was that helped me turn my life around and find happiness. I will share my journey in more detail in the next chapter, but for now I want to focus on the one key factor that had a huge impact on me: gaining knowledge. I started to learn, to soak up knowledge about happiness, the meaning of life and various other topics. I learned about personality, values and what it is that makes us all unique. I learned how to bring change into my life and how to make it last. This knowledge wasn't the only factor that contributed to me finding happiness. It also took a lot of determination and discipline, and luck was probably a bit of a factor as well. But it was this knowledge that gave me the power, inspiration and skills to make the changes I needed to make. However, the really great stuff didn't come from having knowledge of these individual areas, but from being able to put all of it together. The real breakthrough came once I had learned enough about myself to be able to view other insights about happiness and living a meaningful life in the context of who I am instead of blindly following one-size-fits-all advice.

I truly found happiness once I understood that most of the insight and advice you see in books and articles is based on averages, majorities or individual experiences and that hardly any of it always applies to everyone. We read about research findings that say this or that makes people happy or we hear stories from other people about what made them happy and we assume that it applies to all of us. However, the truth is, it simply doesn't. There is no one right way to find happiness that will work for all of us. To truly find lasting happiness we need to create our own path, our own blueprint, designed for our individual personality, values and strengths and weaknesses. The goal of this book is to help you do precisely that.

I'm not a mental health professional. I don't have a Masters or PhD in psychology, sociology or any other related field. I haven't spent hundreds of hours treating patients. I'm just an ordinary person like you — almost. So what qualifies me to write a book about happiness? Most importantly, that I have achieved it, despite the fact that it didn't come easy. Research suggests that it is rare and difficult for people to change their happiness level in a significant and lasting way. However, challenging and unusual as it might be, it can be done. I'm proof of that. For most of my life, up until about eight years ago, I would have rated my level of happiness a 4 or maybe a 5 out of 10 (with 10 being the highest). For the last 3-4 years, I would have rated myself a solid 8 and today I would even say a 9. And the main reason I don't say 10 is that I like the idea that it can be even better in the future.

This book is my attempt to share my experience and insights with others, in a way that is not only easy to understand but, more importantly, practical and actionable. While it is inspired by, and draws heavily on, my own experience, all the insights in this book are backed up by extensive reading and review of existing research. I have spent countless hours reading scientific papers and research findings (and those things are not exactly light reading, trust me). I read numerous books and interviews with, or articles by, leading experts in the field and I've spent many hours reviewing and analysing what I learned. However, despite the research I've done, I don't claim to be a professional or a trained expert, and I certainly don't claim to have all the answers. Luckily, the purpose of this book is not to provide all the answers. It's about asking the right questions, making you think and analyse facts for yourself, giving ideas and tips and guiding you through the process of developing your own blueprint for a happier life. And it doesn't matter if you are currently rating your happiness an 8 or a 4 on the 10-point happiness scale. As long as you are sincerely motivated to improve your life, this book will be of value to you, no matter what your starting point is.

This book is divided into six sections. The first part provides insights into what happiness is in an easy to understand way. We will look at how happiness is different from positive emotions and success, learn about the role of negative emotions and take a look at what top-level factors contribute to our happiness. The second part is all about you. Through a combination of straightforward insights and discussions and engaging exercises, you will learn more about yourself, your personality, your values and your strengths and weaknesses. After that, we will turn our focus back to happiness and review existing research about what may or may not make us happy. You will be encouraged to analyse this information in the context of what you have learned about yourself, and exercises will help you identify the aspects that matter most to you. After that, part four discusses what are considered the Four Pillars of Happiness before part five brings it all together and guides you through a fun and engaging process to develop your own highly individual blueprint for a happier life. The sixth and final part will provide tips on how to put this plan into action and how to continually review and refine your plan to make sure your happiness lasts.

How to Get the Most Out of This Book

The goal of this book is to help you develop your unique and personal blueprint for a happier life and to help you put it into action. That means this book will require your active participation and input. You will be challenged to learn about yourself so you can analyse information in the context of who you are and what is relevant to you. You are the one that will develop your personal blueprint, and it will be up to you if and how you put it into action. But the interactive style of this book will make the process engaging and fun, and, if you do it right, the end result will be more than worth the effort.

Happiness won't come overnight. It will be a journey and you need to be willing to put effort into it and continuously work on it. In many ways, finding happiness is like building your dream home. Before you can even start building, you need to work to save the capital, and you need to develop your plans. As you begin building, things are likely to evolve, either because you change your mind or because something unforeseen happens. Once construction is done, you move in, but it isn't really your dream home until you've made it your own by arranging your furniture, decorating and by starting to make memories in the new house. But then you did it; you are living in your dream home. Happy days! However, chances are within a few years you'll start noticing little things you don't like any more, things break down or wear out and need to be fixed or you realise you need more space.

So you start redecorating and renovating, maybe even adding a whole new part to the house. Over the years, your home will have to change for you to continue to consider it your dream home. Just like building your dream home, finding happiness requires capital, and knowledge is the capital for finding happiness. This knowledge will help you design your plan for a happier life, but once you have a plan, you need to be prepared to make alterations as you implement it. Once you've executed your plan, you might be happy, but over time, the same things that used to bring you happiness don't work any more, and you need to review and update your approach to happiness. Just like living in your dream home is a journey, so is finding happiness. There will be times where you just have it and can enjoy it but, most likely, you will need to make changes and adjustments to keep feeling happy.

Building your Dream Home	Creating a Happy Life
Work hard to save the capital you need	Work hard to learn, gain insights and understanding (knowledge is the capital you need for a happy life)
Develop the plans for your house	Develop your plan for a happier life (your blueprint)
Start building	Start making changes to put your plan into action
Make minor variations on the go as circumstances change (e.g., delays, new contractors, you decide you want a different colour, etc.)	Continuously review and improve your plan as you start putting it into action based on what does or doesn't work and new insights you're gaining.
Move-in day	After your 'building' phase, you will reach a point where you start noticing some improvements in your overall happiness (but you're not done)
Make it your home: move in your furniture, decorate, make memories, etc.	Over time, your happiness increases bit by bit as you put more and more parts of your plan into action and keep at it.
Time to renovate, change, improve.	Just as you might want to make changes to your dream home over time, you are likely to want to make changes to your Happiness Blueprint. As you achieve goals or your life circumstances change, your values and priorities will change as well, and with that, your requirements for a happy life.

Keep in mind that some houses are built in a matter of months while others take years to complete. Happiness works much the same way. Depending on your starting point, your goals and a few other factors you will learn about in the following chapters, some people will achieve happiness more quickly than others. However, regardless of your starting point, if you read the book with the expectation of being super happy by the end of it, you will probably be disappointed. While it has been my experience that simply starting the journey and learning about happiness and yourself will likely have an immediate impact on how happy you feel, this book is only the starting point. It's what you do with what you learn that ultimately makes the difference.

Having said that, there are a few things you can do while reading this book that will improve your chances of quick progress — and of having fun while reading. First and foremost, do the exercises. The exercises are all about helping you figure out what is important to you and how you can apply what you're learning. In other words, the exercises are where we go from general knowledge to highly tailored and actionable insights for you specifically. You can't read up on that anywhere. No one else can tell you what matters most to you. That is the part you'll have to figure out for yourself and the exercises will help you do that. You can download the workbook to help you complete the exercises.

DOWNLOAD THE WORKBOOK

Because of the many exercises and templates in this book, I've put together a free workbook you can download and either print or fill in on your computer. Visit www.lisa-jansen.com/workbook to download it now. The workbook includes templates for all the exercises as well as space to take notes.

Taking notes is also a good idea, or earmarking and high-lighting parts of the book that you feel are especially impor-tant and valuable to you. Because of the interactive nature of this book, it might also be fun to team up with a buddy or even a whole book club and work through it together. That way you can discuss the concepts with another person, and maybe get a better understanding of how someone with a different personality might interpret things. This will help you develop a better idea of your own uniqueness and how it impacts your happiness. However, be aware that parts of this book discuss very personal topics like your core values and your strengths and weaknesses. While open conversations about these concepts can be valuable and inspiring, it's important to respect that not everyone will feel comfortable sharing their thoughts openly. If you do work through this book with a group, I would recommend creating a welcoming environment where everyone feels invited to share and speak up, but no one feels pressured to do so.

Last, but by no means least, don't forget to have fun, be curious and enjoy the journey that this book presents.

Before we move on to learning more about what happiness actually is, let me share my personal journey with you.

My Journey

"Be fearless. But don't be stupid."
LISA JANSEN

"It's now or never."

THAT IS what I wrote in my journal on the day I left Germany bound for New Zealand in early 2007. What might sound like an inspirational statement was actually pure desperation, mixed with a little bit of hope. The journal entry continues with comments like "if I don't make it now, I never will" and "I don't want to live like this any more, this year is my last chance to find happiness." It still brings tears to my eyes reading this. However, uncomfortable as it is for me to remember those thoughts, it also reminds me of how far I've come. That day, I set out to use the next year to turn my life around. It took more than a year, but I got there. Today, the younger me who wrote those words is only a distant memory.

I didn't have an apparent reason to be unhappy. I grew up in an idyllic small town in Germany, I had parents and siblings who loved me, I was well cared for and my family never had to worry about putting food on the table. I was generally healthy, I was smart and even though I wasn't exactly Miss Popular, I did have friends and I was never openly bullied. On paper, my life was pretty good. The one visible sign that my life maybe wasn't perfect was the fact that I was severely overweight. I don't really remember when I started to gain weight, but I remember being the big girl even in primary school. For most of my teens, I was morbidly obese. I managed to lose weight a couple of times, but every time it piled back on quicker than it had come off. At the time I wrote those journal entries, more than 12 years ago, I would have weighed somewhere around 130kg (290lb).

For most of my life I used to think that, if only I could lose weight, if only I could be skinny, I would be happy. In my head, my weight was the only thing that stopped me from being happy and living the life I wanted. It wasn't until many years later that I started to realise that being overweight wasn't the reason I was unhappy, but that it was the other way around. Being unhappy was the reason I was overweight.

Looking back now, I understand that I never felt like I fitted in — and that had little to do with my weight. Things about myself that I'm very proud of today made me feel different and weird at the time, mainly because I didn't understand them. Today I know that I was unhappy because I felt disconnected and lonely and because I didn't love and respect myself, but back then I simply didn't have that level of awareness.

Today, my life is amazing, and I am very happy. It took a lot longer than a year. There wasn't one simple thing, like losing weight, that made all the difference. Happiness didn't just find me one day, and no one else showed up and gave it to me. It required a lot of hard work, trial and error and determination. I had to challenge myself and change the way I thought about life, myself and pretty much everything. However, it was so very much worth it!

It's hard to know precisely what made the difference. I don't remember having a big AHA! moment where I could suddenly see clearly how to find happiness, or even just where to start. However, I do remember one thing that made a huge difference early on.

I was in New Zealand for a study abroad programme. During my second term at the University of Auckland, I took a course called Professional Development taught by the amazing Dr Deb Shepherd. This course ended up being my introduction to what has since become a passion (maybe even a bit of an obsession) for me: personal growth and development.

During this course, I was, for the first time in my life, challenged to learn about myself. I was challenged to observe and analyse how I think, feel and act. For the first time, I purposefully stopped and thought about who I was and who I wanted to be. Up until then, any goals I had were external and tangible; lose weight, get good grades, make friends, get a job, earn money, etc. I had never thought about more internal goals, such as how I think and feel. I had never thought about trying to change my mindset instead of changing my actions and the world around me. One of the most significant things I learned about myself during this course was that I tend to be overly rational and don't connect well with my emotions and gut instincts. This was especially true when it came to making decisions. I would always go with the rational, logical path, often not even listening to, or considering, what my emotions and my instincts were telling me.

Once I had put a plan in place, I would go through with it, no matter how unhappy it made me. I had a plan, and in my head, following the plan was the logical thing to do. Changing the plan meant failure. I realised I had never really learned to connect with my emotions and to put my feelings and mental well-being ahead of any external goals or expectations. Today, I understand that this is partly due to how I was raised and partly just who I am.

Regardless of what caused it, I realised that this overly rational approach was getting in the way of finding happiness. I started to work on connecting more with my emotions and listening more to my instincts, which eventually led to my decision to stay in New Zealand. I was supposed to go back to Germany at the end of the term, but even though that would have been the logical thing to do (I had a degree to finish, my family was there, I had a plan to follow…), it just didn't feel right. I learned to listen to my emotions, and they were telling me to stay. For maybe the first time in my life, I just did what felt right (not what my head told me to do).

Another thing I learned during this Professional Development course was the importance of passion, meaning and purpose. I realised if I wanted to stay in New Zealand, I needed to find something to get involved with, something I would be passionate about and that would connect me with like-minded people. At the beginning of my third term in New Zealand, I joined a student organisation that was all about fostering a culture of innovation and entrepreneurship among students and faculty. This turned out to be quite possibly one of the best decisions of my life. This organisation gave me something to be passionate about, something that made me feel like I mattered and like I was making a difference. It also connected me to a group of amazing people and, for the first time in my life, I felt part of something: I felt connected.

Fast forward to early 2009. I was about to start my final year at university to complete my Masters degree. It had been two years since I left Germany and set out to use the next year to lose weight so I could be happy. I still hadn't lost a pound at this point, but I was definitely a lot happier. I felt connected and I had purpose and goals. Most importantly, I was a lot more connected to my emotions and was starting to learn more and more about who I really am and what matters to me. All of that gave me the strength and determination to finally tackle my big weight challenge.

In 2009 I dropped over 30kg. However, it wasn't just about

losing weight any more. Through getting to know myself better, I had come to realise that I wanted to live an active life. There were so many things I wanted to do that I hadn't been able to because I wasn't fit enough.

I started to have a picture in my head of who I wanted to be, and I knew I needed to be fit and healthy to be that person. Losing weight had turned from a goal in itself to a means to a much more significant and more important goal: living the life I wanted.

My big weight loss years were 2009 and 2010. In late 2010 I reached my goal weight, and I have been within a healthy weight range ever since. But they were also years of personal growth. At the end of 2010, I completed a half marathon, something I never thought I could ever do. Just six months earlier I couldn't run 500 metres without struggling for air. This experience taught me another valuable lesson; the power of doing something you didn't think you could do. I haven't done any more running events since and I don't really enjoy running, but I still consider this one of my most significant achievements. Not because I managed to run (and partly walk) 21 kilometres, but because I overcame my doubts and insecurities and proved to myself how much I can achieve if I just set my mind to it.

I think after that, I took a little break from all the personal growth. I remember 2011 being a great year. I had never felt better about myself, and I very much enjoyed having a more active lifestyle, but I don't remember any major breakthroughs. I was a lot happier than I had ever been in my life and I think after all the change over the previous years, I was simply at a point where I needed a break to get comfortable with the new me. I don't think I realised at the time how much better things could get — otherwise, I might have been in more of a rush to get there.

There were two significant milestones in 2012. First of all, it was the year I started to learn about personality theories and concepts. I don't remember how I got on to the topic, but I remember the first time I did a personality test and reading my profile and then being hooked on the subject. That year, I learned a lot about different personality types and preferences and how they interact with each other. It was the year I discovered that I'm an introvert and what that really means. I learned about my personality and what makes me different from others — something that has had a massive impact on my life and how I view myself. Suddenly I started to understand why I had often felt different and disconnected as a child and why some things that seemed to come easy to almost everyone else (like parties and brainstorming sessions) often felt like hard work to me. I started to understand why I often found it difficult to build real connections with people and what I could do to get better at that. From there, I continued to learn about personal values and what motivates and drives us. I started this journey in 2012 and still don't feel like I've finished it. However, that year I began to understand more and more who I was, what my strengths and weaknesses were and what mattered most to me — and how I could use all of that to create the life I wanted.

The other significant milestone in 2012 was that I started kitesurfing. At the time, I was ready for another challenge. I felt it was time to step out of my comfort zone again. I love the ocean, and I've always dreamed about being one of those fit and active people who do all these cool activities. If someone had told me four years earlier that I would be a kitesurfer, I would have just laughed it off, thinking: "I wish, but that's never going to happen." However, thanks to all the work I had done so far, I had a lot more confidence, and I knew I was up to the challenge. Today, kitesurfing is my favourite thing in the world, but it didn't come easy. Not having any experience with board sports (or sports on the whole) my coordination skills left a lot to be desired and, even though I had the confidence to give it a go, I wasn't very sure of myself once out there. In the beginning, I got dragged around so much that my legs were covered in bruises and I was ready to give up more than once. But I hung in there. I knew this was another step towards the life I wanted, and that gave me the motivation to keep trying. And I got there in the end. Kitesurfing is my favourite activity now because it is lots of fun and, even more importantly, because it connected me to the amazing group of people that I now call my saltwater family. Through kitesurfing (and a lucky work connection) I met a group of people who were living the kind of life I wanted; active, healthy, outdoors and fun. Becoming part of this group over the last few years, to the point where I consider them family, has been what took my life from pretty great to really awesome. While there might have been an element of luck (I ended up working with a guy who was part of this group), none of that would have happened if I hadn't started working on myself years earlier. None of it would have happened if I hadn't learned about myself and who I wanted to be and if I hadn't pushed myself out of my comfort zone to do things like learning to kitesurf.

Since then, I've continued to work on myself. I've learned to trust people more and to build emotional connections with them. I've learned to be vulnerable at times and while it still often doesn't come easy, I've learned how to let certain people in (one area where I still have more work to do). I've continued to learn about happiness and the meaning of life. Most importantly, I've learned to trust myself and to follow my own path in life — even if it means doing life differently.

I found happiness several years ago. Over the last few years, I've learned how to maintain it and how to make my happiness mostly independent of what happens in the world around me. I've learned, and fully internalised, the fact that happiness is an inside job and all about our mindset and attitude. I've found this inner calm and peace that makes me see the good even in challenging situations, and I've found the inner confidence that I can be happy no matter what happens in my life — and, no, I haven't joined a cult or spent five hours a day meditating.

Through everything I've learned and everything I've been through, I have a clear view of what it means to be happy and what it takes to find happiness. When I started my journey towards a happier life, I didn't have a plan, and I didn't really know what I had to do. I thought the secret to happiness was to simply lose weight, but it turned out to be about so much more than that. I didn't know any of that when I started. Instead, I just figured it out step by step. I made many mistakes and took several detours along the way. I've often thought about how much easier and faster it would have been if I had known which steps to take and what to do. This book is my attempt to share my experience and insights with others to help them speed up their journey to a happier life. Throughout this book, I will share how I found happiness, and I will provide the insights that can help others follow the same path. However, this book is about much more than sharing my personal experience. As you will see, it is based on extensive research and reading and takes an analytical and scientific view of the concepts that will be discussed. While I hope my personal story will inspire and motivate you, the goal of this book is to go far beyond that and provide you with easy to understand, engaging and highly actionable insights into happiness and how to find it and make it last.

PART I:

Understanding Happiness

"When I was five years old, my mother always told me that happiness was the key to life. When I went to school, they asked me what I wanted to be when I grew up. I wrote down 'happy'. They told me I didn't understand the assignment, and I told them they didn't understand life."

JOHN LENNON

TODAY, THE concept of happiness is everywhere. Every day, we are bombarded with advertisements for products and services that promise us happiness. Bookstores have entire shelves filled with happiness literature. Countless courses and seminars promise to let us in on the secret to a happy life. Entire marketing and branding departments spend hours designing and developing strategies to promote their products and services as happiness boosters. Happiness is synonymous with smiles and laughter, joy, excitement and pleasure. Little things 'make us happy', we chase goals because we believe they will make us happier and we spend money on things we probably don't need because, in our minds, they will bring us happiness. But why, if it is everywhere in our lives, all the time, are we all still striving for it? If material goods and possessions can bring us happiness, shouldn't we have found it by now? If there are books and courses that will teach us how to be happy, shouldn't we all be happy by now? If achieving our goals is the key to happiness, then why do we always want more once we've achieved a goal? There must be more to it.

What is happiness really about? That's a question many of the most well-known philosophers and scientists, as well as ordinary people, have been trying to answer for thousands of years — and their answers have varied. Eighteenth-century philosopher Immanuel Kant defined happiness as "the satisfaction of all our desires", according to Spanish philosopher José Ortega y Gasset "happiness consists of finding something that satisfies and gratifies us completely" and Friedrich Nietzsche believed that happiness was a power that we could exert over the world around us, defining happiness as: "The feeling that power increases — that resistance is being overcome." Many modern-day academics who research happiness, especially in the field of positive psychology, define a happy person as "someone who experiences frequent positive emotions, such as joy, interest, and pride, and infrequent (though not absent) negative emotions, such as sadness, anxiety and anger".[1] Others argue that happiness, in its truest form, is purely about overall life satisfaction and well-being and is relatively independent of momentary emotions — both positive and negative.

For example, French philosopher Robert Misrahi defines happiness as "the radiation of joy over one's entire existence or over the most vibrant part of one's active past, one's actual present and one's conceived future". Similarly, Sonja Lyubomirsky, a professor of psychology at the University of California and one of the leading researchers in the field of positive psychology, defines happiness as "the experience of joy, contentment, or positive well-being, combined with a sense that one's life is good, meaningful, and worthwhile".[2] Ancient Greek philosopher and scientist Aristotle considered happiness the 'supreme good' because it is the only goal that always is an end in itself, meaning we pursue happiness purely for the sake of happiness and never as a means to an end. Buddhist monk and author Matthieu Ricard argues that happiness is about learning to love ourselves, and defines happiness as "a state of inner fulfilment, not the gratification of inexhaustible desires for outward things".[3]

With so many definitions and views, it can be challenging to understand what happiness is — let alone how to achieve or increase it. One of the reasons happiness is so difficult to define is that it is a subjective and highly individual concept that is experienced in different ways by each of us. In other words, happiness is different for everyone. Therefore, I don't want to force one specific definition of happiness on you. I want you to decide for yourself what happiness is and means to you. However, for the rest of this book to be valuable, it is important that we have a shared understanding of how we view happiness for the purpose of this book so that you, as the reader, know what I mean when I use the term happiness throughout these pages. To achieve this, it helps to take a closer look at the relationship between what is considered happiness for the purpose of this book and three other fundamental concepts of our lives: positive emotions, success and negative emotions.

Happiness and Positive Emotions

What would life be without positive emotions like pleasure and joy? It would probably be pretty dull and boring. We all strive to experience joy, excitement, fun, love, pride and pleasure in our daily lives. They are some of our key motivators and rewards, and it would be easy to assume that the more positive emotions we experience, the happier we are. However, it might not be quite that simple. While certainly related, happiness and pleasure are not the same thing, and happiness is not merely the result of an abundance of positive emotions. One simple example makes that perfectly clear: people get addicted to drugs, alcohol and other substances because they make them feel good in the moment. However, I think we can all agree that most addicts are probably not the happiest people. If being happy were as simple as experiencing lots of pleasure, we would all spend our days eating junk food, having sex and going partying. Most of us don't behave that way because, consciously or unconsciously, we understand that it won't lead to lasting happiness.

Positive emotions like pleasure and joy are momentary feelings we experience as a response to something happening to us or in the world around us. The feeling needs to be triggered by something — even if it's just a thought or a memory that popped into your mind. Happiness, on the other hand, is a state of satisfaction and well-being that is mainly about how we interpret and respond to what happens and less about what actually happens. For example, if you do really well in a competition, you are likely to experience lots of positive emotions like joy, pride and confidence as a result of your achievement. Whether you are an overall happy person will become clearer when you don't do well in a competition. You can allow yourself to feel disappointed and angry for weeks, repeating the event in your head over and over again to figure out where you went wrong, or you might even try to find the blame in other people and their actions. Responding in this way is likely to lead to less happiness. On the other hand, you can accept the result, focus on what you can learn from the experience, remind yourself that you still had fun participating and then focus on doing better in the future. This response is likely to lead to a much higher level of overall happiness with life. In both scenarios, the same thing happened (you lost in a competition). The difference between being happy or unhappy is about how you respond to what happened.

Another key differentiator is the fact that positive emotions are momentary and often wear off relatively quickly, while happiness is a lasting feeling. For example, you might be excited and joyful to meet with an old friend you haven't seen in a long time. Your positive emotions will probably be particularly high at the moment you first see him/her. An hour later you're still feeling great about spending time with them, but it's not as intense any more. A couple of days later, the general feeling of joy is probably gone unless you specifically remember the great time you spent together. Happiness, on the other hand, is lasting. It is a general state of feeling good and satisfied in the moment as well as being confident that this positive state will continue into the future. Of course, happiness can change over time and wear off. However, it's usually a slow and gradual process and is generally caused by a significant event or changes in circumstances. Positive emotions, on the other hand, usually wear off even when whatever caused the feeling in the first place hasn't changed. For example, new shoes or a new smartphone are exciting and bring you joy and pleasure. A few weeks later the shoes or the phone haven't changed at all, but you're likely to get less joy and pleasure from them simply because the excitement and newness have worn off.

In addition, positive emotions like pleasure and joy are often disproportionate to how much we have of whatever caused the positive feeling in the first place. For example, the first glass of wine is much more enjoyable than the fifth and getting a massage once in a while is a delightful special treat, but if you have a massage every day it becomes normal, and you're not experiencing the same level of positive feelings any more.

Maybe the most important differentiator between pleasure and happiness is how much control we can have over them. Positive emotions are an emotional response to something happening, and most of us have little control over when and how we experience them. When something good happens in your life, you don't decide to feel joyful, you just feel it. Experiencing emotions as a result of something happening is usually not a conscious decision but a spontaneous reaction of our brain. We also don't choose how intense we want the feeling to be or how long we want it to last. Yes, we might be able to teach ourselves to be more positive, and we can learn techniques of appreciation and awareness that help us extend how long we feel good about something. However, the initial emotions that we feel in the moment are mostly out of our control. Of course, you could argue that, once we have figured out what brings us joy and pleasure, we can aim to bring more of that into our lives, but as we've learned above, the positive emotions will wear off. The more we have of something, the less joy and pleasure it will likely give us. Happiness, on the other hand, is a lasting mindset, not a spontaneous emotional response. We have a lot more opportunity to shape and modify this mindset. Happiness is about how we interpret and respond to what happens in the world around us, and we can learn to become more aware and have more control over how we view and react to what happens to us. We will learn a lot more about how to control and shape this mindset throughout this book.

The short version of all this is that positive emotions are short-term feelings that are usually caused by external events, while happiness is an internal, long-term state of mind. We can certainly experience more positive emotions by changing external factors in our life, but to change how happy we are with our lives requires an internal mindset change. However, the two are not mutually exclusive. In fact, positive emotions can help us find happiness — if we pursue the right emotions for the right reason. Striving for happiness is challenging for most people because it is such an elusive and abstract concept that takes a long time to achieve. Striving for joy and pleasure, on the other hand, is much easier because they are tangible and more immediate. You can benefit hugely from understanding how positive emotions can help you on your path towards happiness. As the renowned psychologist and author Martin Seligman puts it in his bestselling book Authentic Happiness: "Pleasure can be a powerful motivator, but it does not produce change".[4] Real and lasting change is only possible if positive emotions are used as a means to an end. The important thing is to understand what will ultimately make you happy and how positive emotions can help you work towards that goal. The idea is to pursue positive emotions because they will help you achieve your value-based happiness goals (not for their own sake).

Don't worry if all of this feels a bit confusing and overwhelming at this point. We will discuss these ideas and concepts in more detail throughout the book and examples and exercises will help to make it easier to understand. For now, it's important to understand that experiencing positive emotions like joy and pleasure is a crucial aspect of a happy life. However, all the joy in the world will never automatically add up to lasting happiness. The table below summarises the key differences between positive emotions and happiness.

Positive Emotions	Happiness
Positive emotions are feelings we experience as a response to something happening.	Happiness, on the other hand, is a state of satisfaction and well-being that is fairly independent of what happens in the world.
Positive emotions are an immediate and often automatic reaction to what happens in the world around us.	Happiness is about how we choose to interpret and respond to what happens in the world around us.
Positive emotions are momentary, short-term and wear off over time	Happiness is a lasting state of positivity and contentment about the present as well as the future. While it can wear off over time, it's usually a long and slow decline over time or caused by a major tragic event.
Positive emotions are typically disproportionate to how much we have of whatever caused the positive emotion.	Happiness does not decline if we have more of it.
Positive emotions can be powerful motivators to achieve the change needed to find happiness.	Happiness is the result of changes we make to our mindset and approach.

Happiness and Success

The second clear distinction we need to make is between what we consider happiness in this book and success. I personally believe that finding happiness is the greatest form of success. However, for most people, success is mostly about tangible achievements and the accomplishment of an aim or purpose. When people say things like: "He/She is really successful," they usually don't mean to imply that the person is very happy but refer more to things like career or sporting achievements, being well-off financially, or being a high performer in another area of life. For the purpose of this discussion, we will adopt this mainstream, achievement-focused view of success.

One of the main differences between happiness and success is that the latter is measurable from an external perspective — at least in most cases. As a researcher, you can ask someone about their goals and then observe whether they achieve them, or you can compare a group (like a university class or a sports team) and observe who the high-performers are. From that, you can draw conclusions about how successful (in the traditional sense) a person is. We live in a society where we have fairly well-defined ideas of success. The word is synonymous with high achievement at school or work, above average income and social status, as well as status symbols such as houses and cars. We can look at someone's life and, without ever talking to them, draw certain conclusions about how successful they are — as long as we follow the traditional definition of success (and assuming the person is not drowning in hidden debt). Happiness is much more elusive and internal. It is almost impossible for anyone to judge how happy or unhappy someone else is without asking them. The happiest person is not necessarily the one who laughs the most, has the biggest smile, or jumps up and down with joy the most. While that might be how some people express happiness, not everyone does. There are people who are extremely happy who hardly ever jump up and down screaming and laughing with joy (myself included). On the other hand, we probably all know of someone who seems to show all the signs of being happy, but then we find out they struggle with depression or other challenges and negative feelings. Happiness is not observable from the outside. The only one who truly knows how happy you are is you. The only way we can measure happiness is by asking people. For example, happiness researchers tend to measure participants' happiness either by asking them directly how they rate their level of happiness or by asking a series of questions to then draw conclusions about how happy a participant is from the answers.

Another important distinction is that success often requires being better than others while our happiness does not negatively impact the happiness level of others. In many situations, for one person to be successful (in the achievement-focused way), someone else has to be unsuccessful. Winning a competition means others who set out to achieve the same goal weren't successful, getting a promotion at work usually means someone else didn't get it, scoring that exciting movie role means someone else didn't, being accepted into a prestigious university or other programme means having to be better than the others that applied. We consider those people successful that are better than others in their respective fields. Therefore, by definition, in many situations, one person's success results in someone else being unsuccessful in their endeavours. Finding happiness, by contrast, does not require other people to be unhappy. In fact, one person's happiness is more likely to have a positive impact on the people around them because happy people are often excellent sources of inspiration and support for others. Being happy does not require you to be better or happier than someone else. We can all be equally happy at the same time — what a great world that would be.

Happiness and success are separate concepts. We can be happy without being considered successful, and we can be regarded as successful by most people around us but feel very unhappy inside. It's easy to look at people who are very successful and seemingly have it all and assume they must be happy. The reality is, while we might be able to judge how successful someone is, we cannot judge how happy they are. It is imperative to understand this distinction. Happiness is not about how other people perceive you and think you should feel, and neither is it about achieving certain things — whether they are goals we set for ourselves or the ones society puts upon us. Happiness is purely about how you really feel inside when you're completely real and honest with yourself.

However, it is also important to clarify that happiness doesn't mean an absence of ambition or wanting to be successful. Even though happiness is often defined as a state of satisfaction with life on the whole and overall well-being, that does not mean that happy people are content and do not strive for more. It's part of human nature to have goals and a desire to be successful. If we believe Kant's idea that happiness is "the satisfaction of all our desires", we're basically saying that happiness can only be achieved if we stop wanting more once we get what we wanted in the first place. While some highly skilled and committed individuals might have achieved this state of total contentment and the absence of ambition, for the vast majority of people wanting more and wanting to be successful is just part of life. The good news is, you can be happy and still have the ambition to be successful. However, it's important that 'getting more' does not become the key to your happiness. If you find yourself thinking along the lines of : "If only I can get this promotion, I will be happy" or "as soon as I find a partner and get married, I will be happy," you're on the wrong path. Happiness is not about achievements — that's success.

Success and achievements can certainly play a significant role in finding happiness. Success triggers positive emotions, improves self-confidence, and the pursuit of it can add meaning and purpose to our life — all things that have a positive impact on your happiness, as we will learn later on. Similar to positive emotions, success can help you achieve happiness if you go after the right goals for the right reasons. However, being the most successful business entrepreneur, athlete, artist, mother or father, scientist or activist in the world on its own will not automatically make you happy. It's only when your achievements align with your values that they will contribute to your happiness. That is one of the reasons why learning about your values is part of the next chapter.

The below table summarises the main differences between success and happiness.

Success	Happiness
Success is about achievements and the accomplishment of goals	Happiness is an internal state of satisfaction with life that is not tied to any external goals or achievements.
Success is, to a certain extent, measurable and observable from the outside.	Happiness is internal and cannot be viewed or measured from the outside.
Being successful often requires us to be better than others.	Finding happiness does not require us to be happier or better than others.
By definition, not everyone can be successful in the same area at the same time. (e.g. only one person/team can win a competition, only one actor scores the big movie role, etc.)	Everyone in the entire world can be equally happy at the same time.
Success is partly about how successful others think we are.	Happiness is purely about how we feel internally and has nothing to do with what other people think.

Happiness and Negative Emotions

We have already determined that happiness is not simply an abundance of positive emotions like joy and pleasure, but what is the role of negative emotions like fear, sadness, pain and anger when it comes to happiness?

In the book The Happiness Trap, Russ Harris presents a very compelling case for the argument that one of the main reasons why many people struggle to find happiness is that they are stuck on the idea that happiness requires the absence, or at least minimisation, of negative emotions.[5] Therefore, they try to control their emotions, attempt to remove negative thoughts and feelings from their brains completely, and avoid situations that could lead to negative feelings — and when none of that works, they feel guilty and frustrated (more negative emotions). As Harris, and many others, argue, the problem is that negative emotions are an unavoidable part of life and the more we try to fight them, the more damaging they will be. This is what Harris calls The Happiness Trap. No matter how happy you are, you will experience suffering at some point in your life. Whether it's through the loss of a loved one, the end of a relationship or friendship, being overlooked for a promotion, cutting your finger while chopping vegetables or being hurt or disappointed by another person; I don't think anyone can make it through life without experiencing these, and other, challenging situations and emotions at some stage. Striving for and living a happy, fulfilling life requires us to deal with negative emotions occasionally.

Research has shown that experiencing negative emotions generally does not have a direct impact on how happy we are and how frequently we feel positive emotions. The exception being people who experience an extremely high amount of negative emotions, who have been shown to have fewer positive emotions, and are less likely to be happy. Several studies have found that people can have both higher than average negative emotions and higher than average positive emotions.[6][7] Other studies have found that even very happy people have negative emotions. Among these studies is one by two leaders in the field of positive psychology: Ed Diener and Martin Seligman. In their study, Diener and Seligman compare those participants who are in the top 10% happiest with those who report average and below average levels of happiness.[8] While this study is limited by its small and narrow sample size (222 undergraduate students), the findings do show that even very happy people have negative emotions. Diener and Seligman express relief over this finding, saying that not experiencing any negative emotions would suggest a dysfunctional state of mind.

Another study shows that we can even experience positive and negative emotions at the same time. Researchers from Ohio State University and the University of Chicago conducted an experiment where they asked participants about their feelings immediately after watching the film Life Is Beautiful, moving out of their dormitories, or graduating from college.[9] While the majority of people surveyed reported feeling either happy or sad, many of the participants reported feeling both, indicating that we are capable of feeling both extremes at the same time.

Further support for the theory that negative emotions do not have a direct impact on happiness comes from gender comparisons. It is well established that women are more likely to suffer from depression and studies have shown that women, on average, experience more negative emotions like fear, anxiety, guilt, stress and sadness. At the same time, several studies have shown that women tend to report higher levels of happiness than men.[10] In other words, women seem to experience both more negative emotions and higher levels of happiness than men do.

Experiencing negative emotions does not make us unhappy in much the same way that positive emotions do not automatically make us happy. As we discussed, happiness is not so much about what happens to us (positive or negative) but about how we interpret and respond to what happens. That is one of the reasons why some people are able to find happiness even though they had to deal with great adversity in their lives. One example of this is US Army Sergeant Travis Mills. In April 2012, Sergeant Mills was on patrol as part of his third tour of duty in Afghanistan when an explosive device went off, leaving him critically injured. While his life was saved, he lost parts of both legs and both arms. After extensive surgery, he woke up in a hospital in Germany to the news that he was a quadruple amputee, meaning he'd lost both legs and both arms. Understandably, his initial response was anger, a sense of loss, frustration and shame. I don't think anyone would have blamed him for feeling like this for the rest of his life considering the circumstances. However, after the initial negativity, Sergeant Mills found the strength to move on and focus on all the positive things he still had in his life, like his wife and baby girl. Eventually, he was able to find appreciation for the fact that, unlike so many other soldiers, he was still alive. In an interview, he once said that he didn't think his problems outweighed anyone else's, but I think many of us would have to admit that most of our problems and challenges seem pretty insignificant in comparison. I'm sure Sergeant Mills still experiences the occasional negative emotion due to his situation. He probably still occasionally feels angry or frustrated, like when he can't keep up with his daughter in the playground. However, he is not letting it get in the way of living a fulfilling, meaningful, happy life. Today, Travis is a motivational speaker, actor, author and an advocate for veterans and amputees helping others overcome similar challenges and finding happiness again.[11]

Another equally empowering story is that of Ashley Sullenger and her family. Ashley and her husband lost their 18-month-old baby girl in a tragic drowning accident in 2010. I don't think anyone can even begin to imagine the grief, sadness and loss Ashley would have felt following that event. The loss of a child is probably the worst thing that can happen to any parent, and I think everyone would have understood if Ashley and her husband had become lost in their grief. But they didn't. In an article she wrote, Ashley once said that after a really dark period she eventually realised that she still had a long life ahead of her and that she needed to strive to find happiness again. It must have been incredibly hard to move on after something like that, but Ashley and her husband did it. Today they have a beautiful family, and while I'm sure they still experience periods of grief and sadness over the loss of their daughter, they are living a happy, meaningful life. Moreover, by sharing her story on her blog, Ashley also supports and inspires others who have to deal with great loss.[12]

These stories show that even the biggest tragedies imaginable don't have to prevent us from living happy lives. The loss, the anger and the sadness will probably always stay with us to some extent, but we don't have to let them control us and our life. Stories like those of Ashley and Travis show that the right attitude and mindset can help us find happiness, no matter what. I think these stories also help us to put our own challenges and negative emotions into perspective and can inspire us to find happiness despite the negative events and emotions that might be part of our life. As Ashley's family motto says: "We can do hard things."

NEGATIVE EMOTIONS AREN'T ALL BAD
There is another reason why we shouldn't just avoid and suppress negative emotions. Throughout human history,

negative emotions have been instrumental in keeping us alive. Early humans lived in a dangerous world with threats around every corner. Their brains had to evolve, to be constantly on the lookout for predators and other dangers. Emotions like fear and anxiety trigger our fight-or-flight response. Imagine if our ancestors hadn't felt fear when predators threatened them — the human race would probably be extinct by now. The better humans became at worrying, at anticipating risks and at feeling fear, the more their chances of survival increased. Similarly, emotions like loneliness and sadness make people seek out the company of others and being part of a group significantly increased the chances of survival, as well as reproduction, for our early ancestors.

Of course, today we don't have to worry about being attacked by giant mammoths any more, and we're not as reliant on the protection of a group either. On the whole, our lives are more comfortable and safer than they have ever been. However, that does not mean they are entirely without risks – and our negative emotions still often help to keep us safe. It's fear that's stopping us from walking through a shady neighbourhood on our own and that prevents us from running across a street without looking, no matter how much of a hurry we are in. It's anxiety and worry that makes us think carefully about how big a mortgage we can afford, and it is pain that alerts us to early warning signs that we might be sick and urges us to see a doctor.

Negative emotions are not just valuable in keeping us safe and alive. They can also play a huge role in helping us find happiness. Just like positive emotions tell us something is good and right, negative emotions can tell us what is not right and when we're on the wrong track. While some amount of negative emotion is perfectly normal, an increase in anxiety, doubt, sadness or fear is often an indication that something in our life is not as it should be and that we need to change. However, in this context, it is important to differentiate between an occasional increase in negative emotions in an otherwise relatively positive and overall healthy person and the regular and reoccurring negative feelings that people with anxiety, depression and other mental health problems experience. Depression and anxiety are serious conditions, and I will not claim that I can even begin to understand how they feel or how they can be overcome. If you feel overall negative a lot of the time or experience episodes where you feel overwhelmed by negative thoughts and emotions, and you find yourself worrying to a point where it feels completely demobilising, I would strongly recommend you seek the support of a mental health professional. However, if you are generally a relatively positive person and find you have a good balance of positive and negative emotions, then consider that some negative feelings are your mind's way of telling you that you're off track and that you need to change something. Of course, if you're anything like me, it's just as likely that it's just your mind running wild and your worry is completely unfounded and unnecessary, but it's worth checking in with yourself and finding out exactly what the reasons for your negative thoughts are.

I'll give you a personal example. A few years ago, I had an incredible summer enjoying the beach and all my favourite activities with my friends. After the summer came to an end, I kept having this lingering feeling of sadness and disconnectedness. Life was good at the time. I had a job I enjoyed, I was earning good money, I had just moved into a new place right by the water with stunning views and I had amazing friends in my life and hobbies I enjoyed. Yet, I kept feeling a kind of sadness and disconnectedness. At first, I thought it was just the usual post-summer blues, but after a while, I decided that I needed to figure out what was going on. Was I just having a bit of a low that would go away on its own or was it something I needed to change? I started to listen to myself and especially paid attention to the negative feelings. Once I started doing that, I quickly realised that I didn't really enjoy my job as much as I used to and that the new place, while stunning, didn't really feel like home. I realised that I wasn't getting as much meaning and purpose from my work any more and that I needed to look for new inspiration and motivation elsewhere. All of this ultimately led me to give up my fairly traditional life to live in a campervan, travel around beautiful New Zealand and make more time to enjoy life and more time to write — which led to this book. If I had ignored my negative emotions or not taken them seriously, I would probably still be working full-time in an office, living in an apartment in the city and I'm pretty sure I would be a lot less happy than I am now.

That is an example of how negative feelings can lead to significant life-changing events, but it doesn't always need to be that drastic. Negative emotions can make us aware of the fact that a relationship might be at risk and needs work, that we need to watch our spending to ensure our financial security long-term, that we need to spend more time with our loved ones, that we need to get a health-check and many other everyday situations. Of course, not all negative emotions are calls to action from our mind. Some are just our imagination running wild and result in us worrying over nothing and overthinking everything. However, if you start listening to your negative feelings for a while, you will learn pretty quickly which ones to take seriously and which ones just to sit out.

All of this suggests that negative emotions not only do not prevent us from being happy but can help us find happiness by guiding us away from things that are dangerous or simply not right for us. The key is for us to learn to live with our negative emotions and accept them rather than trying to avoid or suppress them and to learn to listen to them to identify the ones we need to do something about. The most important thing to remember is that both negative and positive emotions are about what happens in the world around us, while happiness is about how we view and respond to what happens.

Success, positive emotions like joy and pleasure and negative emotions like fear and sadness are relatively straightforward and clearly defined concepts (success = the achievement of goals, positive emotions = feeling great about something; negative emotions = feeling bad about something). Happiness, on the other hand, is much more elusive and harder to define. There are numerous definitions, and most people have their own ideas of what happiness means to them. There is no right or wrong definition. However, for this book to be valuable, it is important that we come to a shared understanding of what happiness is. Therefore, for the rest of the book, whenever I mention the term happiness, it refers to:

- A lasting feeling of satisfaction with life on the whole
- Feeling good about one's life today and feeling positive about the future
- A sense that one's life is fulfilling and meaningful
- An inner sense of contentment and confidence that we are capable of handling whatever life throws at us, now and in the future and
- A lasting overall sense of satisfaction with, and love for, who we are and how we live our life

At the same time, happiness in this book does NOT refer to:

- The achievement of specific goals
- Short-term emotions like joy and pleasure
- The absence of negative emotions
- Living up to other people's expectations or ideals

Now that we have a shared understanding of what we mean when we talk about happiness, let's take a look at why we all strive for it.

Why Do We Strive for Happiness?

"Do you want to be happy?" That is probably one of the very few questions that all of us, irrespective of our nationality, race, religion, values, personalities and beliefs, would answer the same way: "YES!". For the vast majority of people, finding happiness is the ultimate goal in life. Ask people anywhere in the world about their biggest goals in life, and you might get responses like start a family, be successful, be healthy, provide for my family, get rich, contribute to my community, or make a difference. If you keep asking long enough, why these are their goals, most people will ultimately say "because it will make me happy". We all strive to be happy. Independent of who we are, where we live, how we were raised and what we believe in, we all want to be happy — and when we're happy, we want to be happier. This is not just a phenomenon of modern times. Happiness is a topic that fascinated and occupied many of the most influential human minds in history. Nearly 2500 years ago renowned thinkers and philosophers such as Confucius, Buddha, Socrates and Aristotle theorised and wrote about happiness. Leading figures in philosophy and theology in the Middle Ages and the Renaissance wrote extensively about the topic, including English philosopher John Locke (1632-1704) who coined the phrase 'pursuit of happiness', in his book An Essay Concerning Human Understanding. The American Declaration of Independence made the 'pursuit of happiness' a fundamental right of the American people, and even Albert Einstein had a theory on how to live a happy life,

Happy people

which, scribbled on a napkin, sold for over a million at an auction in 2017 (so maybe money can buy happiness after all). Interestingly, many of our modern theories and research findings around happiness are surprisingly similar to the thoughts and theories that have been proposed over the last 2500 years. It appears that even though significant effort over many centuries has been put into understanding the concept better, the fundamental ideas and beliefs have not changed much over this time — and neither has the human race's search for happiness. Today, as much as during any time in history, people seem to be compelled to pursue happiness. And there is much evidence that suggests we should do just that.

An ever-growing amount of research shows the numerous benefits of happiness.[13] Happier people are more likely to have healthy relationships and a stronger support network, tend to be more creative and productive, produce a higher quality of work leading to higher income, and they are often more active and have more energy. Happier people also seem to be more likely to show greater self-control and better coping abilities, giving them an advantage in stressful situations. Furthermore, happy people tend to be more cooperative and prosocial, making it more likely that they are well-liked and accepted by others. On top of that, studies suggest that happy people have a better immune system, are healthier and even live longer. We will discuss many of these research findings in more depth later on when we review the science of happiness.

In addition to the rational benefits, it seems likely that we are also genetically and biologically programmed to pursue happiness. Evolutionary psychologists have argued that in the early days of the human race, happiness was an adaptive advantage. Research has shown that happy people are more likely to be social and active, appear more attractive, are better at dealing with stress, are more resilient and have more energy — all skills and traits that would have been essential to survival and reproduction in the early days of the human race and for much of our history. Therefore, it has been argued that happy people were more likely to survive and pass their 'happiness genes' on to their offspring. This theory suggests that, like all evolutionary adaptations, happiness started as a genetic variation, but persisted because it helped us stay alive.[14]

Leading positive psychology researcher and author of the bestseller Authentic Happiness, Martin Seligman, also argues that happiness has a purpose in human evolution and that we are, therefore, genetically programmed to pursue happiness. He explains that, similar to the way that fear leads to an instinctive flight-or-fight response, the pursuit of happiness leads us towards positive outcomes and opportunities — something that would have initiated and motivated much of the progress that the human race has made over the centuries. In other words, while emotions like fear would have kept our ancestors safe when threats appeared, positive emotions and the pursuit of happiness is what motivated them to look for better opportunities and work towards a better future. In Happiness: The Science Behind Your Smile, Daniel Nettle presents a similar argument, saying that the promise of happiness is what motivates us, what gets us out of bed in the morning and what makes us do things we don't want to do. He also makes the point that it is not so much **being** happy, but the **pursuit** of happiness that ultimately ensures we continue to progress and strive for improvement. Nettle argues that the ultimate purpose of the human 'happiness programme' is to keep us striving for more, so we keep evolving and seeking out what's best for us and our survival.[15]

We don't know for sure how early humans felt and what role happiness and its pursuit had in their lives. All we can do is make assumptions based on what we know today about human behaviour, happiness and how the human race has developed. While we don't know to what extent happiness was a key motivator for our ancestors, we can surmise about the role it might have played and, more importantly, the role it currently plays. The idea of a better and happier life is what motivates us to keep working, keep looking for opportunities to improve ourselves and our lives and to keep making progress. Therefore, irrespective of the role it had in the past, the pursuit of happiness is certainly a key motivator and source of growth in today's society. Without it, our lives and the world we live in would look very different.

So, do we pursue happiness because of the benefits it brings or because we're genetically programmed to do so? It's likely to be a combination of both. While the argument around the benefits of being happy is compelling, we can't ignore the fact that many people are not fully aware of these research findings, and yet they pursue happiness in much the same way. That suggests there is at least some genetic element that makes us seek happiness, regardless of how much we know about its benefits. However, something I have experienced myself and observed in many others is that those people who proactively learn about happiness, its benefits and how to achieve it seem to be more determined and more proactive in their pursuit. They are also the ones who often have the best understanding of what will bring them happiness and are clear about the fact that an internal state of happiness is their ultimate goal, while less aware people often chase more tangible things like money, success, status and recognition as means to finding happiness.

The pursuit of happiness seems to be ingrained in all of us. While it means different things to different people, we all strive to be happier. The question then becomes: what determines how happy we are?

What Determines How Happy We Are?

In part three of this book, we will take a closer look at specific factors that may or may not help us be happier and we will review scientific research findings for each of them. However, we first need to address the bigger question of what ultimately determines how happy we are.

In recent years, an increasing number of highly regarded researchers, authors and thinkers in the field have started to adapt the Happiness Formula developed by Martin Seligman to answer this question. Seligman is often referred to as the founder of positive psychology, which is the field of research that focuses on what makes us happy. Up until the late 90s, most researchers and scientists were focused on understanding the dark side of happiness: mental illness, depression and anxiety. The primary goal at the time was to help people who suffer from these conditions to overcome them or learn to deal better with them. In other words, researchers were focused on helping people go from a 0 or 1 on the 10-point happiness scale to maybe a 4 or 5. While this was, without a doubt, incredibly valuable and essential work, it didn't give us many insights into what might help us go from a 4 to an 8 or from a 7 to a 9 on the happiness scale. Martin Seligman and other like-minded colleagues identified this gap and started to focus their research on the upper end of the happiness scale. The field of positive psychology was born. Seligman has written more than 250 scholarly publications and 20 books, including international best-sellers: Authentic Happiness, Flourish and Learned Optimism. In 1998, he was elected president of the American Psychological Association. Needless to say, he knows a thing or two about the science around happiness.

In his 2002 book, Authentic Happiness, Seligman introduces his Happiness Formula. Don't worry. This formula is nothing like those complicated, weird-looking things you might remember from your maths classes. Seligman's formula basically just identifies the three key elements that make up our overall happiness; our set range, our life circumstances and factors under our voluntary control. Of course, there is much complexity in each of these three areas and fully understanding happiness and what makes us happier takes a lot more than merely applying the formula to our life. However, it is a great starting point and, for the purpose of this book, a good way to bring structure to the discussion. So let's take a closer look at this Happiness Formula.

The Happiness Formula

Seligman's Happiness Formula looks like this (see, nothing too scary):

$$H = S + C + V$$

- H stands for an enduring level of happiness
- S is your set range (Genetics)
- C is the circumstances in your life (External), and
- V represents factors under your voluntary control (Internal).

Let's take a look at the individual elements.

ENDURING LEVEL OF HAPPINESS
By referring to the sum of the equation as "an enduring level of happiness", instead of just "happiness", Seligman wants to make sure that his audience understands that this formula is not about generating momentary positive emotions, like joy and pleasure. In line with the definition of happiness we are applying in this book, Seligman's formula is about finding

long-term, lasting happiness and satisfaction with life on the whole.

According to Seligman, this lasting happiness is influenced by three primary factors; genetics, life circumstances and our voluntary actions.

Is Happiness Genetic?

Seligman and other researchers suggest that a pre-determined set-range, dictated by genetics, partially governs our happiness. They argue that we might experience spikes and lows that take us outside of our range for a short time, but before long, we end up back within our genetically set range. As Seligman states: "Roughly half of our score on happiness tests is accounted for by the score our biological parents would have gotten had they taken the test".[16] Studies with identical twins who were separated at birth further support this argument. These studies show that identical twins are likely to report similar levels of happiness even years after they had been separated and even though they were raised by different people in different environments.[17] Further reinforcement for the argument that our happiness is partly genetic comes from a 2016 study that claims to have identified genetic variants that are associated with subjective well-being, depressive symptoms and neuroticism.[18] The researchers found three genetic variants for happiness, two that can account for differences in symptoms of depression and 11 that could account for varying degrees of neuroticism. However, the results of either of these studies are not fully conclusive and need to be interpreted with care. In the case of the twin research, not all twins showed similar levels of happiness, suggesting that genetics are not the only factor that impacts our happiness. In the case of the genetic research, the authors themselves point out that there are some limitations to their study and that more research is needed to understand what, if any, genes impact our happiness.

Nevertheless, several other studies suggest that happiness is partly influenced by genetics.[19] However, it has also been shown that our genetics are not the only thing that determines how happy we are. It is very likely that, for genetic reasons, happiness comes more naturally to some of us than others. In that regard, happiness is much like sports. Most of us can learn any sport. If we put in the effort, we might even get very good at it. However, some will have more natural talent while others will have to put in a lot more work to get to the same level — and the Olympics might be out of reach for some of us. However, no amount of genetic talent guarantees a spot at the Olympics. Even the most talented athletes still have to work hard to be the best they can be. Happiness works much the same way. We all can be very happy, but some of us might have to put in more effort than others. That brings us to another critical point. None of the studies into the effects genetics has on happiness (nor most other research areas around happiness) take into account how much effort an individual person has made to improve their happiness. Maybe specific genes are more likely to make us work on ourselves and proactively try to increase our subjective well-being, which then makes us happier, rather than genes directly making us happy.

Overall, genetics are likely to play some role in our happiness. However, I would argue that it is better to look at it as a genetically SUGGESTED range rather than a SET range. It is my firm belief and experience that there are ways to achieve high levels of happiness, even if your genetic range might be relatively low. Some of us just need to work a bit harder to achieve it. Moreover, let's not forget, genetics is only one of the three elements of the happiness formula.

Is Happiness Determined by our Life Circumstances?

The term "life circumstances" summarises everything that happens to us and the overall environment we live in: the country we're born into, our hair and skin colour, how tall we are, what kind of education we have access to, how well we're doing career-wise and how much money we earn, as well as our relationships and our health. This category is also sometimes referred to as "environmental" or "external" factors. These are the aspects of our life that are either entirely or partially out of our control. Some of it is merely up to chance (like the country we were born in or winning the lottery) while other aspects are, partly or fully, dependent on what other people do (like getting married or being successful at work). We all are probably connecting our happiness to our life circumstances in some ways. Things like income, job satisfaction, health, education, age, relationships and similar factors, are such significant parts of our life that it is hard to imagine they do not impact our happiness in some way. Most of us have goals or expectations around our life circumstances that we believe will improve our happiness; get the promotion and be happy, make lots of money and be happy, meet your soulmate and be happy, win a competition and be happy...

In part three of this book, we will review the scientific evidence around how certain life circumstances impact our happiness. You will see that there is evidence suggesting that some aspects, for example, relationships and health, can potentially have a fairly significant impact, while the findings for other areas, like income, career success and education, are more complex and inconclusive.

However, overall it seems as though life circumstances only have a relatively limited impact on our happiness. A renowned researcher in the field, Sonja Lyubomirsky, and her colleagues suggest that life circumstances only make up about 10% of our happiness.[20] It seems as though even significant improvements in life circumstances have only little, and often short-term, impact on how happy we are. For example, studies of lottery winners have shown that the unexpected income leads to an immediate lift in happiness. However, this is momentary. After a relatively short time, lottery winners will report the same or very similar level of happiness as they did before.[21]

Contrary to what most of us might have assumed, it appears that our life circumstances only have a somewhat limited impact on our happiness.

Is Happiness Determined by our Voluntary Actions?

While life circumstances are those factors that are mostly external, voluntary actions are those that are mainly internal. Voluntary actions are the things we choose to do. They are fully within our control. It is completely up to us whether we do them or not. We're not dependent on luck or anyone else to make voluntary actions part of our life. They include activities we decide to make part of our life, like regular exercise, spending more time with friends or family, spending more time in nature, or reading more. Voluntary actions also include how we choose to view the world, to what extent we feel grateful for what we have, how mindful and kind we are and what goals we set for ourselves. Voluntary actions are fully within our control. However, that does not mean that they always come easily and naturally. While we can control them, it can sometimes be challenging to do so and can require practice, patience and determination.

Voluntary actions are also sometimes referred to as internal factors because they are about our inner thoughts, choices and mindset, rather than what happens in the external world around us. As was argued earlier in this chapter, one of the critical differences between long-term happiness and short-term positive emotions is that emotions are a response to what is happening around us while happiness is mostly about how we interpret and respond to what happens. This distinction demonstrates how vital voluntary activities are for our happiness. While we have limited control over what happens in the world, we can control how we respond, and the right voluntary actions can help us respond in a way that is beneficial to us and our happiness. At their core, voluntary actions are about believing that happiness is within our control and that we can find greater happiness by making choices and taking actions that do not rely on anyone else other than ourselves. Voluntary actions are about changing ourselves and our mindset, not about changing the external world around us.

For those of us seeking to increase our happiness and long-term life satisfaction, voluntary actions are where the real magic can happen. It's been estimated that voluntary factors make up around 40% of our overall happiness. Whether or not that specific number is correct, most researchers agree that voluntary actions have significantly more impact on our happiness than life circumstances tend to have. This is especially true for people whose life circumstances provide for the basic needs around comfort and security. We will spend more time discussing a range of voluntary activities in part three of this book, including reviewing what scientific research suggests can help us be happier and how we can put that into action.

In summary, there are three key elements that, combined, make up our lasting happiness; our genetics, our life circumstances and voluntary actions we choose to incorporate into our life. To determine to what extent each of these three factors can help us find happiness or increase it, we need to consider two questions:

1. How much impact does each factor have on our happiness?
2. To what extent can we change and control each factor?

Exactly how much impact each of the three factors has on our happiness is one thing researchers argue about. It is highly likely that it varies from person to person. As a rough indication, Sonja Lyubomirsky and her colleagues have suggested that about 50% is genetic, 10% is our life circumstances and 40% is voluntary activities.[22] However, these numbers are rough estimates at best, and they could potentially vary hugely for different people. Nevertheless, we can assume that for most of us, our genetics and voluntary actions have much more impact on how happy we are than our life circumstances.

Answering the second question is more straightforward. We know we can't control or change our genetics (at least not at the time this book was written). We also know that we have limited control over our life circumstances. While most of them are not completely out of our control, they generally require some amount of luck and the involvement of other people. For example, you can, of course, control how much effort you put into your education, but you are, to some extent, limited by the educational institutions and options available to you based on where you live and what you can afford. Similarly, you can put a lot of effort and energy into having great relationships with your family, but you rely on them to do their part as well, otherwise you won't be able to have that loving connection you're looking for. Voluntary actions, on the other hand, are fully within your control. That doesn't mean they are always easy, but it does mean that it is up to you and the choices you make whether or not you incorporate them into your life.

The diagram below shows what we have to work with in terms of finding and increasing happiness. Our genetics might have a fairly significant impact on our happiness, but we have essentially no control over them. Therefore, we can disregard this factor for the purpose of this book (no point focusing on something we can't change). Environmental factors have some impact on our happiness, and we have some control over them, so there might be some potential there. However, voluntary actions seem to have more impact on our happiness and we also have more control over them, suggesting that they offer more opportunity for us to find and lift our happiness.

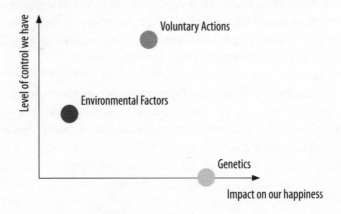

However, with all of this it is important to remember that we are all unique. There is no 'one-size-fits-all' approach to finding happiness and the extent to which each of these three elements impacts our happiness could vary significantly for different people. Part three of this book will take a closer look at both voluntary actions and environmental factors and will outline how they might impact your happiness and what you can do to be happier. What you learn about yourself in the next chapter will enable you to review that information in the context of your individuality and will help you identify the aspects that are most important to **you**.

Your Definition of Happiness

Before we wrap up this chapter, it's time for the first exercise. Consider everything you've learned in this chapter, as well as everything you already knew from your own experience and other books or articles you've read, and write your definition of happiness. Focus on what you want to experience and how you want to feel, more so than specific goals you want to achieve. Your definition can be anything you want it to be, from one word to several sentences or a list of bullet points. It could be a quote, a song, or even an image or drawing. You can be creative, poetic or descriptive — whatever works for you, as long as it represents what happiness means to you.

EXERCISE: YOUR DEFINITION OF HAPPINESS

Write your definition of happiness based on what you know and believe so far.

This chapter should have given you a better understanding of happiness and some of the science and theories behind it. In part three, we will return to happiness to look at what research and common knowledge suggest may or may not make us happier. However, for you to be able to evaluate and analyse that information based on what is relevant to you, it's important to first get to know yourself better.

PART II:

Getting To Know Yourself

"Knowing yourself is the beginning of all wisdom."
ARISTOTLE

HOW CAN we aim to create a happy life if we don't know who we are, what matters most to us and what our core values and beliefs and our strengths and weaknesses are? Research has shown that being true to yourself is key to happiness,[23] but how can you be true to yourself if you don't really know yourself?

These questions are often overlooked in happiness literature and advice. A lot of the time, specific tactics and techniques are recommended to make us happier, or bold statements are made about what does or doesn't make us happy, without any regards to the fact that we are all unique. What might work for some of us won't work for others. For example, studies have suggested that people with rich, busy social lives, who spend little time on their own, tend to be happier than people who spend more time alone.[24] While that might be perfectly true for the majority of people, especially extroverted ones, it might not be true at all for more introverted people. I, for one, spend a lot of time on my own and I am very happy with that. Similarly, religion and spirituality might be excellent sources of happiness for people with open-minded, spiritual personalities while others with more rational characters find scientific facts and techniques more helpful. For us to truly find lasting happiness, we can't just follow generic one-size-fits-all advice.

We need to take into account that what works for the person next to us might not be the right approach for us. As highly regarded positive psychology researcher Sonja Lyubomirsky and her colleagues point out: "Any one particular activity will not help every person become happier. People have enduring strengths, interests, values, and inclinations that undoubtedly predispose them to benefit more from some strategies than others."[25]

Understanding who you are, what your strengths and weaknesses are and what you value most enables you to create a truly meaningful and fulfilling life. It allows you to pursue a career that suits your preference, to find hobbies that motivate and inspire you, to surround yourself with people who bring out the best in you and much more. Knowing yourself well also makes it easier to structure your days, tasks and life in general in a way that works for you, giving you the best chance at being productive and successful. Moreover, let's not forget that having a good understanding of ourselves often also gives us a better understanding of other people, which results in better relationships and makes it easier to engage and interact with people. Most importantly, knowing yourself will help you discover what will truly make you happy and will enable you to develop strategies for finding happiness that are tailored to who you are, thus giving you a much better chance at making it happen.

I consider investing time into getting to know myself and learning about different personalities and personal values one of the best things I've ever done for myself. In many ways, it woke me up. It gave me the insights and awareness to create the amazing life I have today, and it continues to help me make the right decisions. I think most people would agree that my lifestyle is not exactly traditional or conventional. I'm in my mid-30s, I live in a motorhome, I only work part-time and I've no intentions to settle down anytime soon. It might not be normal, but it's 100% right for me. If I hadn't learned about myself, if I hadn't taken the time to understand my personal values and strengths, I would probably still be unhappy, overweight, working 50 hours a week and feeling alone and disconnected. For me, a big part of learning about personality and values was understanding my uniqueness and individuality. It made me realise that one-size-fits-all hardly ever works, and that almost everything in life needs to be tailored to who we are and what we value. It enabled me to stop following mainstream advice, and instead learn to listen to myself and do what's right for me, regardless of what everyone else is doing. Knowing myself and understanding the different personality types has made everything in my life easier and better and I believe it can do the same for you.

This chapter will help you get a better understanding of who you are. By learning more about yourself now, you can then review what you learn about happiness throughout this book in the context of who you are and what makes YOU happy (as opposed to what tends to make the average person happy). There are three key areas we will work through in this chapter.

1. Understanding your personality
2. Identifying your personal values
3. Highlighting your personal strengths and weaknesses

It is important to understand that the focus of this chapter is to get to know yourself—not to criticise or change yourself. Therefore, I urge you to be as open-minded and honest as possible. Don't be afraid to admit weaknesses or aspects of your personality you might not like right away. Sometimes it's the things we don't appreciate at first that turn out to be our biggest strengths. We will spend some time at the end of the chapter looking specifically at those things you've learned about yourself that you don't like or consider weaknesses to try and find out if maybe there is something positive in them after all. For now, just be real and honest and try not to judge things you learn about yourself as good or bad.

This chapter is highly interactive with several exercises, so get ready. If you get right into it and stay open-minded, I promise it will be a lot of fun. I will refer to online resources several times, so I suggest you work through this chapter when you have some quiet time and access to the internet. I apologise if you do not have internet access. I would have loved to include the full resources and exercises in this book. However, you probably wouldn't have been able to carry it (or it wouldn't have fitted on to your e-reader). I want to provide you with the best available assets and materials, and this seemed to be the best way to do so. However, I have, wherever possible, included summaries and 'offline options' that enable you to get a lot of value out of this chapter even if you don't have internet access.

One more thing about the tests and exercises included in this chapter. It's important to remember that these are subjective and might not always be 100% accurate. In general, you know yourself better than any test ever will. I suggest you take the exercises and tests as sources of inspiration and guidance, not as set truths. However, these tests can often highlight aspects of yourself you might not have been aware of until now. Furthermore, much research has shown that we often tend to overestimate our own skills and strengths, and that we might not be as good at judging ourselves as we would like to think. Therefore, I encourage you to give everything a fair chance and consider the possibility that it might be true before you discard it. Just because something doesn't feel familiar right away, doesn't mean it's not true. The more open-minded you are as you work through this chapter, the more value you will get out of it.

Ready to get to know the real you?

Your Personality

The first step of getting to know yourself is learning more about your personality. Everything that comes after this — your values and beliefs and your strengths and weaknesses — are usually closely related to your personality, so this is an excellent place to start.

We all have a distinctive personality. Our personality determines who we are internally; how we feel, what we think and how we perceive and interact with the world around us. In general, personality is defined as "the combination of characteristics or qualities that form an individual's distinctive character." By definition, personalities are unique — like fingerprints, we all have them, but no two are the same. Our personality largely determines things like how outgoing we are, whether we are careful or if we like to take risks, whether we tend to be optimistic or pessimistic, if we like to make plans or be spontaneous, how creative we are and much more.

We all have a unique personality from the day we are born. One of the most fascinating things for me over the last few years has been watching my friends' kids grow up. There are several girls that are roughly the same age, and even when they were infants you could tell that they had different personalities. Two of them are sisters born only 18 months apart into the same family and roughly the same environment, but their characters couldn't be more different. One is often quiet and seems to be internally focused. She can play by herself for hours, and you can often see her sit somewhere and think or daydream. You often wonder what is going on in that amazing mind of hers. The other one is a little rocket. She is loud and wild, always running around and wanting to engage with people. They are both amazing little humans in their own unique ways but definitely have distinctive personalities. I'm sure you can think of similar examples among the kids you know. While personalities develop further as kids grow up, we all have some level of unique personality from the day we are born.

A critical aspect of personality is that it is relatively consistent — especially once we've reached maturity. That does not mean that we always feel or behave exactly the same way in any given situation. However, there usually is a recognisable pattern and regularity to how we act and feel. For example, someone with a fairly cautious personality would evaluate all new situations carefully, be acutely aware of the risks and identify potential problems early in any given situation. The same person would not suddenly jump into a new adventure without a care in the world, feeling thoroughly excited and optimistic. They might decide to take more risks, and they might look like they are jumping in head over heels, but inside they would still worry and be on the lookout for problems. However, it's important to distinguish between personality and situational behaviour. Just because you are feeling anxious in a specific situation doesn't mean that you're an anxious personality. Just think of someone who feels anxious and worries a lot when faced with the idea of climbing up a high tower but doesn't usually worry much in any other situation in life. This person doesn't have an anxious personality, they just have a fear of heights. Similarly, someone might care deeply about a small number of close friends or family, but that doesn't automatically mean they have a caring personality. On the other hand, feeling high levels of empathy and responsibility towards people in general, no matter who they are, indicates a caring personality. As we will learn soon, most personality traits represent a range and we might express certain characteristics more strongly in some situations than others, but overall, personality traits are those thoughts, feelings and behaviours we have and show consistently and regularly regardless of the specific situation.

Personality explains why different people behave and respond very differently in the same situation. The same stressful situation brings some people to the brink of tears while others are calm and composed. Some people crumble under stress while others do their best work. The same book is interesting and inspiring to some while others find it irrelevant and boring. The thought of an upcoming trip to an exotic location makes some people buzz with excitement while others mostly worry about all the things that could go wrong and all the details they need to organise. Someone new moving into the neighbourhood causes some to bake cakes and throw a welcome party while others observe the newbies suspiciously from behind the curtain for a few days before they decide to say hello. Personality, by definition, means that no two people are the same. Our different personalities are what draw us together sometimes (opposites attract) and what drives us crazy at other times. In many situations, different personalities make groups more productive, fun and successful but at the same time, a lot of interpersonal conflicts are primarily caused by our different personalities causing us to interpret and approach things differently.

Personality and Happiness

Given that personality makes us who we are and has a massive impact on how we live our lives and how we engage with others, it is worth looking at how personality impacts happiness. As it turns out, personality is a factor many happiness researchers have considered. Most of this research has focused on understanding if, and how, individual personality traits impact happiness. In short, researchers set out to investigate whether people with certain personality traits are more likely to be happy than others. While studies have shown different results, most researchers, practitioners and thinkers in the field do agree that there is a correlation between happiness and personality. Two traits, in particular, have been shown repeatedly to be reliable predictors of happiness: extroversion and neuroticism.

EXTROVERSION

Extroversion is the term used to describe the tendency to prefer being surrounded by people over spending time alone. Extroverts are people who thrive in social situations and who feel energised when spending lots of time around people. Introverts, on the other hand, are people who need less external stimulation, often find spending lots of time with people exhausting and draw energy from spending time alone. An important distinction to make is that extroversion and introversion are not the same as being outgoing or shy. Instead, it's mostly about how we get energy. Extroverts gain energy from spending time with people while introverts get energy from spending time alone (and often find spending time around people exhausting — which doesn't mean that they don't enjoy it). As with all personality traits, there is a scale. While most of us have a clear tendency to be either more extroverted or more introverted, there is a big difference between someone who is slightly more introverted than extroverted and someone who is almost completely on the introverted extreme of the scale. We will learn more about this a bit later when we discuss specific personality types.

Several studies have suggested that, on average, extroverted people tend to be happier than introverted people.[26] [27] [28] One possible explanation for this is that extroverts are more likely to spend time with people and engage in social activities, which increases happiness. Another possible reason is that introverts, by definition, spend more time in their heads, analysing and interpreting things which might make them more prone to doubts and negative thinking. It's also possible that finding happiness is harder for introverts because many of us live in extroverted environments. It's estimated that up to two-thirds of the population in the western world are extroverts, putting introverts in the minority. Many western societies are designed by and for extroverts. Often, introverted behaviour is seen as 'weird' or 'wrong' and is discouraged. Think about the child that plays quietly in her room until the mother comes to ask what's wrong and why she isn't playing outside with all the other kids. Think about the teenager who doesn't like big parties and is called lame and no-fun (or even worse things) by his peers. Think about the employee who prefers to have time to think independently instead of engaging in team brainstorming sessions but is told she needs to be more engaged and outspoken. Of course, there are also times where extroverts are forced to be more introverted, like when it's time to work quietly and independently at school or work. However, on the whole, extroverted behaviour is often more expected and accepted than introverted behaviour. With that in mind, it might not be overly surprising that introverts, on average, report lower levels of happiness.

Regardless, it is important to understand that introverts can be just as happy, if not more so, than extroverts. I'm living proof of that, and I know many more introverts that are very happy people. From my own experience I believe that, for introverts even more so than extroverts, self-awareness and self-knowledge are crucial to finding happiness. It's likely that the introvert's version of happiness looks different from the average person's idea of happiness. Learning about ourselves, understanding what it means to be introverted, as well as getting a better understanding of other aspects of personality, are hugely beneficial in designing a life that will make us happy. I believe that when it comes to the pursuit of happiness, introverts have many advantages that are often underestimated. For starters, we are usually very thoughtful and deliberate people, meaning we can analyse information independently and make the right decision for us without being pulled in a million different directions by external factors and other people's opinions. Maybe even more importantly though, we do not rely on external stimulation to be happy. One of the best things about being an introvert is the ability to be comfortable on our own. For extroverts, interaction with people is vital to finding happiness. If you take that away from them, they will struggle. They are reliant on other people to feel happy while introverts can achieve the same feeling with much less input from others.

So if you already know, or find out once we get to the exercises, that you are an introvert, don't feel like you're doomed or will never be able to be as happy as more extroverted people. Remember, all the study findings are only averages. In each study, there were happy introverts and unhappy extroverts. Being introverted is no reason not to be happy. Your path to happiness might just be a bit different.

NEUROTICISM

The term neuroticism is used to describe people who are prone to moodiness, sadness and who are generally emotionally unstable. Those people who are high in neuroticism tend to experience frequent stress, worry a lot and regularly experience dramatic shifts in mood. They tend to be in a negative and anxious state of mind more often than people who score lower in neuroticism. However, we have to be careful not to confuse neuroticism with merely experiencing negative feelings occasionally. Negative emotions are part of life. We all experience them. If something sad or frustrating happens in your life and you experience the related negative emotions, you're not automatically a neurotic personality. Neuroticism is about the tendency to emotionally overreact. People who score high in neuroticism don't just experience negative emotions when something sad or upsetting happens. Feelings like worry, fear, anger, frustration, guilt and other negative emotions tend to be their default response no matter what happens. They are the kind of people that can take compliments and well-intended statements and turn them into upsetting insults. They go on an amazing holiday and afterward talk about all the things that went wrong and that they didn't enjoy. They get a fantastic job offer, but their first thoughts are about all the stress of moving to a new city and all the things that could go wrong. Their partner is home late once, and in their heads, they fabricate a story where s/he has an affair and is about to leave them. Most people who score high in neuroticism feel stressed very quickly and are less likely to handle that stress well. They also often feel lonely and disconnected and easily feel threatened by relatively minor frustrations and challenges.

Extremely high scores in neuroticism are problematic and can lead to mental disorders, depression and chronic anxiety. If you find that you score very high in neuroticism when we get to the exercises, it might be worth considering talking to a mental health professional or seeking help in other ways. However, less extreme scores do not always have to be all bad news. Neurotic people are often the first to see potential problems and challenges, which can make them a real asset at work as well as in our social lives (who wouldn't like an early warning about what could go wrong?). They also are often more cautious and can be an excellent balance for someone who tends to get into trouble by taking too many risks. Nevertheless, several researchers have suggested that people who score higher than average in neuroticism tend to be less happy, on average, than those who score low in neuroticism.[29] [30] [31]

However, as with extroversion, there are a few factors to consider and having a relatively high neuroticism score does not automatically mean you can't be happy. First of all, the research findings did not conclude that all people low in neuroticism are happy and those high in neuroticism are unhappy. Instead, they merely suggest that the former, on average, tend to be happier, which does not mean the latter are not happy. Secondly, as always, the research reports on averages, and there are exceptions. There are people who score high in neuroticism and happiness, just like there are others who score low in both areas. Maybe the most important aspect though is that most experts in the field do believe that neuroticism is something we can work on and improve over time. Someone who scores high in neuroticism is probably not going to change completely overnight, but there are a number of things that have been shown to decrease neuroticism over time. Mindfulness and regular exercise are two activities that have been reported to reduce neuroticism. We will discuss both of them and their positive impact on our overall happiness later in the book.

In addition to neuroticism and extroversion, researchers have also looked at how other personality traits impact happiness, but findings have not convincingly suggested any other strong correlations. However, it is possible that a range of other personality traits and nuances do impact our happiness. Most researchers are using the Big Five Model of personality traits, which we will discuss soon, to assess the correlation between personality and happiness. That means, they are limiting themselves to five distinctive personality traits. While these five have been argued to reflect what the majority of our character is made up of, it is likely that different combinations and nuances impact our lives and happiness in different ways.

Furthermore, most existing research takes a fairly narrow view, usually comparing our personality traits with our level of happiness at a specific point in time or over a relatively short period. This has led to insights around the impact of certain personality traits on happiness. However, one question that science has not yet been able to answer is what is most likely to make individual personality types happier. For example, while research suggests that, on average, extroverted people are happier than introverted, we know very little about what is most likely to lift the happiness of an introverted person and whether it would do the same for an extrovert. Similarly, we know that people with high neuroticism are, on average, less happy than those with low neuroticism, but science and research can't tell us much about what makes a neurotic person happier and how that might be different to what makes a less neurotic person happier. The same is true with any of the other personality traits and types. We know a bit about how they relate to happiness in the average population but hardly anything about which, if any, techniques and tactics are most likely to have a positive impact on the happiness of people with certain personality traits. In short, there is no exact science that can tell you, if you're personality type A, here is what will make you happy and here is what will make you miserable and if you're personality type B, it's this. Even if researchers would set out to investigate this, I would be very surprised if they would find exact results given the complexity of personality. We are all unique. Even people of the same broad personality type who have similar values will be different in some ways. That means, when it comes to understanding what will actually make us happier, we can't rely on science or experts to give us the answers, we need to figure it out ourselves — which is what this book is all about.

Can Personality Change?

One of the big questions around personality is to what extent it can change and evolve based on our experiences, life circumstances and actions. Does personality change or is it set for life? The answer is not a simple yes or no. Most theories agree that our personalities are primarily shaped by a combination of our genetics and experiences we have at a very young age and that significant portions of our personalities are shaped during our childhood years. However, that does not mean that our personalities won't and can't change any more once we've reached adulthood. In fact, research has suggested that certain personality traits are likely to change as we get older. For example, on average, we tend to be less extroverted and open as we get older but more agreeable.[32] While this might not apply to everyone, it does indicate that there can be some flexibility and fluidity in our personalities.

Another important aspect to consider in this context is that assessing whether or not we have certain personality traits is hardly ever a simple yes or no question. Instead, we need to look at it as a range where we are a particular personality type to a certain degree. For example, it's not as simple as saying you're either an extrovert or an introvert and assuming that all introverts are equally introverted and all extroverts are equally extroverted. Instead, we can be introverted or extroverted to degrees. Think about it as a percentage where 100% is being extremely extroverted and 0% is being extremely introverted. Most of us are neither 100 nor 0%. We're somewhere in the middle. From a personality theory and research perspective, everyone who scores less than 50% is considered an introvert and everyone who scores more than 50% is regarded as an extrovert. Similarly, consider openness, another personality trait we will learn more about soon. You're neither open or not.

Instead, you might score 60% or 30% in openness. When we think about whether personality can change, it seems unlikely that someone moves from 20% to 80% in any personality trait throughout life — unless he or she suffers from major traumatic experiences or potential brain damage. However, smaller changes, like moving from 45 to 55%, are a lot more likely.

It is also possible that different aspects of our personality are more prominent at different stages in our life, which can impact how we view ourselves. For example, during our teenage years and early 20s, we're still getting to know ourselves and the world, we're learning and experimenting and we're 'trying on' different versions of ourselves. During this phase, we might consider ourselves as very open. As we get older, we are more settled and might realise that our true personality is less open, and that what we went through earlier in our life was just a phase. Even though our true character might not have changed much at all, our perception and awareness of it have changed, which can make us feel like we are a different person.

Another aspect to consider is effort. What if we put in effort? What if we identify specific aspects of our personality and work towards changing them? That is the question Nathan Hudson and Chris Fraley set out to answer.[33] They conducted two experiments with around 130 university students participating in each. At the beginning of the 16-week experiments, the participants were asked to decide which personality traits they wanted to change and to come up with strategies for how they might achieve that change. Participants attended weekly online sessions where they were reminded of their goals and completed writing assignments to measure their progress. The personality of each participant was measured via the Big Five model both at the beginning and at the end of the study. The findings from both experiments showed that participants were, in fact, able to change their personalities. For example, participants who wanted to become more extroverted did rate higher in extroversion at the end of the study than they had done in the beginning and also reported more daily activities that matched this personality change. However, the researchers also point out that the changes in personality were fairly minimal in both experiments, further supporting the previous argument that we are unlikely to experience extreme changes. Nevertheless, the study results are encouraging for those of us who want to change aspects of our personality, and it is possible that putting in the effort for more than 16 weeks (the lengths of the above experiments) would lead to more significant changes.

The argument that personality can change is also supported by Dr Chris Boyce, from the University of Manchester's School of Psychological Sciences and his colleagues.[34] Boyce and his team analysed data from 7500 Australians who had answered questions about their personality and overall life satisfaction twice, with four years in between. The goal of the study was to find out if personality changes over time and if so, how these changes impact life satisfaction compared to the impact external factors like changes in income, employment or marital status have. The results are very encouraging for those hoping personality can change. Not only did they find that personality could and did change over the four-year time span, they also found that these personality changes had a positive impact on life satisfaction — twice as much as the external factors did.

While it is likely that some aspects of our personality are genetic and do not change, it seems that there are aspects we can change, at least to some degree. For the context of this book, that is good news given the direct correlation between personality and happiness. However, from my personal experience, I would argue that when it comes to increasing happiness, accepting and leveraging your character might be more valuable than trying to change it. Personality factors should generally not be considered 'good' or 'bad', and I think the notion that certain personality types are better and happier than others is problematic. I argue that a better approach would be to accept that your personality impacts what does or doesn't make you happy under the assumption that all personalities can be equally happy — their path to get there is just different. I'm an introvert. Despite what research suggests, I'm very happy, and I'm sure I'm happier than many extroverts around me. However, that wasn't always the case. For a long time, I was not happy with my life, I often felt out of place, disconnected and like I didn't fit in. I haven't found happiness by setting out to change my personality to become more extroverted. What helped me find happiness was learning about my personality, learning to listen to myself, learning about my strengths and how to leverage them and then designing a life that makes me happy — even though that is probably quite different to the kind of life most people would choose. Today, I consider being an introvert one of my biggest strengths. I'm happy, not despite being an introvert but because I'm an introvert. However, I also do say that part of becoming a happy introvert has been finding a small group of close friends and being more socially active with them, which could be interpreted as being more extroverted than I used to be before, so there might be an element of personality change as well.

Regardless of whether you want to lift your happiness by changing your personality or by understanding, accepting and leveraging it, you first need to learn more about what personality type you are and what natural preferences you have. To do so, we will now get to the more interactive and fun part of this chapter. In the following, we will look at two common methods to determine your personality type, and you'll get the chance to do the tests to find out what you're made of.

Personality Types

There are countless ways to determine and analyse different personality types. Over the years, many researchers, theorists and authors have come up with different ways to dissect, order and interpret our personalities and have come up with models and tests that help us determine our personality type and understand what that means. In this book we will focus on two specific personality models: The Big Five or Five Factor model and the Myers-Briggs Type Indicator (MBTI®). These two have been chosen for specific reasons. The Big Five is the model most commonly used by researchers to study personality in the context of happiness. As we will review a number of research studies that used the Big Five model later on, it makes sense to get familiar with the terminology and to find out what your Big Five personality type is. The MBTI tool, on the other hand, is very popular with the general population and is often used in workplaces and self-development programmes. While similar in some ways, they take a very different approach in other areas — especially when it comes to analysing individual people's overall personalities. With one being more academic and the other being easier to understand and interpret, the combination of the two should enable you to get a good idea of different personality traits and your specific type and preferences.

A WORD OF WARNING

A quick word of caution before we dive into personality tests. The purpose of these tests in general, and especially in the context of this book, is not to label yourself or put yourself in a box, or even worse, label others. This is a really important point, so I urge you to take a minute to take this in. The goal here is not to give your personality a name or a label. The goal simply is to get to know yourself better. These tests, their results and concepts can help you do that. However, make sure you see them as indications, inspirations and guidance, not as facts. Personality tests are not like tests at school where you either fail or pass and you get a grade that tells you exactly how well you did. Think about it more like our physical traits. For example, we often 'label' people by their hair colour. Someone is either blonde, brunette, black or ginger. However, consider how many different shades of each colour there are and how little our hair colour tells someone about our overall appearance. A woman with dark blonde hair might be called blonde by some and brunette by others. If you would describe someone with 'she's blonde,' your audience might have a rough idea about her hair colour, but there is no way they could pick her out of a crowd based on that description (unless everyone else has black hair). Personality traits are similar. They can mean slightly different things to different people, and one individual trait says fairly little about who someone really is. So don't get too caught up with the individual terms, types and labels. Focus on their overall meaning and descriptions and analyse for yourself what aspects most apply to you.

Furthermore, it is essential to understand there are a number of factors that might impact how you 'score' in personality tests other than just your natural personality. The environment you grew up in, experiences you've had during your childhood as well as more recently, the main people and role models in your life (past and present), what state of mind you're in when you're doing the test and many other factors impact your results. For example, you might have a natural preference for a certain personality trait, but all other members of your family prefer the opposite extreme, which means you grew up in an environment where 'normal' was not your natural preference. This would very likely have had an impact on your personality development and is likely to impact how you respond to certain questions in the tests. Similarly, we are all influenced by society telling us how we should feel, think and act, which can make it hard to differentiate between who we really are and who we think we should be. Given all of these influences, I encourage you to take your time with the following exercises, listen to yourself and answer questions honestly. Focus on how you actually feel or think, not how you think you should feel or think. Remember that no one other than yourself will see your answers (unless you choose to share them).

It is also perfectly normal to feel like you're a different personality in different situations. I'm a very different person at work from the one outside of work. At my job, I'm organised, structured, outspoken and often take a lead role. When I'm with my friends, I tend to be a lot more easy-going, spontaneous, and am usually happy for others to take the lead. Whenever personality tests ask questions around whether I'm organised or easy-going, I'm often unsure how to respond. This seems to be a common issue. I've heard from many other people that they often find certain questions demand alternate answers in different situations. If you experience this challenge as you proceed with the personality types below, I have two suggestions for you. First, try to look beyond your superficial behaviour and look for your underlying motivation, thoughts and feelings instead. Think about how you really feel in certain situations and what your actual thinking patterns and approach are. For example, while I am a lot more easy-going outside of work and don't actively make plans, I often catch myself planning unconsciously in my head. I map out the day in my head by thinking about how long activities will take, what time they might finish, what I might do afterward and what time I'll be back home in the evening. At work, I do this a lot more proactively and usually have a written schedule and plan for projects that I like to stick to. Outside of work it's just in my head and I'm less set on sticking to the plan, but I do still plan (just quietly in my head). When it comes down to deciding whether I'm more organised or more easy-going, I often feel like I'm one in some situations and the other in different situations, but when I really pay attention to my thoughts and approach, I realise that I am planning and organising even when I'm in my more easy-going situations. It might be similar for you, so if you find yourself faced with questions where you feel you're either in different environments, spend a bit of time thinking about how you really feel, think and act (consciously and unconsciously), and you might be able to identify your true preference. If that doesn't work for you, my second suggestion is to focus on the situation where you feel more real and comfortable. For example, as much as I enjoy my work, I do think there is more pressure to act a certain way and I also often put myself under pressure to perform at my best and deliver outstanding work. Outside of work I feel less pressure and constraint and feel more comfortable to be my true self. Therefore, if in doubt even after analysing my underlying thought-patterns, I generally assume my outside-of-work preferences are a stronger indication of my real personality (unless of course the question specifically relates to work or to situations I'm much more likely to experience at work). While this second suggestion might help you answer questions where you feel you have a preference for either option at different times, I would strongly recommend starting by trying to figure it out using the first suggestion. The reason for this is that the first suggestion encourages you to carefully evaluate your thoughts, feelings and behaviour and it might make you discover aspects you weren't aware of before. Jumping ahead to the second approach, because it seems easier, means you risk missing those hidden nuances and details of your personality and could end up with a distorted view of who you really are.

With all of that out of the way, let's start looking at different personality types and preferences.

The Big Five

The Big Five, also often called the Five Factor Model, has its roots in academic research. Over several decades, researchers have developed and refined models that would enable them to determine someone's personality and then analyse it in the context of other factors — including happiness. Since the late 20th century, more and more researchers have agreed that personality can ultimately be narrowed down to five specific traits. In the now commonly accepted Big Five model, these five traits are openness, conscientiousness, extroversion, agreeableness and neuroticism (OCEAN). An important aspect of the Big Five model is that these traits represent a range between two extremes. The model is not intended to give yes or no answers (you are open, but you're not agreeable). Instead, its goal is to indicate where on the scale between, for example, being extremely open and not being open at all, someone sits. Let's take a look at each of these five factors. As you read through the descriptions below, I encourage you to rate your preference for each of the five factors to start getting an idea of your personality.

OPENNESS
Openness is also often referred to as Openness to Experience because it refers to a person's willingness and excitement around engaging in new activities and experiences. Someone who scores high in openness is more likely to be excited about new opportunities and exploring unconventional thinking and beliefs. They are often inventive people who prefer variety over

routine and thrive in intense and euphoric situations. A person who scores low in openness, on the other hand, is more likely to feel nervous and uncomfortable in unknown circumstances and tends to be more cautious and sceptical about new ideas and beliefs. They are likely to prefer routine and familiar environments and are often more pragmatic people.

Where on the Openness scale do you think you are?

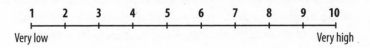

CONSCIENTIOUSNESS

Conscientiousness refers to the desire to do one's jobs well and thoroughly, with a high level of awareness of actions and their consequences. People who score high in conscientiousness are usually very self-motivated, goal-oriented, punctual, dependable and tidy. They often set ambitious goals and are highly motivated to achieve them. They don't shy away from hard work and are determined to succeed in every aspect of their life. However, they do often struggle in less organised environments with lots of ambiguity. People who score lower in conscientiousness are usually less organised and are more impulsive and spontaneous. They are often late and need more external pressure to be motivated and achieve goals. They are also less aware of consequences and often act on a last-minute whim.

Where on the Conscientiousness scale do you think you are?

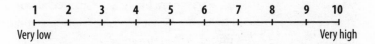

EXTROVERSION

The extroversion trait in the Big Five model has two sides to it, one that is readily observable from the outside and one that's a lot more internal. Firstly, extroversion is associated with outgoing, confident behaviour. Secondly, extroversion refers to drawing energy and stimulation from being surrounded by people while the opposite, introversion, refers to drawing energy from solitude and needing less external stimulus. People who score high in extroversion are usually very social individuals who like spending time with people, enjoy meeting new people and generally tend to have large social circles. They are often talkative and good at engaging others in conversations. They thrive in social environments but often find it hard to spend time alone and motivate themselves without external incentives. People who score low in extroversion in the Big Five model are referred to as introverts. Introverts tend to prefer spending time alone over spending much time around people, and they often have a smaller, but very close, group of friends. Introverts often tend to be quieter and can be shy around new people. However, it's important to note that extroversion and introversion are not the same as being outgoing or shy. Introverts often don't engage with new people not because they are too scared or insecure, but because they don't want to invest the energy.

Where on the Extroversion scale do you think you are?

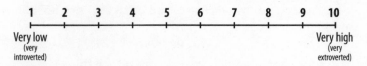

AGREEABLENESS

In the Big Five model, the term agreeableness is used to describe someone's tendency to be friendly, supportive and open towards others and new ideas. People who score high in agreeableness are usually very compassionate and co-operative, always happy to support and help others and tend to trust people easily. They generally enjoy teamwork and do well within teams. They can be considered more likeable than less agreeable people which is not to say that they actually are better people. While often perceived as likeable, their tendency to avoid conflict and arguments at all cost can be problematic in groups and relationships. People who score low in agreeableness are usually less concerned with pleasing others and are less focused on being likeable and making friends. However, this does not mean they aren't liked or don't have friends, it simply means they are less focused on pleasing others. For less agreeable people, their own interests and goals are more important than the needs of others, which can make them seem selfish at times. They are often competitive and can be argumentative. Interestingly, agreeableness is one of the factors in the Big Five model that has been shown to be fluid and often increases as we get older.

Where on the Agreeableness scale do you think you are?

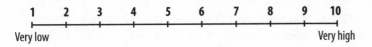

NEUROTICISM

We've already discussed neuroticism earlier in this chapter. In the context of the Big Five model, it is mainly about how emotionally stable someone is, whereby neuroticism is used to describe someone who is relatively unstable. People who score high in neuroticism often worry a lot and have a tendency to overthink, overreact and see negative aspects before positive ones. They often find it more difficult to deal with everyday challenges and stresses and can easily become frustrated and angry if things don't go their way. They also often feel threat-ened and might have a tendency to take criticism very person-ally. People who score low in neuroticism, on the other hand, tend to be more emotionally stable and less prone to worry. They tend to be good at dealing with stressful situations and generally see the positive before the negative.

Where on the Neuroticism scale do you think you are?

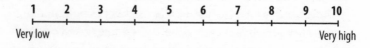

EXERCISE: WHAT'S YOUR BIG
FIVE PERSONALITY?

Now that you have a basic understanding of the five traits of the model, it's time to find out how you score on each factor. There are two ways to do this. You might want to do both exercises or just pick one. The second option requires access to the internet so if you don't currently have that, stick with the first one. At an absolute minimum, I strongly suggest you give yourself a score for each trait if you haven't already. While this is a very limited view, if you are considerate and honest, it does give you an indication of what your tendency for each person-ality trait might be. However, working through the exercises below will provide you with much additional insight into your personality, so I recommend taking the time to work through at least one of them in detail.

EXERCISE I: THE FRIENDS AND FAMILY METHOD

1. If you haven't already, go back to the previous pages, and give yourself a score for each of the five factors. Make sure you

think about what the individual traits mean and how you are most likely to behave, think and feel. Be honest!

2. Ask at least four other people to give you feedback and a rating on each of the five traits. This can be friends, family members, colleagues or other people who know you relatively well and engage with you regularly. The workbook includes a template you can give to people to provide their rating (you can download the workbook for free at www.lisa-jansen.com/workbook). Make sure you pick people who are currently part of your life (not someone who knew you well two years ago but doesn't spend much time with you any more). You can ask more than four people. If you find that the responses from the initial four people you asked are very different from each other, it's probably a good idea to get input from more people to even things out a bit.

3. Look for outliers. For example, if you asked four people for feedback and three of them gave you the same or very similar scores, and the fourth person gave you a very different score, this is called an outlier and is worth a closer look. It is essentially up to you if you keep the score or remove it. Think about whether it would be a better reflection of your personality to keep it or not. Does the person know you well? Do they maybe have a different perspective from everyone else? Have they maybe misunderstood what the trait means or how the scoring works? Investigate and consider. If you feel the score is likely to be inaccurate, remove it (don't include it when working through the below steps).

4. For each trait, add all the scores you got from others (not including the one you gave yourself and ones you have removed as 'outliers') and then divide it by the total number

of scores you added up. This will give you an average score for each trait. The more people you've asked for feedback and the more diverse this group is (family, friends, colleagues) the more accurate are the scores likely to be in determining your tendency for each of the Big Five personality traits.

5. Compare the average scores you got from friends and family to the ones you gave yourself. If you find significant differences for a trait (or several), it might be worth exploring this a bit more. Consider who you asked for feedback. Are they people that tend to experience only one specific side of you? For example, it's likely that you behave differently among your family from how you behave with strangers or at work. So if all or most of your scores are from family members, that might be a one-sided and limited view of your personality. If you did ask a diverse group of people, ask some of them why they scored you that way. That information might help you better assess if they have misunderstood something about your personality (or the questions) or if you maybe need to adjust your view of yourself slightly.

6. Based on the steps above, decide on your 'final' score for each of the five traits. Make sure you consider the scores you got from others and be honest with yourself. However, remember, it's your personality, and in the end, nobody knows you better than you know yourself.

EXERCISE 2: THE ONLINE TEST

1. If you haven't already, go back to the previous pages and give yourself a score for each of the five factors. Make sure you think about what the individual traits mean and how you are most likely to behave, think and feel. Be honest!

2. Go online and find a Big Five personality test. Below are three I recommend but there are many others to pick from if you don't like the look of these. You can do several of them if you wish to.

   a. **The Truity Test: https://www.truity.com** You will find the Big Five personality test under 'Take a Test' in the menu. The Landing page shows a price of US $29, but you can actually get to your results for free. When you get to the end of it, you will be asked to create an account. Ignore this and click on the 'No thanks, just show my results.' Make sure you copy the results into a Word document or similar and save them somewhere so you can access them again later.

   b. **Open Psychometrics Project: https://openpsychometrics. org** This one does not look as flash as the above, but it works just as well and is entirely free.

   c. **Psychology Today: https://www.psychologytoday.com** This test comes with a price tag of US $6.95 (at the time of writing). The test is well hidden on the Psychology Today website. The quickest way to find it is a Google search for 'Psychology Today Big Five Test.' The reason I'm including it here despite it not being free is that I personally found it particularly interesting and accurate. You get a very detailed report that gives you a good overview of how you scored on each trait and what the individual scores, as well as the combination of all your five scores, mean. I am in no way associated with Psychology Today and have nothing to gain from anyone purchasing this test.

3. Once you have your results, take some time to review and analyse them. Do you agree with them? Are they similar to the scores you gave yourself? If not, and you've only done one of the above tests so far, it might be worth trying another one to get some more clarity.

4. Based on what you've learned from the online test(s) as well as your own score, decide on your 'final' score for each of the five traits.

At this point, you should start to develop a better idea of who you are. The Big Five model is a great way to get an initial understanding of your personality based on the five primary traits. However, one of the limitations for ordinary people like you and me is that it can be hard to analyse our results. While it is relatively easy to understand our preferences and tendencies for the five traits individually, the model doesn't tell us much about what the combination of our five scores means. One of the reasons I like the Psychology Today test is because they do give you an overall summary. However, the other tests and the model, in general, don't tell us, for example, what the combination of a high score in Openness and a low score in Agreeableness means for our overall personality. It's up to us to put the pieces together and figure it out. This is why I like the Myers-Briggs Type Indicator (MBTI®) test in combination with the Big Five model.

Myers-Briggs Type Indicator

The Myers-Briggs Type Indicator (MBTI®) finds its origins in the theories developed by Swiss psychiatrist and psychoanalyst Carl Jung at the beginning of the 20th century. Jung explored the idea that four main psychological functions — sensation, intuition, feeling and thinking — determine how we experience and engage with the world around us. Jung's work and publications would later become the foundation on which mother and daughter duo Katharine Cook Briggs and Isabel Briggs Myers developed the MBTI. Their goal was to make Jung's theories and concepts understandable and applicable for the general public. With that in mind, they created a tool that would help people thrive by understanding their own and others' personalities and enable them to leverage each other's strengths. Today, the MBTI is one of the most widely used personality tests. While less popular with scientific researchers than the Big Five model, the MBTI is frequently used in workplace team building and professional development exercises as well as personal growth workshops and relationship counselling and courses.

The MBTI is built around four opposing concepts, often referred to as dichotomies. Each of the eight extremes is associated with a letter, and the test helps people identify their four-letter personality type. The four dichotomies with their two opposing concepts result in a total of 16 distinctive personality types. However, as with the Big Five model, the MBTI views personalities on a spectrum. Only a very few people are on the extreme ends of any of the four dichotomies. Most people are somewhere along the scale, with a slight or moderate preference for one extreme over the other. Numerous authors have dedicated entire books to the MBTI and what is referred to as Type Watching — the ability to identify the MBTI's personality preferences in oneself and others. There are also many resources available online for those who wish to learn more about the MBTI and the 16 personality types. For the purpose of this book, we will keep it limited to a short description of the four dichotomies and will then jump into exercises to help you identify your type.

THE FOUR MBTI DICHOTOMIES

1. **What world do you prefer:**
   Extroversion (E) vs. Introversion (I)

We've already talked about extroversion and introversion in the previous sections. In the context of the MBTI, extroversion and introversion are seen as the part of our personality that indicates which world we prefer; the external world with other people and things or our internal world with our own thoughts and ideas. As we've discussed before, extroverts tend to be more outgoing, enjoy spending time with lots of people and often prefer group work and brainstorming sessions over working on their own. Extroverts often solve problems by talking about them with other people. Introverts, on the other hand, usually prefer spending more time alone, tend to think things through on their own before they talk or act, prefer having a few close friends over a large social circle and generally need less encouragement and motivation from the external world.

Understanding where you are on the spectrum can help you design your life based on your preference, which will ultimately help you lead a more fulfilling and happier life. For example, if you are an introvert, it's critical that you create space for yourself in your life. Whether at home, at work, or with your friends, it will be necessary for you to have 'time-outs' and the chance to reflect and think on your own. If you are an extrovert, you'll want to make sure you have lots of opportunities to engage with others and get the external stimulation and encouragement you need. Of course, to which extent you need either, space or stimulation, depends on how introverted or extroverted you are.

Before you rate your level for introversion or extroversion, remember that it's not about being shy or confident. While many extroverts come across as very confident, I also know some that are quiet and shy, just like there are introverts who are confident and outspoken. The real question to ask yourself is not so much about how comfortable or confident you feel around people, but what being around people and being alone does to your energy. Think about the last time you spent a longer period of time with a group of people. How did you feel after a few hours of constant communication and interaction? Did you feel energised and excited? Then you're probably more of an extrovert. If you felt exhausted and were looking forward to getting some time on your own, then you are probably more of an introvert. Another question to consider is when you perform at your best. Do you feel like you do your best work when you have time to reflect and think things through on your own (introvert) or do you feel like you do your best work when you engage with a group and have lots of discussions and opportunity to bounce ideas off each other (extrovert)? Remember, it's not about picking one of two extremes. It's a scale, and you might be only very slightly more introverted than extroverted or the other way around. So, where on the scale do you see yourself?

What world do you prefer?

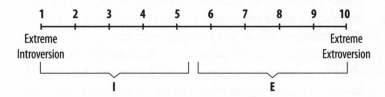

2. How do you gather information: Sensing (S) vs. Intuition (N)

The next pair of preferences in the MBTI is about how you gather information. Do you prefer to focus on the direct information you take in (sensing), or do you prefer to interpret and add meaning (intuition)? In short, sensing is about facts and intuition is about possibilities.

Sensing people usually tend to focus on what they can actually see, smell, hear, touch and taste — the information our five senses provide. For them, gathering information is about identifying what is real and present. They prefer concrete and specific data, tend to take things literally and are often considered 'here and now' people. Intuitive people, on the other hand, are more focused on the meaning and possibilities hidden within facts and information. They tend to live in the future and prefer abstract theories and big-picture thinking over practical experiences and facts. Sensing and intuitive people tend to have different memories. Think about a past experience. Do you remember actual facts about the experience, like what time it was, what the weather was like and who was there, or is your memory more about how you felt and what the experience was like overall? The former tends to be how sensing people remember experiences while the latter is how intuitive people tend to remember them. Another indicator is that people who score high in intuition tend to be more interested in trying new things while people who score higher in sensing tend to prefer tried and tested methods.

Sensing people are often described as realists, practical, factual and as living in the present. They are acutely aware of their surroundings and often have high attention to detail. Intuitive people are often characterised as more future-oriented, imaginative, inventive, idealistic, profound and as someone who easily sees possibilities. While sensors are sometimes at risk of being so focused on facts and the present that they miss opportunities, intuitive people are sometimes at risk of being dreamers who are so caught up in future possibilities that they never actually make anything happen in the present. Where on the scale do you see yourself? Are you more interested in what actually is (sensing) or in what could be (intuition)?

How do you gather information?

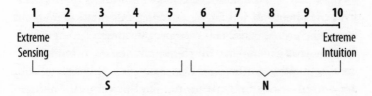

3. How do you make decisions: Thinking (T) vs. Feeling (F)

The third dimension of the MBTI is about how you make decisions. Do you tend to focus on facts and what is fair when making decisions (thinking) or are you more concerned with personal issues and the people involved (feeling)? Interestingly, this is the only MBTI dimension that seems to have a clear gender bias; the majority of men are thinkers, and the majority of women are feelers. However, that is just an average, and there are many feeling men and thinking women (myself included).

It's important to distinguish the terms thinking and feeling from intelligence and emotion. Being a thinker does not mean that you don't have emotions and being a feeler does not mean you can't be rational and logical. It's about which is dominant when you have to make decisions; what you feel or what you think? Most of us make some decisions as feelers and others as thinkers, depending on the circumstances. However, most of us also have a natural preference for one or the other.

People who have a preference for thinking tend to make decisions based on the facts available and their logic. Their main concern when making decisions is 'what is fair?' They often weigh the pros and cons carefully and tend to believe that they make the best decisions if they manage to stay objective and leave their personal feelings out of it. They also often believe that being honest and telling the truth is more important than being 'nice', which can sometimes make them seem blunt and even inconsiderate — especially to very feeling people. People with a preference for thinking often enjoy working in technical and scientific fields where logic is highly valued. They tend to have a natural gift for finding the most efficient and logical solutions and often spot inconsistencies very quickly. People with a strong preference for thinking over feeling can sometimes be at risk of overlooking the impact their decisions have on people and can seem uncaring and indifferent.

Those people who have a preference for feeling tend to make their decisions based on what is best for the people involved. They consider doing right by people as more important than doing what's fair. They often spend time looking at a decision from different people's points of view instead of weighing the factual pros and cons. Their main goal is to keep everyone happy and overall harmony in the group. They often find that being considerate and supportive of others is more important than telling the truth and generally tend to make decisions with their heart more so than their head. Feeling people often appear warm, caring and supportive but can also be at risk of being too nice, too idealistic and even mushy.

Here is a simple example to help you figure out your preference. Imagine you had the difficult job of deciding who out of a group of workers should be made redundant. If you have a clear preference for thinking, you're likely to consider things like, who has been on the team the longest, who is the most productive, who shows the most commitment, whose skills and experience are the most important to keep in the business and similar rational facts. If you have a strong preference for feeling, you are likely to be much more concerned with personal aspects like who would struggle the most if they lose their job, who has a family to look after, who would struggle to find new employment, who is the most friendly and caring and similar emotional, people-focused aspects. Do you see the difference? Thinkers want to do what's logical and fair while feelers want to do what's best for the people. Of course, these are the extremes and most of us would consider aspects from both sides. But most of us also have a natural preference for one over the other.

People with a preference for thinking are often described as logical, firm, rational, objective, truth-seekers, impersonal and critical while those with a preference for feeling are described as passionate, driven by emotion, gentle, caring, empathetic, easily hurt and avoiders of conflict. Where on the Thinking vs. Feeling scale do you see yourself?

How do you make decisions?

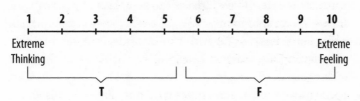

4. How do you engage with the world: Judging (J) vs. Perceiving (P)

The fourth and final pair of preferences of the MBTI is about how you engage with the world — the behaviours that others tend to see. In dealing with the outside world, do you prefer to get things decided (judging) or do you prefer to stay open to new information and options (perceiving)?

People who have a preference for judging generally seem to be organised and structured and seem to prefer a systematic and well-planned lifestyle. They tend to push for decisions to be finalised rather than engaging in endless discussions and evaluations of options. Having a preference for judging is not the same as being judgemental, it just means that you prefer to have decisions made rather than staying open to options. Judging people often like to make lists of things that need to be done, often appear very task-oriented and tend to prioritise getting a job done over having fun. People with a preference for perceiving, on the other hand, seem more flexible and spontaneous. They tend to stay open to new options and information instead of just making a decision and going with it. Most perceiving people like to keep plans to a minimum and prefer to respond to whatever happens in the moment. While judging people are often very good at planning work and hardly ever need to rush to the finish line, perceiving people tend to leave things last minute and are highly motivated by approaching deadlines. Judgers can be at risk of making decisions too quickly and missing out on valuable new information, while perceivers can be at risk of being forever open to new insights and never actually making a decision and getting on with things.

It's important to remember that this dimension is about how you interact with the world — which might, at times, be different from how you feel internally. You might feel curious and open-minded internally, but the way you engage with the outside world is more structured and decisive, which would mean you have a preference for judging despite your internal state feeling more perceiving. Alternatively, you might be very non-committal and flexible in the way you engage with others (perceiving), but internally you have a pretty good plan of what you're doing when and where. This dimension is about how others experience and see you, not how you feel.

If you have a preference for judging, others are likely to

describe you as decisive, organised, a doer, scheduled, controlled, responsible and someone who likes making plans and then seeing them through to the finish quickly. If you have a preference for perceiving, you've likely been described as spontaneous, relaxed, flexible, disorganised, non-committal, carefree and someone who often changes tracks halfway through and who dislikes routines. How do you think you're engaging with the world?

How do you engage with the world?

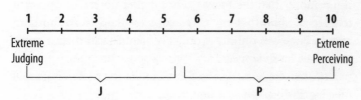

CONCERNS & CRITICISM

Popular and widely used as it may be, the MBTI also has its fair share of critics, and it is essential to consider some of their arguments before going ahead and determining your type. The primary concern raised regularly is that the MBTI scores put people in a box. By labelling ourselves and others as either A or B on the four dichotomies, we easily ignore the fact that the concepts are a scale, not two extremes. The MBTI types do not take into account that there is a big difference between someone who scores a 1 on the Judging-Perceiving scale and someone who scores a 5. Both get 'typed' as a J, but their preferences are, in fact, quite different. I am an INTJ, and for a while, I worked closely with another INTJ. On several occasions, I would think to myself: "How are we the same personality type?" Though we clearly had a few things in common, we were so different in other ways that it was sometimes hard to believe we were the same type. It is highly likely that, even though we got the same four-letter result, our actual positions on each of the four scales are quite different. This issue of putting people in a box is a valid concern and should be taken seriously. However, it doesn't necessarily diminish the usefulness of the tool as such. What it means is that we need to be careful when interpreting our results and that we need to look beyond just the four-letter result. Focusing where precisely on each of the four scales we sit, and how strong or weak our preferences are, can tell us just as much, if not more, than the four letters. Furthermore, it's important to keep in mind that any personality test, especially those we can do ourselves online, is only ever an indication and guide, not a fact set in stone.

The other frequently voiced criticism of the MBTI is its lack of scientific background and validation. Firstly, neither Katharine Cook Briggs nor Isabel Briggs Myers had any official training in psychometrics or psychological assessments. Briggs completed a degree in agriculture and Myers one in political science. Therefore, while both were certainly highly educated women, especially for their time, critics argue that neither had the formal training to develop a scientifically valid instrument. However, one only needs to look at the growing number of highly successful ventures founded by high school drop-outs or people without any university degrees whatsoever to know that you don't always need a formal education to create something significant and successful.

Further criticism from the scientific community is the claim that there is hardly any scientific evidence that proves that the scores on the MBTI can predict significant life outcomes such as job performance and satisfaction. While it is true that the MBTI is not very widely used in scientific research, two researchers, Robert McCrae and Paul Costa, have shown that the preferences measured by the MBTI are very similar to four of the five traits in the widely used and scientifically accepted Big Five model.[35] Given these similarities, it can be argued that the MBTI scores are almost as good at predicting life outcomes as the Big Five model is.

It is my personal belief and experience that the MBTI can be hugely valuable, especially when analysed in the right context and with some objective care. As for so many people, the MBTI was my introduction to personality typology and personality tests. Several years ago, I was researching personal growth and development when I came across one of the free online versions of the test. Always curious, I took the test right away — totally unaware of what it would set into motion for me. As you read in my personal story earlier in this book, starting to learn about myself has been instrumental in finding real happiness. I still remember reading my INTJ profile for the first time, and all of a sudden, so many things started to make sense. The more I learned about my type and my preferences, the more I understood who I am, what makes me happy and why, and how I can interact better with others at work and in my personal life. I am very careful not to use the types or elements of them as labels or excuses, but having the internal awareness and knowledge has helped me tremendously. I absolutely believe it can do the same for you. So, time to find out your MBTI type.

Below are two exercises to help you determine your type, the friends and family method and the online test method. I encourage you to do both, but you can, of course, just pick one. If you don't want to do either exercise right now, I would at least encourage you to give yourself a rating for each of the four dimensions and maybe spend a little bit of time learning more about your self-identified type. Check the resources at the end of this section to find out where to learn more about your type.

EXERCISE: WHAT'S YOUR MBTI TYPE?

EXERCISE I: THE FRIENDS AND FAMILY METHOD

Before you get into this, it's important to understand that certain aspects of the MBTI are somewhat difficult to judge from the outside. In particular, whether we're thinkers or feelers when it comes to decision-making is hard, maybe even impossible, to assess from the outside. Similarly, introversion and extroversion still tend to be misunderstood as shy and outgoing by many people, so someone might rate you as extroverted because you seem confident and outspoken (in the area of your life that he or she is part of) and they might not be aware of how much you depend on solitude to recharge your batteries and how reserved you might be in other situations. Keep this in mind as you proceed with this exercise. Even more so than for the Big Five, other people's opinion can only give you an indication and maybe a starting point, but they won't be a reliable judge of your full personality.

1. If you haven't already, go back to the previous pages and indicate what you think your preference for each of the four dichotomies is. Make sure you think about what the individual concepts and extremes mean and how you are most likely to behave, think and feel. Be honest! There is no right or wrong, and no type is considered better than the other.

2. Ask at least four other people to give you feedback and a rating in each of the four areas. They can be friends, family members, colleagues or other people who know you relatively well and engage with you regularly. Use the template from the workbook. Pick people who are currently an active and regular part of your life. You can ask more than four people.

If you find that the responses from the initial four people you asked are very different from each other, it's probably a good idea to get input from more people to even things out a bit.

3. As you did in the same exercise for the Big Five model, look for outliers — any scores that stand out as significantly different from all others. Think about whether it would be a better reflection of your personality to keep them or not. Does the person who gave the outlier score know you well? Do they maybe have a different perspective from everyone else? Have they perhaps misunderstood what the trait means or how the scoring works? Investigate and consider. If you feel the score is likely to be inaccurate, remove it (don't include when working through the steps below).

4. For each trait, add all the scores you got from others together (not including the one you gave yourself and the outliers you removed in step 3) and then divide it by the number of scores you added together. This will provide you with an average rating for each concept. The more people you've asked for feedback, and the more diverse this group is (family, friends, colleagues), the more accurate the scores are likely to be.

5. Compare the average scores you got from friends and family to the ones you gave yourself. If you find significant differences for any one of the four areas (or several), it might be worth exploring this a bit more. Ask people why they scored you the way they did. That information might help you better assess if they have misunderstood something about your personality or if you maybe need to adjust your view of yourself slightly. If you are still unsure about your preference, you might want to read up on the different types a bit more. The official Myers-Briggs Foundation website offers a

vast amount of resources and information about the different types.

6. Based on the steps above, decide on your type. Make sure you consider the scores you got from others and be honest with yourself. However, remember, it's your personality, and in the end, nobody knows you better than you know yourself. The personality type that most feels like you, is most likely who you are.

7. Below each letter, indicate how weak or strong this preference is over the other extreme. For example, if you find you have a strong preference for Judging over Perceiving, add an S below the J. Add an M for moderate preference and a W for weak preference.

EXERCISE 2: THE ONLINE TEST

1. If you haven't already, go back to the previous pages and indicate what you think your preference for each of the four dichotomies is. Make sure you think about what the individual concepts and extremes mean and how you are most likely to behave, think or feel.

2. Go online and find an MBTI test. Below are three I recommend but there are many others to pick from if you don't like the look of these. You can do several of them if you want to.
   a. **The official MBTI Test: https://www.mbtionline.com** This is the only official Myers-Briggs Assessment available online. All other tests are based on the MBTI but are not the actual assessment (which doesn't necessarily make them less valuable). The assessment comes with a price tag of US $49.95 (at time of writing). In general, I prefer

recommending free recourses, but since this is the only online test endorsed by the Myers-Briggs Foundation, I wanted to include it. It's a great resource with lots of additional insights and learning opportunities. The only thing that can be a little bit annoying is that you need to click through the whole learning journey in the end before you get to see your results.

b. **Human Metrics: http://www.humanmetrics.com/personality** A free online personality test that is based on Carl Jung's and Isabel Briggs Myers' personality type theory. The test will identify your four-letter type, including how strong your preference for each letter is, as well as a detailed overview of what your type means and what your strengths and weaknesses are.

c. **My Personality — https://my-personality-test.com** This is another free alternative to the official Myers-Briggs assessment. While not the 'real thing', it also determines your four-letter type based on a series of questions. There is an option to buy a premium profile at the end, but you don't need to do this, you get your results and a short profile for free, and you can use this to learn more through other free resources.

Regardless of which test you choose, make sure you pay attention to the degree to which you prefer one extreme to the other. For example, I am an INTJ. However, while my preference for introversion over extroversion is strong, my preference for intuitive over sensing is only very small. It's important to pay attention to this as there is a big difference between someone who is a 100% introvert and someone who is only slightly more introverted than extroverted. Both would have personality types that start with the letter I, but they are likely to be very different people. In fact, the person who only has a slight preference for introversion is more likely to be similar to someone who has a slight preference for extroversion than they are to someone who is very introverted, even though they share the same personality type letter with the latter. So make sure you not only focus on which letter combination you are, but also on how strong your preferences are.

3. Once you have your results, take some time to review and analyse them. Do you agree with them? Are they similar to the type you selected for yourself? If not, and you've only done one of the above tests so far, it might be worth trying another one to get more clarity. If you're still unsure, maybe try having a conversation about it with someone who knows you very well to see what they think. If you find you have very weak preferences in one or more areas, it might be worth also reading up on the profile of the four-letter type you would be if this weak preference would swing the other way. For example, if the test suggests that you are an ENFJ, but your preference for feeling over thinking is weak, also read the profile for the ENTJ type to see if it feels like a better fit for you.

4. Based on what you've learned from the online test(s), as well as your own score, decide on your four-letter type. Make sure you take your online test results seriously and give it some thought (especially if the results are different to how you assessed yourself). However, in the end remember that it's your personality and no online test will know you better than you know yourself. The personality type that most feels like you, is most likely who you are.

5. Below each letter, indicate how weak or strong this prefer-ence is over the other extreme. You can include the actual

percentage from your test results or simple use S for strong, M for moderate and W for weak.

LEARN MORE ABOUT YOUR TYPE

Now that you have identified your type, I would encourage you to take some time to learn a bit more about it. There are many great online resources with detailed descriptions of each type. Here are some I can recommend, and a simple Google search will show many more.

a. 16 Personalities — https://www.16personalities.com/
b. Human Metrics — http://www.humanmetrics.com/personality/type
c. TypeLogic — http://typelogic.com/

At this point, you should have a pretty good understanding of your personality. How does it feel? Do you feel like you're getting to know yourself better? Have you discovered things you weren't aware of before? Did you maybe gain a better understanding of why you are a certain way?

Learning more about your personality can be incredibly valuable, but it's also important to remember that who we are and what makes us happy is about more than personality. Other aspects that are very important are our personal values and beliefs. So that's what we will discover next.

Your Personal Values

How can we expect to find happiness if we don't know what is truly important to us, what matters most, what inspires us and what truly fulfils us? The short answer is: we can't! That is why it is so important to learn about our values as part of our journey to a happier life.

Our personal values determine who we are as much as our personality traits do, if not more so. While our personality preferences determine how we tend to think, feel and behave, our values are our broad life goals and priorities that determine how we perceive and view situations and how we react. The two concepts are similar in many ways. Both are somewhat stable throughout our lives. They are not completely fixed, but only tend to change slowly over time. Both also determine how we interact with the world and how we behave, and both have a significant impact on what will make us happy. However, they are distinctive concepts, and it's important to understand these differences before proceeding. The key distinction is that personality traits are descriptive variables while values are motivational values. What that means is that personality traits describe how we tend to feel, think and behave, while values are what motivates us and what we believe is important.

We all have values, but not all of us are fully aware of what these values are — something we're about to change. Our values are a key driver in decision-making. They are often the reason why we do one thing even though we feel like doing something else. Our values help us channel and direct our emotions to make sure we do what's best for us in the long-term, not what seems like the most fun in the moment. For example, imagine you're out for drinks with a few friends. You feel like another glass of wine, but you've already had two, and you need to drive home. You decide not to have another drink, even though you want to, because you value safety, following the law, or having your driver's licence more than you value having another drink. Here's another example. You might find a wallet with money in it. Even though you might need the extra cash right now, you decide to hand it in because you value honesty and doing the right thing more than you value some extra cash. However, values don't always make us do what's generally considered the smart or right thing. We can all probably remember a time where we went to a party or some other fun activity even though we knew we should be working or studying for an important test. We made that choice because, at that time, we valued having fun or being accepted and considered 'cool' by our peers more than we valued doing our job or passing that test.

Values vs. Social Ideals and Expectations

One of the hardest aspects of determining your personal values is being able to differentiate between your values and social ideals and expectations. Most of us live in societies where certain values are expected to be adopted by everyone. Values like honesty, integrity, being nice to others, respecting your parents and teachers, or helping people in need, are often so embedded in our cultures and societies that they can feel like rules and laws instead of values. We grow up with them and are taught about right and wrong in alignment with these values. However, as valid and important as they may be, such generic social ideals and expectations are different from our personal values. It can be challenging to look beyond how you think you should feel and behave and truly identify what matters most to you personally.

One thing that is important to remember in this context is that this section is about identifying your highest personal values. Just because things like honesty and kindness might not make it on to your list, doesn't mean you don't value them. All it means is that there are things you value more. Social ideals and moral expectations are essential in making our societies work — imagine the chaos we would be living in if no one cared about honesty, integrity, kindness, respect and supporting each other. I think we can all agree we would rather live in a world where the majority of people value and respect these social ideals. However, that doesn't mean they need to be your highest values. You might value family, creativity, learning or freedom more than honesty or kindness, which doesn't mean you're not honest or kind. It just means you value other things more.

Personal values, much like personality, are highly individual. While we might enjoy shared values with a group, like our family values, cultural values or company values at our workplace, our personal values are unique to us. Our families and the societies we live in might influence our values, but they can't and shouldn't define them. Just like your personality is about who you are internally (not who others think you are or want you to be), your values are about what truly matters most to you — not what parents, teachers, colleagues, friends or society think you should value. No one can or should tell you what your values are or should be. Only you can look inside yourself and find out what is most important to you.

Keep all of this in mind as you work through the exercises to identify your personal values. Remember that this is not about meeting expectations or pleasing others. It is about who you are and what you truly value the most. You never have to share your values with anyone if you don't want to. Just knowing them yourself will be incredibly valuable as you work towards a happier life.

Why is Knowing Our Values So Important?

Knowing and understanding your personal values is a crucial aspect of living a meaningful life. Our values impact our lives in many important ways — whether we're consciously aware of it or not. Let's look at five important reasons to learn about your values.

1. We make decisions based on our values

Our values are a key factor in our decision making. From seemingly small everyday choices to big life-changing decisions, our values are often the primary factor that determines what we decide. For example, imagine you are offered a new role at work. It would be a big step up for you and would come with a fancy title, a nice new office and more money. However, it would also come with long hours and a lot more responsibility. Do you take the job? How do you know what the right choice is? How do you know what will ultimately make you happy? Now imagine you had spent time identifying and understanding your personal values. You recognised that family and being an active and involved parent is one of your top values, while status and money are not that important to you. Do you think it would be easier to make the right choice with this new-found knowledge of what matters most to you? Here is another, everyday example: it's dinner time, you're hungry and tired from a long day at work or looking after the kids. The easy dinner option is to stop at the fast-food restaurant on the way home. You know it's not healthy and you probably shouldn't, but it just seems like the easiest and best option at the time, and it would mean that you have time to play with your kids instead of cooking a healthy dinner. Now imagine you had identified your personal values and realised that the health and well-being of yourself and your family are your highest value. The one thing that matters more to you than anything else is that you are fit and healthy and that your kids grow up being healthy. How would this awareness impact your dinner decision? Or turn things around — what if you knew that spending quality time with your kids was your highest value? Do you think being aware of your personal values would help you make the right decisions?

I've been overweight for most of my life. I lost weight several times over the years, but it always piled back on three times faster than it came off. That was up until about six years ago.

Six years ago, I lost a lot of weight, and I have been within a healthy weight range ever since. What changed? I won't lie to you, it didn't just get easy all of a sudden. I didn't figure out some big secret. My challenges around food and eating didn't go away. I still struggle with it a lot. I still love chocolate, I'm still an emotional eater and even though I eat healthily most of the time, I still overindulge regularly. I've gained a few pounds several times since I reached my goal weight six years ago. The difference now is that I am able to stop and get back on track before things get out of control again. Why? Because I'm very aware of my personal values and the fact that health and fitness is one of my highest. Through having learned about my core values, I have come to understand that it is extremely important to me to feel fit and healthy, to be able to do all my favourite activities and to feel comfortable with, and proud of, who I am. I fully understand that giving in to my cravings too much will mean I won't be that person and I will ultimately be unhappy. That doesn't mean that I always make the right choices. I do overeat occasionally, and I do gain a bit of weight at times. However, I always make the right decisions before it's too late and my weight spirals out of control again. That is the power of knowing, understanding and living your values. It helps you make the right decisions when it matters most.

2. Not living by your values is likely to be a great source of stress and worry

Living by your personal core values essentially means living the life you're meant to live. The life that is right for you. Consequently, not living by your values means you're not living 'your' life — you're not true to yourself. It probably comes as no surprise then, that not living by your values is a great source of stress and other negative emotions.

Our personal values are one of the reasons why different people respond so differently to the same situation or decision. For example, think of people with highly demanding jobs. They work long hours, have lots of responsibility and don't get much time for things outside of work. Some people truly thrive in this kind of environment. They love the work and challenges and are feeling fulfilled and happy with the situation. Others react differently. While they might be able to keep up with the demands of the job and appear to be doing well, they feel stressed, tired and unhappy on the inside. Chances are, a key difference between those two people are their personal values. The first person is likely to value hard work, achievements, professional success and status. For her, the life she is living aligns well with her values. While others might look at it and think she works too much and has no work-life balance, she is perfectly happy with it. She's living her values. The second person is likely to have other values. He might value family time, outdoor activities, reading, travelling or just quiet time. While he is absolutely capable of doing the demanding job, he is not living life around his core values, which is why he isn't enjoying it and is feeling stressed.

Here is another example. Imagine a couple, Ben and Amber. Amber values fun, excitement, creativity and spontaneity. Ben also values fun and excitement but his highest values are financial security and being able to take care of his family. One day, Ben and Amber decide to buy a house together. Getting a bit carried away, they buy one that's at the very top end of their budget, meaning money will be tight. For Amber, that's not a problem. She loves the house and the excitement of being in a new place, and she doesn't worry much about money. Ben, on the other hand, finds the whole situation very stressful. He constantly worries about not being able to pay the mortgage and what would happen if either one of them would unexpectedly lose their jobs or if they had a significant unexpected expense. In hindsight, Ben would have probably been much happier if they had chosen a more affordable house while Amber would probably have been just as excited and happy with that. If Ben had understood and lived by his values, he could have avoided this situation and the constant worry and stress that resulted.

3. If you don't live by yours, you're at risk of living by someone else's values

Something drives your motivation and behaviour. Something determines how you live your life and what choices you make. Values are our key drivers and motivators in life. If it's not your own values that drive your life, then there is a good chance that you're living by someone else's. We are all influenced by the people and society around us, but there is a difference between being influenced by them and living fully by other people's values instead of our own. Imagine a relationship (romantic or otherwise) where one person is very aware and outspoken about their values and beliefs, and the other person doesn't really know theirs. You can easily see how the one who is aware of their values becomes the stronger and more dominant person in the relationship. They are likely to take the lead in a lot of decision-making as well as other aspects of the relationship. If you're the person who doesn't know your values, you're likely to just follow. Even if things don't feel right to you at times, you can't explain why and how you would rather do something, so you struggle to win (or even initiate) any arguments. Eventually, it feels easier just to give in and follow. Before you know it, you're living a life based on someone else's values and beliefs — and as we've learned above, not living by your values is often a great source of stress and other negative emotions.

On the other hand, if you learn about your values, you are in a much better position to understand what matters to you and why and how you want to do things. This would potentially enable you to have better conversations and discussions with the other person, and together you can design a relationship around both of your values.

4. Knowing your values enables you to live life to the fullest

I think we all dream about living happy and fulfilling lives. However, how can you live life to the fullest when you don't know what 'the fullest' looks like for you? Personal values are like your internal compass. When understood and used correctly, this compass can point us towards the activities, people and choices that will bring us the most fulfilment and happiness. Knowing what you value most helps you pursue the right things in life and avoid investing energy into things that won't bring you happiness.

This fourth point is especially relevant if your values are maybe slightly unusual or just different from the people around you. We all get influenced by the opinions, actions and ideals of the people in our lives and the environment we live in. Additionally, most of us live in societies with well-established, traditional ways of living our lives. The majority of people seem to follow similar paths in life, and there is often a lot of internal and external pressure for us all to do the same. It can be challenging to break free from that and truly live life your way. Even if you are happy living a relatively traditional life, there might be other little things where you feel pressure to follow instead of doing it your way. Learning about your values and how to live by them gives you the awareness and motivation you need to be true to yourself and swim against the stream when needed. It gives you the knowledge and reason to live life your way, which will ultimately lead to a meaningful and happy life. I know this from personal experience. In the last few years, I've made some unusual choices, like giving up my apartment to live in a campervan and working only part-time hours. I'm in my mid-30s, an age when most people are focused on either starting and growing families or progressing their careers, or both. Understanding my values helped me realise that kind of life is not right for me (for now) and even more importantly, gave me the encouragement and confidence to follow my own path — even when it's difficult at times. While life has not been without challenges, I can say without a doubt that I feel more fulfilled, happier and true to myself than ever before.

5. You will be better at prioritising

Most of us are living busy lives, and we often feel like there is not enough time in the day to get everything done. Your values can help you prioritise and de-stress your life. Knowing and living by your values enables you to look at your task list and decide what is truly important and what isn't. For example, let's assume your to-do list contains things like mowing the lawn, finishing a big work assignment, calling your mother, playtime with the kids and getting a birthday gift for your best friend. If your top values are family time and getting ahead at work, you might prioritise your work assignment and playtime with your kids, and leave mowing the lawn and cleaning the house for another day (or even pay someone to do it). However, if your highest values are about maintaining a well-kept home for your family and caring for your friends, you might prioritise cleaning and buying a birthday present, and spend less time playing and finishing your work assignment.

Knowing your personal values helps you differentiate between what you think you should do (because what will the neighbours think if you don't mow the lawn soon or what if your kids think you don't love them because you didn't play enough with them) and what is really important to you personally and what will really enrich your life. When it comes down to squeezing 20 hours' worth of tasks into a 14-hour day, using your values to help you prioritise can be a real life-saver.

In summary, understanding and living by your values is incredibly important because it helps you find happiness! Living by your values helps you make the right decisions, prioritise the right things, enables you to be true to yourself, helps you avoid getting into situations that cause stress and worry and overall promotes living a fulfilled life. Understanding your personal values is just as important for finding happiness as understanding your personality is. So, time to find out what your highest personal values are. Remember, this is not about identifying everything you value, but it's about recognising what is most important to you.

Identifying Your Core Values

Identifying your personal values is a less scientific process than identifying your personality preferences. There aren't any online tests where you can answer a few questions and it spits out your values. One of the reasons for this is the fact that there is an endless number of possible values. Measuring our preferences for individual values, as tests do for personality, is basically impossible. While our personalities can be narrowed down to a few unique areas, the same can't be done for values, unless you want to answer thousands of questions to determine your preference for hundreds of possible values.

The good news is, most of us are already living by our highest values — at least some of the time — which means we can identify them by looking inside ourselves. Think about situations and times in your life when you felt good, authentic, confident and content. Most likely, those are the moments when you were living by your highest values. Values are in our heart and soul. It's up to us to look inside ourselves and figure out what matters most. However, there are a few questions that can kick-start your thinking and help you narrow it down. That's what the below exercise is all about.

EXERCISES: IDENTIFYING YOUR CORE VALUES

This personal values exercise consists of three parts. The first part is a series of brainstorming exercises; in the second part we will look for themes and in the third part we will narrow it down to your top values.

As you work through these three parts, try to respond as intuitively as possible. Don't overthink it. There are no right or wrong answers, and as we have discussed before, it's important you focus on what you think and feel, not what you think you should think and feel. Ready? Here we go.

PART I — BRAINSTORMING:
This first part of the values exercise is about brainstorming and writing down your thoughts. No decisions are made till Part III of the exercise, so you have nothing to lose from just going for it and writing down whatever comes to your mind.

1. Write down what is important to you. This can be absolutely anything. Also, write down why each is important to you.

What's important to you?	Why is it important to you?

2. Write down at least three things you like about other people. Write down what that means to you and why you like it.

What do you like about other people?	What does it mean to you? Why do you like it?

3. Write down at least three things you like about yourself. Write down what that means to you and why you like it.

What do you like about yourself?	What does it mean to you? Why do you like it?

4. Think of at least two occasions when you felt really productive and full of achievement. Write down what you were doing and what you think made you a high achiever in that situation.

When did you feel super productive?	What made you a high achiever?

5. Write down at least three activities or things you feel really passionate about and love. Write down why you feel passionate about them (how do they make you feel)?

What are you really passionate about?	Why do you feel passionate about it?

6. Think of at least two occasions where you didn't do what you felt like doing and did the 'right' or 'sensible' thing instead. What was the situation and what stopped you from doing what you wanted to do?

When did you NOT do what you felt like doing?	What stopped you from doing what you felt like?

7. Write down at least three things (or people) that inspire you. How and why do they inspire you?

What inspires you?	How and why does it inspire you?

8. Write down at least two things that you enjoy talking about with friends and family. Why do you enjoy talking about them?

What do you enjoy talking about?	Why do you enjoy talking about it?

9. Write down at least two things you find yourself thinking about regularly. What occupies your mind the most? What do these thoughts mean to you?

What do you think about?	What do those thoughts mean to you?

PART II — FINDING THEMES AND COMMUNALITIES

Now that you have a whole bunch of ideas around what matters to you, it's time to identify some common themes and recurring ideas.

1. Go back through your answers for each of the nine questions above and identify the underlying values involved. In some cases, it might be obvious, in others, you might have to read between the lines. For example, you might enjoy talking about music. This could indicate that you value music, or it could be that you like talking about music because you're really knowledgeable in this area and what you really value is knowledge or learning. Don't rush this part. Spend a bit of time thinking through your answer for each question and then note down what values you can identify that matter to you. If you struggle with this part, it might help to do a quick online search for 'list of personal values' to get some ideas of what values to look for. But remember, your values can be anything and your personal ones might not show up on any generic list.

Question	Value(s) you identified in your answer
1	
2	
3	
4	
5	
6	
7	
8	
9	

2. The above is a list of all the things you value. Go through the list and highlight common themes, similarities and repeating values. Which are the ones that stand out as maybe more important than others?

PART III — IDENTIFYING YOUR HIGHEST VALUES

Now it's time to identify your top values. I would recommend aiming for 3-6, but it is ultimately up to you how many you want. These will be the things that matter most to you and that you want to use to guide your decision-making and direction in life.

1. From your above list, identify the 3-6 values that feel most important to you. Which are the core values you want to live your life by?

2. Test your values. Close your eyes and imagine yourself living life based on them. Imagine making decisions based on those values — especially difficult decisions. Does it feel right? Can

you see yourself doing it? Or does it feel weird and unrealistic? If it's the latter, you probably want to spend a bit more time thinking through your values and maybe reshuffle a few things. It's important that you can actually see yourself living by them and being happy.

3. Once you have your 'final' core values, take a minute to write them down and add short descriptions of what they mean to you.

Your Core Values:	What does this value mean to you?

Living Your Values

Now that you have identified your values, it's time to live by them. Your core values should inform your decision-making, help you prioritise and generally guide you towards the people, activities and situations that bring the most fulfilment and happiness into your life. For most people, this part is relatively straightforward. As we've discussed, most of us already live by our values — consciously or unconsciously — and gaining full awareness of what our highest values are will likely impact our lives without us even putting much effort or thought into it.

The biggest challenge is not getting sidetracked by other

people's opinions and expectations and our own thoughts around what we should do or feel (rather than what we really value). It can be hard to stay true to your values at times, especially when there is a lot of internal or external pressure to act differently. For example, if you're a man in your 30s or 40s, there is likely to be a lot of pressure for you to focus on your career, get promotions, earn more money and provide for your family. However, if your highest personal values are about family and spending time with your kids, you're probably much happier when working less, making less money, but spending more time with your kids, and maybe even being the stay-at-home parent while your wife (who values her career more) goes back to work. However, since that is not the most common and socially accepted path, you might experience pressure from others, as well as yourself, to follow the traditional route. It's situations like these where living by your values can be challenging and sticking to them takes strength and determination.

I find that it helps to remind yourself regularly of your core values. Depending on your situation and the decisions and challenges you're facing, it might be worth re-reading them monthly or weekly, or even daily. Also, make sure you keep them handy, so you can easily refer back to them when you have to make difficult decisions and want to make sure they align with your core values. If you're creatively minded, you might even want to visualise them and display them somewhere in your home.

Challenges can also arise when your values clash with someone else's who is a vital part of your life — for example, your spouse or child. What if both parents highly value child-care and want to be the stay-at-home parent? Or, if both value their career and want to be the one who goes back to work? What if you value order and tidiness but your child values creativity and the freedom to explore and experiment (by making a mess)? What if you value travelling and learning about new cultures, but your spouse values the security of home and spending time with local friends and family? I'm sure you can all think of other examples where what you wanted most was in direct conflict with what someone else wanted most. Usually, the best way to handle these situations is making compromises. Make sure you fully understand each other's values and why they are so important to each of you, and then look for compromises. In some cases, you might both be able to get some of what you want. For example, you could both work part-time and split career and child-care responsibilities. In other cases, a direct compromise might not be possible, and it comes down to making an 'I give you what you want this time, but you give me what I want next time' agreement. Of course, there are situations where compromises are not possible or acceptable. In those situations, it comes down to reconsidering exactly how important the specific value is in the context of the overall situation and other values. If there really is no compromise, it might be a sign that the relationship is not meant to be and both people involved would be happier going their separate ways (hard as that might be).

Living by your values is mostly a matter of awareness and conscious decision-making. Being true to yourselves and living by your values is key to living a happy and fulfilled life. That is why learning about your values is so important in the context of this book. The awareness you've gained in this section will enable you to consider all the insights and ideas around happiness that will be provided throughout the rest of this book and put them into the context of what matters most to you. Our values are as unique as our personalities. No two people have exactly the same values or personalities. Consequently, no two people will find happiness in exactly the same way. Make sure you keep your values handy as you continue reading, so you can easily refer back to them when needed to make sure you stay true to what matters most to you.

LEARNING MORE ABOUT PERSONAL VALUES

If you want to learn more about personal values, I highly recommend the book The Values Factor by Dr John Demartin. That book was my introduction to personal values, and I have re-read it twice since. It is very deep and comprehensive, so you will need some persistence, but especially the first half and the last few chapters are very valuable to anyone who wants to learn more about personal values.

Your Strengths and Weaknesses

Finding happiness essentially comes down to two things:

1. figuring out what makes you happy and
2. getting it.

Your core values are very much about what makes you happy. Your personality, on the other hand, is a bit of both. Your personality preferences impact what will make you happy, but understanding your personality also gives you a better chance at coming up with a plan that will help you get whatever it is that will make you happy. There is another area that can be incredibly valuable in helping you get whatever it is that will bring you happiness, and that is understanding your strengths and weaknesses.

Your strengths are all the things you are good at and that come natural to you. This can be anything from a particular activity, like being a good cook or basketball player, through to something more generic like being athletic, intelligent, funny or finding it easy to connect with people. Your strengths might be physical (athletic, strong, good-looking), intellectual (smart, quick learner, knowledgeable), practical (good cook, writer, teacher, leader), emotional (highly likeable, caring, high emotional intelligence, positive) and much more. Strengths can be just about anything that you feel you're good at. While weaknesses are often positioned as the opposite of strengths, it's important to understand that weaknesses are not simply all the things you're not good at. It's only when these things have a negative impact on your life that they become weaknesses. For example, I am not exactly a good cook, but I wouldn't consider it a weakness because it doesn't impact my life. I've mastered a few simple recipes and learned enough to be able to cook the occasional meal for friends, and that's all I need. I don't have any ambition to be a better cook. Therefore, I wouldn't consider it a weakness. On the other hand, a lack of patience is a weakness of mine. I'm often the 'I want it all and I want it now' type and I find it hard to be patient with myself and others. This occasionally causes problems because I put myself under a lot of pressure, set myself up for failure and have probably, on occasion, been too demanding of others in work situations. My lack of patience has a negative impact on my life while my lack of cooking skills doesn't. That is why I consider the former a weakness and the latter simply something I'm not good at.

To summarise:
- STRENGTHS: Everything you're good at that comes natural and easy to you
- WEAKNESSES: Everything you're not good at that has a negative impact on your life.

It would be easy to jump to the conclusion that happiness comes from focusing on our strengths and avoiding our weaknesses. However, it might not be that black and white. Personally, I don't like the word weaknesses. I prefer to call them 'areas for development'. There are many things I'm not good at where I have no intentions to invest effort to improve (like cooking for example), but they are not weaknesses. As we discussed above, something is only a weakness once it negatively impacts our life. Because of that negative impact, we shouldn't just ignore them. Instead, we should learn to live and work with them. That doesn't mean that we should aim to 'fix' or 'remove' all our weaknesses, but we should at least be aware of them and minimise their impact. That is why I like to think of them as areas for development. They are not areas for improvement or removal from our lives, but simply areas for development. This implies we're aware of them and we're working on it. Remember my patience example above? If I had just ignored it or removed situations that require patience from my life, I would not have been anywhere near as successful in my career and life as I have been. I would have had to stop working with other people, or I would have clashed with colleagues all the time because my expectations were too high. I would probably never have even tried to learn to kitesurf (my favourite activity) because I would have wanted to avoid the patience required to learn. Many of my favourite activities and best friendships have required patience at some point, so if I had avoided them, or not found the necessary patience, I wouldn't have any of them in my life today. Patience is still not something that comes naturally to me. However, merely being aware of the fact that it is one of my areas for development helps me respond better in situations when it is required and be kinder to myself and others when things take a bit longer than I would like them to. Don't avoid or ignore your weaknesses. Be aware of them, accept that they may never be your biggest strengths, but set out to be the best you can be in all areas of your life.

By spending some time thinking through your strengths and weaknesses and making yourself aware of them, you give yourself a much better chance of identifying the strategies, tactics and activities that will help you achieve your happiness goals. It enables you to fully leverage your strengths and work on or work around your weaknesses. For example, imagine one of your goals for achieving happiness is to spend more quality time with your kids. By learning about your strengths and weaknesses, you have come to understand that creative storytelling and coming up with fun things to do are among your strengths, but one of your weaknesses is that you are pretty unorganised and often forget things. You now know, the key to achieving your goal to spend more quality time with your kids lies in making sure you make the time — not making sure you come up with great things to do, that part comes easy to you. You can focus your energy on sticking to your schedule and organising your days better without having to worry much about what to do with your kids when the time comes.

Being fully aware of your strengths and weaknesses will be very valuable once you start designing your Happiness Blueprint later in this book. It means that you will be in the best possible position to decide on strategies and tactics for achieving your goals.

Before we dive into identifying your strengths and weaknesses, there is one more important aspect to consider, and that is the fact that the two are often very closely related and, in many cases, have the same underlying foundation. It's important to see ourselves and others as whole constructs, not individual pieces we can mix and match together. Often, the things that are our biggest strengths are also what cause our most significant weaknesses. For example, someone might be an extraordinarily analytical thinker who excels at understanding logic and rational decision-making. The same person might often get criticised for not being empathetic and understanding of other people's feelings. However, if this person were more emotional and caring, they probably wouldn't be the extraordinary thinker that they are. Being a great rational decision-maker requires our brain to work a certain way and being empathetic requires our brain to work a different way. Rational decision-making, by definition, requires emotions to be put aside. That doesn't mean they can't learn to be (or at least appear) more empathetic and caring, but it would probably require quite a bit of effort and never truly come easy. Similarly, someone else might be highly regarded for being very caring, kind and nurturing and for having the ability to relate to people quickly. He or she might then get criticised for being overly emotional and not being able to make rational decisions. Being really good at one thing often automatically means not being very good at other things simply because the two require opposing skills and mindsets. We all have strengths and weaknesses. It's important to view ourselves and others as a whole and to consider that our weaknesses and our strengths are closely related. Expecting ourselves, or others, to change one without any impact on the other (get rid of the weakness but keep the strengths) is often impossible.

With all of that in mind, it's time to figure out what your strengths and weaknesses are.

EXERCISE: IDENTIFY YOUR STRENGTHS AND WEAKNESSES

Most people are already well aware of their strengths and weaknesses. Often, the hard part is not identifying them, but admitting them. Remember, you don't need to share the exercises included in this book with anyone else. It's all just about helping you increase your awareness of yourself. The best way to do that is by being totally honest without worrying about being judged or misunderstood. So as you work through the exercise below, take some time to reflect and think, and make sure you're honest with yourself — and that applies to both weaknesses and strengths (some people will find it easier to admit weaknesses than identify strengths).

1. Start with what you already know. In the table below, or in the workbook, write down all the strengths and weaknesses you can think of. What are you good at and what are areas for development? Don't hold back at this point, just write down everything you can think of.

2. Think back to what you learned about your personality earlier in this chapter. What strengths and weaknesses are typical for your personality type? Which of those resonate with you?

3. Think through the questions below to expand your list of STRENGTHS. For each question, think about your answers and the underlying strengths involved. Again, don't hold back, write down everything that comes to mind.
   a. Think about situations where you did really well and were successful. What were you doing? What contributed to your success?
   b. What are activities you thoroughly enjoy and can do for hours without getting tired?
   c. What do others compliment and recommend you for? What are the things your friends, family, colleagues or other people in your life think you do well?
   d. Think about especially happy memories and situations where you were particularly happy. What were you doing and what contributed to your happiness?
   e. Think of a time when you felt particularly proud of yourself. What happened and what were you proud of? What helped you achieve that?

4. Think through the questions below to expand your list of WEAKNESSES. For each question, think about your answers and the underlying weaknesses involved. Note down everything you can think of.

    a. Think about situations where you did not achieve something you set out to do or did not get the result you wanted or needed. What were you doing and what got in the way of it being a success?

    b. What have others (managers, family, colleagues, friends) criticised you for and suggested you could work on?

    c. Think about situations where you had to work really hard to achieve something. What were you doing and why was it so hard?

    d. Think about activities that take a lot of your energy and often leave you feeling exhausted and drained. What are the activities and why do you find them draining?

    e. Think about situations when you feel stressed or anxious. What is happening and what is causing the stress? Do you find other people seem to get less stressed in similar situations? Could this be due to a weakness on your part?

    f. Can you think of a time when you felt disappointed with yourself? What happened and why did you feel disappointed?

5. Optional: Ask people for feedback. If you don't feel confident you can objectively identify your strengths and weaknesses by working through the steps above, it can be very valuable to ask others for feedback. If you do, make sure you ask several people with different connections to you (friends, family, colleagues) and encourage them to be honest. Be prepared to hear some things you might not like. Don't take them personally. We all have weaknesses, and it takes a strong person to be brave enough to ask for them openly. Moreover, once you know, you can start working on them.

	Strengths	Weaknesses (aka Areas for Development)
Write down anything you can think of		
What does your personality type suggest? Which ones do you relate to?		
What do you come up with while working through the questions above?		
What do others say?		

6. Review everything you've written down above. Go through and highlight the strengths and weaknesses you think have the most significant impact on your life or that represent the biggest opportunities.

You should now have a fairly good understanding of what your strengths and weaknesses (areas for development) are and which ones you should pay most attention to as you develop your Happiness Blueprint later in this book.

Before we wrap up this chapter on getting to know yourself, it's worth taking the time to think about those aspects you've discovered that you don't like and don't feel very positive about — they might not be as bad as you think they are.

Turn Negatives into Positives

Doing exercises like the ones in this chapter to learn more about your personality, values and strengths and weaknesses can be intense and a bit overwhelming, especially if you've never really thought much about all of this before. Hopefully, you found it valuable and you have discovered a lot of positive and exciting things about yourself. However, you've probably also identified a few things that you don't like all that much. Maybe learning more about yourself has highlighted some weaknesses you weren't aware of before, or maybe there are aspects of your personality you worry will hold you back in life, make you less popular and less successful. While I hope these exercises have given you a new level of awareness and confidence, they might also have given you some new doubts and potential insecurities. That is entirely normal and a part of the process. Nobody is perfect. We have all doubts, insecurities and things we are not good at. It's part of being human, and most of us are able to accept our shortcomings without too much trouble. However, for some of us, it's easy to get caught up in the negative and forget or minimise all the great things we have going for us. Others might not be overly caught up in negative aspects overall, but are stuck on one or two specific negative thoughts and are at risk of missing out on opportunities and the chance to live life to the fullest because of it. Regardless of how much those potentially negative aspects impact you, we all can benefit from spending some time reviewing them and looking for the positive in what feels like negatives.

We are often quick to pass judgment, on others as well as ourselves. We become aware of something that feels like it could be a potential problem or shortcoming, and right away we label it as something negative, a weakness, or something that will hold us back. Once we've applied that label, it becomes hard to assess something objectively and see potential opportunities or strengths in it. I firmly believe that for many of us, a key to a happier life lies in fully accepting ourselves for who we are and in being able to see the positive in the negative. Let me give you an example. For a long time, I used to consider my introversion as something negative. I often wished I could be more extroverted. I felt like introverts were disadvantaged in the world, that it was holding me back and that I was missing out on friendships and fun experiences simply because I didn't have as much energy for spending time around people as others had. The need to spend time alone often made me feel weird and at times even unproductive. I worried about others judging me, thinking I was distant, a loner and no fun. Through learning about myself and what it means to be introverted, I slowly started to realise all the great stuff that comes with being an introvert. Today, I consider my introversion one of my biggest strengths. It's one of the reasons why I'm good at my job because I can work independently and just get things done. It means I'm good at deep thinking and reflection, which has been a crucial skill on my journey to a happier life, and it means that I'm highly independent and don't rely on other people to feel good and to be entertained. The time I spend alone is now the most productive time of my days and most importantly, being an introvert is one of the reasons why I have formed such close relationships with a small number of people rather than trying to balance a large group of friends.

There is a good chance that you also have something that you consider a negative or weakness right now that could be one of your best attributes if you spend some time understanding and developing it. Furthermore, as we've learned, our strengths and weaknesses are often caused by similar underlying traits and preferences and the same is true for other aspects of our personality and who we are. That means, while something you have identified as 'negative' might be just that, it might, at the same time, be closely connected, or even the cause of, something you consider a positive. For example, one of my good friends often doubts and criticises herself for reacting, and occasionally overreacting, emotionally and taking things too personally. She sometimes feels she would be better at dealing with life and feel less stressed if she could be more rational and objective. However, the fact that she is a very emotional and sensitive person also makes her an amazing friend, sibling, daughter and partner. It is also a real asset in her job, where she has to deal with a lot of diverse people and can fully leverage her ability to relate to them emotionally and show genuine empathy.

The purpose of this short section is to encourage you to spend a bit of time thinking about those things you've learned about yourself that you consider a negative and to then try and see the positive in them. It's not about changing anything or trying to improve in certain areas. It's simply about becoming aware of the fact that not everything that looks like a negative aspect is always just that. Why is this important for finding happiness? For two main reasons: firstly, understanding how things you have labelled as negative or undesirable might have a positive impact on your life will be very valuable later in this book when you start thinking about exactly what will make you happy and how you can achieve that. Secondly, as we will learn in the next chapter, positive thinking and the ability to see the good in the bad has been shown to be a vital skill of happy people, and this is a great place to start practising.

EXERCISE: FIND THE POSITIVE
IN THE NEGATIVE

There isn't any methodology or science to this exercise. It's simply about you taking some time to find the positive in what you consider negatives.

1. In the template below, or in the workbook (or just on a piece of paper) write down everything you have learned about yourself (or already knew) that you consider harmful, a shortcoming or something you worry will hold you back. Write down everything you don't like about yourself. Only write one item per line.

2. Go through them line by line and for each, try really hard to come up with something positive. Think about how it impacts your life in the broadest sense. Consider if the same underlying trait causes things you love about yourself. Think about what it enables you to do that you wouldn't be able to do without this trait. You should be able to see something positive for each negative, even if it's a bit of a stretch in some cases.

3. If you struggle with the above, ask for help. Find a friend or family member who you trust and who is good at positive thinking (a very optimistic person who tends to always see the good before the bad). Ask them to work through your list with you. Often the objectivity another person brings can help you see positive aspects you would not have been able to identify on your own.

4. Go back and highlight or underline those parts that you feel are especially important and relevant and that you want to make sure you stay aware of as you continue to work through this book.

List everything you don't like about yourself or consider a shortcoming or negative in some other way.	Come up with something positive about each negative. Try hard and ask for help if you get stuck.

One important thing to clarify is that this exercise is not about removing, ignoring or overlooking our shortcomings and possible negative aspects of our personality. The idea is not for you to now go ahead thinking you've turned all your negatives into positives. The negative still exists. There is a chance that some of them should have never been considered shortcomings in the first place and working through the exercise above has made you realise that (like my earlier introversion example). However, even in those cases, there is probably still some negative element — otherwise, you would not have categorised it as such in the first place. The purpose of this exercise was not to make the negatives go away. Instead, it was about creating awareness of them and their potential positive impacts on your life, so you can use that information as you continue learning about happiness in this book and when you design your blueprint for a happier life. Both our positive and our negative traits make us who we are, and it's important to consider both together as a whole. Being aware of your shortcomings and their impact means you can work on them if you think that will help you be happier, and it means you can avoid strategies and tactics that require skills you might not be good at and instead focus on those that do play to your strengths.

We have covered a lot of ground in this chapter. Hopefully, you have learned a lot about yourself or have been reminded of aspects you were already aware of. Before we move on, it's time to pull it all together and write your personal profile.

Your Personal Profile

We have discussed a lot in this chapter and chances are you might feel a bit overwhelmed by it all — but hopefully excited and energised as well. Everything you've learned will form the foundation for your Happiness Blueprint. As you know, the goal of this book is to help you design your individual plan for a happier life based on your specific personality, values, preferences and strengths and weaknesses. In the next chapter, we will review the scientific research into what may or may not make us happy. A key goal will be for you to review and analyse that information in the context of who you are, and to identify those elements that are particularly important and relevant to you. To be able to do that, it helps to summarise everything you've learned about yourself on one or two pages that you can easily refer back to throughout the rest of this book to refresh your memory when needed. Therefore, the last exercise in this chapter is about developing your personal profile.

EXERCISE: CREATE YOUR PERSONAL PROFILE

The goal of this exercise is to combine what you've learned about yourself in a simple way on one or two pages that you can easily refer back to. You can do this in any way you like. I'm including a template for you to use if you wish to. However, you don't have to follow the template. If you're a creative person, you might want to create something with images and colours; if you enjoy writing you might simply write a one-page profile of yourself; if you like to keep it short and simple, just write down some bullet points. Whatever works for you, as long as it gives you a good overview of who you are, including:

- your values
- the key things that define you
- what you like about yourself and what you don't like about yourself
- your strengths and weaknesses and
- who you are and who you are not.

Your Personal Profile Template

Hello, my name is....	
Here are three things that define me:	The three things that are most important to me are...
Here are some things I like about myself:	And here are some things I don't really like about myself:
I'm good at lots of things, including...	But, there are also some things I'm not so good at, for example...
My MBTI Personality Type is:	
That means I am...	And I'm not...
This is how I would describe myself in one sentence:	

Make sure you keep your profile handy as you continue working through this book. As I've mentioned several times, no one other than yourself can tell you what will genuinely and lastingly make you happy. It's up to you to figure that out. The next two chapters will provide insights and information to guide and inspire you, but it is up to you to review these insights in the context of who you are. Keeping your profile close by will help you do so. Refer back to it whenever you feel like you need a reminder or when you're not sure if and how something you learn applies to you.

That brings us to the end of the 'Getting to Know Yourself' chapter. By now you should have a pretty good understanding of who you are. Hopefully, you had some fun working it all out. However, remember that you are a living, breathing, human being who is constantly changing and evolving. Some of the things you have discovered about yourself tend to not change much at all throughout your life, for example, your level of extroversion vs. introversion, but others are likely to change over time, especially your strengths and weaknesses and your values. I love doing exercises like these, so I tend to re-do them at least once a year. I have noticed that my personality doesn't change much at all. I am and always have been an INTJ when doing the Myers-Briggs personality test and every time I read the description I relate to it strongly, which tells me it must be true. On the other hand, my values have changed quite a bit over the past five or six years, and I've noticed my strengths and weaknesses change depending on my life circumstances and the challenges I face. However, there is also a lot of consistency and the key pillars of who I am don't tend to change much — and when they do, it's very slowly. I can highly recommend doing exercises like these regularly to make sure you're aware of any change and can adjust accordingly. This also is important to keep in mind as you develop your blueprint for a happy life. You change, life changes, so it makes sense that what makes you happy changes as well. That is why there is a whole chapter at the end to help you review and improve your blueprint over time.

However, we've got two more sections to work through before you can start designing your blueprint. Now that we know who we are, it's time to shift focus back to happiness.

The Scientific View of Finding Happiness

"The grand essentials to happiness in this life are something to do, something to love, and something to hope for."
GEORGE WASHINGTON BURNAP, THE SPHERE AND
DUTIES OF WOMAN: A COURSE OF LECTURES

I N PART I of this book, we looked at what happiness actually is. We discussed the different definitions and viewpoints, looked at how happiness is different from experiencing positive emotions and success, and we learned that experiencing negative emotions does not automatically make us unhappy. We also scratched the surface of what determines how happy we are and learned that it is a combination of our genetics, environmental factors and voluntary activities. Now it's time to get more specific and take a look at what exactly research suggests may or may not make us happy. The goal of this chapter is to give you a better understanding of what may contribute to your happiness and to help you consider these insights in the context of what you have learned about yourself in the previous chapter. As you work through this book, your goal should be to identify the factors and insights that are most relevant to you, and that are likely to have the most significant positive impact on your happiness. These insights will then form the foundation of your Happiness Blueprint later on. Therefore, I would recommend taking notes as you read through this chapter, so you remember the things that matter most to you when it is time to design your blueprint. There will also be exercises to help with this at the end of each main section.

Before we get into it, remember that, for the purpose of this book, we have defined happiness as a lasting feeling of satisfaction with life on the whole and feeling good about one's life today and feeling positive about the future. This book is not about experiencing a lot of momentary positive emotions like pleasure and joy, or being successful in the traditional sense, but about increasing your overall love for life. Consequently, this chapter will not talk about the little things you can do to experience joy, like having ice cream, going for a walk on the beach or listening to your favourite song. Instead, we will focus on what can potentially help us achieve that long-term, lasting happiness and life satisfaction that we're all striving for.

Before we get into it and start reviewing scientific research finding, there are a few things you should know about research.

THINGS TO KNOW ABOUT RESEARCH

A core belief behind this book is that we are all highly unique individuals and that there is no one-size-fits-all recipe for a happy life. I cannot stress enough how important it is to keep this in mind as you read through this chapter. I will refer to several research studies whose findings suggest that certain life circumstances, activities, or beliefs lead to a happier life — or a less happy one. When analysing these findings and assessing which ones are relevant for you, it is valuable to understand a few things about how research works. First of all, hardly any research studies take individual personalities, values and beliefs into account. There is very little research that looks at what may or may not make us happy, based on our unique personality. Secondly, you will struggle to find research where the findings always apply to all participants. Often, the results are valid for only a relatively small majority of participants. For example, researchers might investigate the impact that getting a dog has on happiness. They interview 500 people who recently got dogs and learn than 60% feel happier since they got the dog while 40% feel the same as before or even less happy (dogs can be hard work after all). After some more analysis and after making sure that there are no other factors that might impact the results, the researchers conclude that there is a direct correlation between getting a dog and happiness because the majority of study participants reported feeling happier since having a dog. However, this is not true for 40% of the people in the study. This is a highly simplified example. Most researchers put substantial effort into making sure their findings are robust and accurate. Nevertheless, it is important to consider that in almost all studies, some participants prove that the average results do not apply to everyone.

Another factor to consider is that research often looks for what makes the average person happier — which does not mean that others are unhappy. In a research project that compares people who have a certain trait with another group of people who don't have the trait, researchers might conclude that the group that has the trait is, on average, happier. However, group A being, on average, happier than Group B, does not mean that Group B is not happy. They are just not quite as happy as group A — and in some cases, there is only a slight difference. For example, researchers might hypothesise that people who regularly go to music concerts are more likely to be happy than those who don't. They collect data from 1000 people from each group and find that, on average, concert-goers rate their happiness as 7.8 on the 10-point scale and people who don't regularly go to concerts, on average, rate their happiness as 7.3. The researchers conclude that people who go to music concerts are happier. However, those who don't go to concerts still rate their happiness pretty high and only minimally lower than the concert-goers. With the difference between the two groups this small, it is entirely possible that the results would be different with a larger sample size — or just a different one. And even if the difference between the two groups would be bigger, for example 9.0 versus 7.5, an average happiness score of 7.5 still suggests that most of the people who don't enjoy concerts are happy.

Furthermore, we need to consider how data is often analysed and, to some extent, manipulated. I still remember an introductory statistics class I had to take at university as part of my economics degree — the same kind of statistics class psychology and sociology students take. One of the first things we learned was to 'clean up our data' by removing outliers that mess up our findings. This was done to make it easier to work with our data-sets. The assumption is that if the majority of the data falls in the same area, those few unique outliers that don't, can be ignored. This is a common procedure in research and is not considered cheating at all. However, if you're one of those 'outliers', it means your viewpoint is not considered in the research findings and the results won't be relevant to you.

Another thing to consider when evaluating research findings is that the cause and effect relationship between happiness and the traits investigated in the studies can be unclear. While something might lead to a happier life, it's also possible that happier people are more likely to show the trait. For example, coming back to our earlier example of getting a dog. It's possible that bringing a dog into our life makes us happier (at least for the average person). However, it's also possible that happier people are more likely to get a dog. Similarly, it's possible that going to music concerts makes people happy. However, it is just as likely that happy people are going to more shows. Researchers work hard to determine the exact cause and effect relationship between the factors they investigate, but often it's not possible to be 100% certain about it.

One final piece of advice I would give when reviewing

research findings is to pay close attention to the study participants. While researchers are usually careful to specify in their publications exactly who participated in their study, this information is often left out by mainstream media reporting on the findings. This can be problematic if the participants are a highly specific group of people, rather than a sample that represents the average population. For example, once you start taking a closer look, you realise that a lot of research has been done with university students as the subjects. This makes sense given that researchers usually work and teach at universities and, therefore, have easy access to students. However, it is important to consider that being a university student is a very distinctive time in a young person's life and it is usually before they have really found themselves and their path. Therefore, what might be true for students is not necessarily true for all of us. The same applies to studies where participants only include any other specific group such as elderly people, a specific age range or any other characteristic. Findings from studies with narrow or highly specific groups of participants can be valuable to all of us, however, I do challenge you to look beyond just the superficial findings and understand where the insights came from. That way, you will be in a much better position to assess their relevance to you.

Researchers all over the world work hard to identify and share insights. Many of these insights have been incredibly valuable for both individual people and societies. However, there are some limitations to most studies that we need to be aware of when analysing research findings with the goal of determining which ones are most relevant to us and can help us live a happier life. Research findings have their limitations, and it would be very risky to assume all of them apply to you. This chapter will give ideas and insights into what makes people happy and what doesn't. However, they are purely intended as ideas and suggestions, not concrete advice or facts. Hopefully, the knowledge you have gained about yourself in the previous chapter will enable you to put this into context and identify those areas that are most relevant to you. Nevertheless, I do urge you to stay open-minded and give all the ideas and insights presented a fair chance before you disregard any of them as not relevant to you. No one said the path to a happier life is easy, and sometimes it means giving new, uncomfortable things a go.

Before we get into discussing individual factors, let's put some structure in place. Remember Martin Seligman's Happiness Formula that we discussed in part 1? Let me refresh your memory. Seligman argues that happiness is essentially made up of three factors; your genetically set range, your life circumstances and voluntary activities.

$$H = S + C + V$$

Since we can't do much about our genetics (at least not yet), we will ignore the S in the formula for now and focus on the C and V.

C = Life Circumstances (External Factors — Aspects that we have limited control over)

V = Voluntary Activities (Internal Factors — Aspects that are fully within your control)

In the following, we will look at a number of life circumstances and voluntary factors and review what researchers have found when investigating their effects on happiness.

Life Circumstances

Is happiness determined, or at least influenced, by life circumstances such as wealth, relationships, education and other external factors? Let's see what existing research findings suggest.

Money and Materialistic Goods

Money can't buy happiness! Or can it? Let's face it, most of us live in a materialistic world where money does matter. Not surprisingly, several studies have shown that poverty leads to unhappiness and, on average, the populations of wealthy nations tend to be happier than the populations of impoverished countries. However, it's not as simple as saying more money equals more happiness. First of all, some people and nations live in poverty but report higher levels of happiness than wealthier people and countries. One only needs to look at The World Happiness Report which sets out to identify the happiest nations on an annual basis. The top five or 10 are usually no surprise, wealthy nations like Switzerland, the Scandinavian countries, New Zealand and Australia can all be found at the top of the list. However, in the 2018 report, you can find Costa Rica in 13th place and the United States in 18th place even though the per capita GDP of the United States is about 40% higher than that of Costa Rica. Similarly, the United Arab Emirates and Qatar, the two nations with the highest GDP per capita, are ranked at 20 and 32 respectively, which means there are several nations that are less wealthy but happier. Furthermore, The World Happiness Report also shows that, while income per capita in the United States has more than doubled since 1972, happiness (or subjective well-being) has remained roughly unchanged. The same seems to be true for other countries, including France and Japan.[36] While this indicates that wealth does not have a direct and linear impact on a nation's happiness, we also can't ignore the fact that out of the poorest 20% of countries only one (Tajikistan) can be found in the top 100 of happiest nations. This suggests that, at least on a national level, there is a relationship between wealth and happiness. However, data suggests there is a limit as to how much wealth leads to more happiness. In his analysis of data from the World Values Survey in his book Authentic Happiness, Martin Seligman shows that there is a correlation between a country's overall purchasing power and average life satisfaction. Interestingly, this is only true until the gross national product exceeds US$8000 per capita. Any added wealth above this level seems to have minimal impact on life satisfaction. However, Seligman also points out that there are exceptions to the rule, with Brazil, mainland China and Argentina scoring much higher on the happiness scale than their wealth would predict, and other countries, especially Japan and those in the former Soviet bloc, being less happy than their wealth would suggest.[37]

What is the conclusion from all this? If we look at wealth on a national level, poverty seems to have a negative impact on happiness, but more wealth only has a positive impact on happiness until the population's basic needs are met. After that, more wealth does not automatically result in more happiness. However, it does seem as though, on average, people living in wealthier countries might have an advantage when it comes to finding happiness, even though there is no happiness guarantee, no matter how wealthy your country is. In this context, it's also worth considering the cause and effect relationship. Just because wealthier nations, on average, seem to be happier, that does not automatically mean higher wealth is what's causing happiness. Wealthy nations are also often the ones less impacted by natural disasters, they are often in more comfortable climates, they often provide better education and generally a more comfortable lifestyle. It's just as likely that those factors are what makes people happier, and not merely the fact that they have more money to spend.

What if we look at the correlation between money and happiness at a personal level? If we look at people within the same country, are those with more wealth more likely to be happy? Who better to ask than two Nobel Laureates? In 2000, psychologist Daniel Kahneman and economist Angus Deaton published a paper in which they argue that there is a positive relationship between more money and happiness. However, there is a limit. Kahneman and Deaton analysed data from more than 450,000 responses to the Gallup-Health-ways Well-Being Index, a daily survey of 1000 US residents conducted by the Gallup organisation. Based on their calculations, happiness increases with wealth up to a point where the person has an annual income of about US$75,000 which, at the time, was about 10% more than the average income in the United States. Any additional increases in income beyond $75,000 did not seem to have a direct impact on happiness.[38] In other words, if you have below average income and are struggling to get by financially, there is a good chance that more money will make you happier. However, if you're already living a fairly comfortable life, more money might not be the main thing to pursue to increase your happiness.

What about the super-rich? It's easy to look at the rich and famous and their lifestyles and assume that they must be happy. After all, how can you not be happy if you have a personal helicopter to take you anywhere you want, the cash to buy whatever you desire and don't ever have to work a day in your life again if you don't want to? Ed Diener and his colleagues took a scientific lens to the question of whether the super-rich

Phyllis was very unhappy

are really happier than the rest of us.[39] They compared the subjective well-being of people from Forbes' list of wealthiest Americans (individuals with a net worth of $125 million and more) with the subjective well-being of a group of ordinary people from the same geographical area. The wealthy people reported slightly higher levels of subjective well-being than the 'ordinary' people did. However, it was only a slight difference, and there were several unhappy wealthy people in the study. Furthermore, none of the wealthy participants believed that money was a major source of their happiness.

If you find that surprising, consider this next research finding: winning the lottery is unlikely to make you any happier in the long run. A famous study done in the 1970s showed that people who had won the lottery only rated their happiness minimally higher than a control group that did not win anything (4 out of 5 vs. 3.82 out of 5). What's more, the lottery winners reported getting significantly less pleasure from ordinary, everyday events and tasks.[40] However, other studies suggest that winning the lottery might have a positive impact on mental health,[41] so it's not all bad news for the lucky winners.

Surprising as these findings might be to some, researchers believe there is a simple explanation. They suggest that chasing money purely for its own sake is likely the reason why some wealthy people report being unhappy and lacking fulfilment. In the research project titled The Dark Side of the American Dream, Tim Kasser and Richard Ryan suggest that pursuing money and financial success as the primary goal and value in one's life has a negative impact on well-being and mental health. However, that does not mean that striving for financial success is always a bad idea. It just shouldn't be the main goal or a goal in itself. For someone who knows herself and her values well and who has a clear purpose in life, money can enable her to live a better, happier life based on her values. For someone who wants to provide the best possible life for his family, more money can enable him to offer a new level of security and comfort which then makes him happier. Kasser and Ryan argue that it is those people who build wealth just for the sake of it, without any clear purpose, who will struggle to find happiness no matter how much money they manage to amass.

If more money doesn't necessarily result in more happiness, what about the things money can buy? Do they make us happy? Unfortunately, not really. Researchers have shown that people tend to overestimate the value materialistic goods will give them in the long term. While the fancy new car or apartment might make you happy in the moment, the effect wears off over time, and you feel pretty much the same way about your new car or apartment as you did about the old. Interestingly, when asked to predict the value that material items will bring them, as opposed to the value experiences will bring, most people tend to attach a higher future value to the material items. However, studies have shown that once we have the item and have had the experience, we actually attach a higher value to the experience and consider it more worth our money than the material item.[42] In other words, spending your money on experiences like travel, quality time with friends and family or your hobbies is more likely to bring you long-term happiness than investing your money in materialistic goods.

Something else that might be worth spending your money on to increase your happiness is time. A group of researchers around Ashley Whillans and Elizabeth Dunn showed that using your money to buy time, for example, by paying others to do your chores, was linked to greater life satisfaction in seven studies with more than 6000 participants. The researchers backed up these findings with an experiment. Sixty working adults from Vancouver, Canada were each given two payments of $40 on two consecutive weekends. On the first weekend, the participants were randomly assigned into two groups. Group one was told to spend their $40 on something that would save them time, the other group was told to spend the money on a materialistic item. On the second weekend, the groups switched, so that at the end of the experiment, each person had spent $40 on a purchase to save time on one weekend and $40 on a material item on the other weekend. Each participant received a phone call at 5pm on each of the two respective spending days. They were asked about their feelings, the positive and negative effects of the purchases and the time stress they experienced on that day. The findings showed that the majority of participants reported higher positive effects and less stress on the day they made the purchase that saved them time and less positive effect and more stress on the day they purchased the materialistic item.[43]

However, new evidence has shown that some material purchases can, in fact, have a positive impact on our happiness — if the purchase aligns with your personality and values. Researchers from the University of Cambridge analysed the spending of more than 600 individuals in the UK based on their bank transactions.[44] The study participants also filled out a questionnaire about their personality (using the Big Five model we discussed earlier) as well as their life satisfaction. The researchers then compared the participants' spending with their personality type to identify to what extent spending fitted the individual's personality. Their findings suggested that those people who spent their money on things that fitted their personality, on average, reported higher levels of life satisfaction. Moreover, the extent to which spending fitted their personality had a stronger impact on happiness than the individual's total income or their total spending, suggesting that spending money on the right things is more important to our happiness than having lots of money or buying lots of stuff.

In summary, it seems that increasing our wealth beyond what we need to live a secure and comfortable life won't automatically make us any happier, no matter how much money we have. There is increasing support for the hypothesis that it's not so much about how much money we have or don't have, but about why we strive for it and what we do with it. Therefore, the question you should ask yourself is not whether money will make you happy. Instead, ask yourself what your real values and purpose are and if/how money will enable you to live according to them. For me, freedom and independence are among my highest values. At times, I am very focused on earning more money because I know it enables me to be free at other times. Having created a situation where I am financially secure and don't need to worry about how I am paying the bills next month has undoubtedly been an ingredient to my happiness. Whenever I feel that financial safety buffer is getting too small, I go back to working hard for several months because I know I need to feel somewhat financially secure to enjoy my freedom and independence at other times. However, it's not the money that makes me happy, but what it enables me to do — for example, spending time writing this book. So as you think about your own situation and whether you want to make earning more money part of your Happiness Blueprint, think carefully about exactly why you feel you need the money. What will it enable you to do that you can't already do? How will that genuinely contribute to your happiness? How will it allow you to live a more meaningful life based on your values and beliefs?

Whether or not building wealth will make you happier comes down to your current situation as well as your personality and values. If you are currently struggling to make ends meet and have to worry about providing for yourself or your family, then earning more money has the potential to improve your happiness significantly. If you can already live relatively comfortably with your current income, it comes down to your personality and values. Ask yourself how important long-term financial security is for you? How much do you value material goods and other things that money can buy? What are your core values, and do you need more money to live by them? For example, if you value travelling but you currently can't afford it, more money can help you be happier because it would enable you to have more of your core value in your life. On the other hand, if you value family time or the freedom to do whatever you want with your time, chasing after more money probably won't make you any happier. It might even make you less happy because the extra time you spend working to earn more money is time you can't spend on what you value most.

Work

Regardless of the exact impact money might have on our happiness, you can't argue with the fact that it is an essential aspect of our lives and our society. While there might be a small number of people that live in self-sufficient communities where money doesn't matter, the majority of us rely on it to live our lives. Work is how most of us get that money. If you work a standard 40-hour week, you spend almost a quarter of your time at your job. If we assume you sleep seven hours per night, that's about a third of your waking hours. Add to that commuting time and overtime, and the percentage is even higher. For many of us, work is the single one thing that takes up most of our time each week — and raising children and looking after a household is very much considered work in this context. With it taking up such a large chunk of our time and being such a critical part of our lives, it's important to look at if, and how, work impacts our happiness.

Let's start by looking at the relationship between work satisfaction and overall well-being. Does high job satisfaction mean we're happier? Findings from research into this question are not entirely conclusive. Researchers argue that there are three possible relationships between job- and life-satisfaction.[45] The first one is called the 'spill-over model'. In this scenario, happiness at work has a direct spill-over effect on overall life satisfaction and vice versa. The second model, 'segmentation', implies that there is no direct relationship between work and life satisfaction, meaning a person might be very happy with life overall but not happy with their job or the other way around. How we feel about one does not impact how we feel about the other. The third and final theory is called 'compensation'. In this model, people try to compensate for unhappiness in one area by pursuing happiness and satisfaction in the other. It is highly likely that the model applied in any given situation varies from person to person, with some of us more likely to experience the spill-over effect and others more likely to experience segmentation or compensation. However, in a study of a random sample of workers, 68% fell into the spill-over category, suggesting that for many of us there is a positive relationship between job satisfaction and overall life satisfaction.[46] Therefore, it's worth looking at how we can increase our job satisfaction and how we can improve the chances of our work having a positive impact on our happiness.

Two researchers, Jan-Emmanuel De Neve and George Ward, have done excellent work in this area. They have analysed data from The World Happiness Report and the Gallup World Poll to look at the relationship between happiness and work.[47] Their findings provide a number of interesting insights. Maybe not too surprisingly, the most robust result is that unemployment very likely leads to unhappiness. Around the world, people in employment rate their overall life satisfaction significantly higher than unemployed people do. Those people who are unemployed also report higher levels of negative emotions and experiences in their day-to-day lives. De Neve and Ward also found that workers in labour-intensive industries like construction, mining, manufacturing, transport, farming, fishing and forestry reported lower levels of happiness in every region around the world, both regarding overall life satisfaction as well as day-to-day emotional states. However, before you jump to the conclusion that blue-collar jobs make us unhappy, you have to consider the possibility that the cause and effect is the other way around, and unhappy people are more likely to seek employment in these industries rather than working in these industries being what makes them unhappy. And as always, it's worth remembering that these are averages and that not all unemployed people and blue-collar workers in the sample were unhappy. Another, probably not very surprising, finding is that, in developed countries, self-employed people are reporting higher levels of overall life satisfaction. However, they also report higher levels of daily negative emotions like stress and worry — something that is to be expected given the level of responsibility they have for themselves and potentially others.

De Neve and Ward also looked at job satisfaction around the world to determine what makes some jobs more enjoyable than others. Their findings suggest that, on average, people in well-paid jobs tend to report higher levels of happiness and report being more satisfied with their lives and their jobs. However, the researchers also identified a number of other factors that are strong predictors of happiness. The one that stands out the most as a particularly strong predictor for happiness is work-life balance. This suggests that even people with less ideal and fulfilling jobs can increase their happiness by finding a meaningful purpose outside of work and balancing the two effectively. Other aspects that seem to impact job satisfaction are variety at work and regularly needing to learn new skills, the extent to which a person believes their job is secure, the level of autonomy the employee has, as well as how much support they receive from colleagues. On the other hand, work that is generally considered high-risk seems to be associated with lower levels of well-being.

Another well-known researcher in the field, Amy Wrzesniewski, argues that job satisfaction might be less about external characteristics of the job, like pay and industry sector, and more about how we perceive our work. In a 2001 research paper published together with Jane Dutton, she argues that past research has often been too focused on external factors and did not take the role the employee can play into account. Wrzesniewski believes that even people in very restricted and routine jobs have some influence on how they perceive and approach their work.[48] The thinking behind this is that, while certain aspects of our jobs might be set in stone, most of us have the opportunity to shape aspects of what we do or how we do it, meaning we have an opportunity to shape our job to bring us more fulfilment and satisfaction. Several real-world examples support this theory. In one study, hospital cleaning staff were interviewed to determine their job perception and their overall job satisfaction.[49] The researchers noticed significant differences in how these workers described their jobs and their skill levels, allowing them to separate participants into two groups. The first group were those cleaners that were strictly focused on the actual job description, motivated to only do the bare minimum required and who interacted as little as possible with others. The study found that the cleaners in this group did not like cleaning in general, believed that the skill level required for the job was low and did not show much initiative to engage with other members of the workplace or to try to change the tasks of their job. The cleaners in the second group, on the other hand, had a different view of their work and looked far beyond the actual job description. They had the exact same job, but they modified tasks, voluntarily took on tasks outside their specific job description and they frequently interacted with a wide range of people, including patients, visitors, colleagues and other hospital staff. Members of this second group had positive feelings towards their job and the tasks, thought of it as highly skilled work and showed commitment and a sense of ownership by initiating and engaging in activities that helped patients and visitors, as well as their colleagues and other staff in the hospital. This process of shaping one's job in a way that provides more fulfilment and satisfaction is called 'job crafting', and its positive effect on job satisfaction has been shown in other examples as well. From hairdressers to engineers, nurses, information technicians and kitchen employees, job crafting has been proven as a method to help individuals get more satisfaction out of their jobs. If you are interested in learning more about job crafting, how it works and how you might be able to apply it in your job, I strongly recommend reading Amy Wrzesniewski and Jane Dutton's paper Crafting a Job: Revisioning Employees as Active Crafters of Their Work (you should be able to find it on Google).

Job crafting is all about bringing meaning and purpose to a job and connecting it to your personal values. The theory that finding one's job meaningful is key to high levels of job satisfaction has also been backed up by the findings of a survey of more than 2000 Australians aged between 16 and 70.[50] When asked what they define as 'a good job', it being well-paid was the top response (66%). However, the next three top responses all refer to the importance of meaning and purpose. According to the survey respondents, a 'good job' needs to be fulfilling (61%), something I'm passionate about (57%) and meaningful (53%). Several other surveys and studies have also shown that finding meaning and purpose in the work is a key factor of job satisfaction for a growing number of workers. In short, meaningful work increases job satisfaction, which is then likely to have a positive impact on our overall happiness. In this context, it helps to remember that there are two ways in which we can ensure our work is meaningful. Firstly, we can find a job that is meaningful to us and aligns with our values and strengths. Secondly, we can be proactive and take the initiative to shape and modify the job we have to go beyond the actual job description and make it more meaningful to us.

Let's assume you have found a job that suits you and that you're at least not completely unhappy with. Will achievements such as promotions, pay rises and awards make you happier? Interestingly, recent research suggests that it might, in fact, be the other way around and that happiness leads to career success. After an in-depth review of cross-sectional, longitudinal and experimental research into happiness and job satisfaction, a team of researchers working with Lisa Walsh from the University of California came to the conclusion that happiness precedes and leads to career success rather than success at work leading to happiness.[51]

Regardless of what the latest research says, most people who had a significant promotion, or another career achievement, would probably argue that it did make them happier. However, the fundamental question is how long that increased happiness lasted. Remember, we're not talking about short-term pleasure and joy here, but about lasting happiness and life satisfaction. While promotions and pay rises, similarly to winning the lottery or buying new materialist goods, make us feel good in the moment, this happiness usually wears off quickly, and we're back to our previous level of happiness. Researchers often refer to this phenomenon as hedonic adaptation and more mainstream literature also calls it the hedonic treadmill. It describes the often-observed tendency for people's happiness to spike or drop immediately after positive and negative events, but that this effect is short-term and will level off quickly. Before long, most people are back to the same level of happiness they reported before the event. Hedonic adaptation is often listed as one of the main reasons why external events like career success, as well as more money and materialistic goods, don't seem to have a lasting impact on our overall life satisfaction.

In summary, if you believe increasing your job satisfaction is key to a happier life, looking for meaning as opposed to promotions and achievement seems to be the way to go. Finding work that is meaningful to you or finding ways to bring more meaning into your job seems to be much more likely to result in lasting happiness than chasing pay rises and promotions which might make you happy in the moment, but the effect will most likely wear off quickly.

To decide whether your work situation is something you should look at to increase your happiness, ask yourself to what extent your work aligns with your core values. Do you feel your work is meaningful and helps you live by your values? If not, does your work enable you to live your values outside of work by allowing enough time and providing enough income? Overall, do you enjoy your work and can you see a long-term future in the profession? If you answer 'No' to all these questions, ask yourself how important that is for your happiness. Some people are perfectly happy even though they don't enjoy their work and don't get much fulfilment out of it. For some people, work is just work, and they are happy regardless of their job situation. For others, work is an important aspect of their lives and their identity. If you're the latter and you're currently not fulfilled with your job, it might be worth considering a change.

Relationships

While money, materialistic goods and career success might impact happiness to varying degrees, surely good relationships with our families, friends and spouses should make us happier, right? The short answer is yes — but even when it comes to relationships, it's not a one-size-fits-all situation.

On the whole, numerous studies have shown that people with a rich, busy social life are happier than those who spend a lot of time on their own. One often cited study in this area was done by Ed Diener and Martin Seligman. Their study of 222 undergraduate students found that those students who rate their happiness the highest had stronger social relationships and were overall more extroverted.[52] However, before you rush out the door to find a whole bunch of new friends to socialise with, there are a few things you should consider. First of all, a rich social life was not an absolute predictor of happiness. Several people in Diener and Seligman's study reported low levels of happiness even though they had a great social life. Furthermore, a rich social life does not necessarily mean more friends and more people to socialise with. It could well be that those people who rate their social life as active have a small, but very close, group of friends. We also can't ignore the fact that this study was limited to university students who are likely to be of an age where friends and social lives are particularly important and active. The same research with people in their 40s might have shown different results. Finally, and this ties right back to what motived me to write this book, Diener and Seligman do not take different personalities into account. While a rich social life and little alone time might be a critical element to a happy life for an extrovert, social activity might not be significant at all for an introvert. Many introverts enjoy alone time and prefer to have a less active social life. This is also backed up by another study which, while showing support of the 'extroverts are happier' hypothesis, also clearly shows that there are numerous happy introverts.[53] Therefore, it seems that a rich social life does not automatically lead to happiness and that it is highly likely that some people are happier with a less busy social life.

A factor that does seem to have an impact on happiness is our relationship with our family. Several studies have found that people with close, supportive families tend to be happier, on average. For example, in order to get a better understanding of the importance of family support for our happiness, Rebecca North and her colleague conducted a study that compared the impact of family support on happiness with the impact family income has.[54] The researchers collected data from 274 married adults across a 10-year period. They found family social support had a substantial positive impact on long-term happiness, significantly more so than income, which only had a minor impact on lasting happiness. Several other studies have also shown that strong family relationships seem to have a positive impact on happiness. However, not all of the happy people in any of these studies had strong family relationships, and not all of the unhappy people didn't feel close to their families. You don't have to have a great relationship with your family to be happy. However, research findings do suggest that it can help. But it is also worth remembering that family isn't necessarily limited to the people we're genetically related to. Sometimes family are the people you choose to make your family.

Other types of relationships that researchers have looked at are romantic ones, especially marriage. Michael Argyle does a great job in reviewing and summarising the research into happiness and marriage (as well as happiness and other environmental factors).[55] According to Argyle, most existing research into the matter clearly shows that married people tend to be happier than unmarried people — with those not married but living together being happier than singles but singles being happier than divorcees and widows. However, it's important to note that the cause and effect relationship is not clear. Are married people happier or are happy people more likely to get married? The research also doesn't differentiate between those people who are single by choice and those who are just waiting for the right person to come along to get married. I wouldn't be surprised if the 'single by choice' group scores much higher than the group that wants to get married in the future. Furthermore, Argyle also points out that marriage is the one relationship that is often the greatest source of negative emotions like conflict, stress and anger, so marriage will not automatically lead to increased happiness for everyone and in some cases, it can even lead to a decrease in happiness (especially when it ends in divorce).

Another interesting study into the effect marriage has on life satisfaction was carried out by a group of researchers around Richard Lucas from Michigan State University.[56] This study is particularly interesting because it involved more than 24,000 participants and because it looked at the long-term effects of marriage, meaning it compared the self-reported level of happiness from years before getting married to the level of happiness many years after getting married. The researchers concluded that, on average, people experience a spike in happiness right after getting married, but most people seem to adapt to marriage after a few years and their self-reported levels of happiness are back to where they were before getting married (there is that hedonic adaptation again). However, Lucas and his colleagues also found that there were substantial differences between the individual participants in this study. Some participants, especially those that experienced high increases in happiness directly after getting married, still reported being significantly happier years later. On the other hand, other participants reported significant decreases in happiness as the years progressed. It's probably no surprise that marriage can be a great contributor to happiness, given it is one of the strongest social connections, a great source of support and because love is one of the strongest positive emotions we experience. Nevertheless, research suggests that marriage alone does not necessarily make us any happier, and there certainly is no guarantee that getting married will lead to lasting happiness.

However, overall relationships do seem to have an impact on happiness. Further support for this comes from Bangladesh. While Bangladesh is one of the poorest countries in the world, research has shown that its people report higher levels of happiness than many other, wealthier nations do. Researchers have concluded that one of the likely reasons for this is the importance of community and relationships in the Bangladeshi life and culture.[57] Bangladeshi people might not have the material comforts and security most of us enjoy, but their strong interpersonal relationships seem to more than make up for that when it comes to happiness.

In the end, it is important to remember that it is the quality of relationships that matters, not the quantity. Exactly what types of relationships and social life will make you happy is highly dependent on your personality and your values. The key to happiness is to understand who you are and to design your relationships around it. If you are an extrovert, building relationships probably comes easily to you. Your challenge might well be knowing when to stop making new friends and instead, nurturing the relationships you have. If you're an

introvert, you might find it harder to establish close relationships. However, being an introvert myself, my recommendation
would be not to hide behind it and get too comfortable on
your own. Enjoying your own company doesn't mean spending
all your time alone is what will make you happiest. I tend to
spend much time on my own and having 'me-time' is key to
my happiness and overall well-being. However, the one thing
that's even more valuable to my happiness is my amazing group
of friends. I might not see them all the time, and I definitely
spend more time alone than I spend with them, but I wouldn't
be anywhere near as happy as I am if I didn't have them in
my life. For most of us, some close relationships, even if it's
just a small number, can have a huge impact on our happiness.
So even if it doesn't come easy, it might be worth considering making 'deepening relationships' part of your Happiness
Blueprint — it's done wonders for me.

Major Tragic Events

Another area worth looking at is unexpected tragic life events,
mainly because they are bound to affect all of us at some stage.
Life is full of surprises and unexpected events so it's worth
understanding how they might impact our happiness. In this
case, we will focus on significant unforeseen tragic events under
the assumption that they are more likely to have a substantial
impact on happiness than minor tragedies have.

I don't think anyone makes it through life without experiencing some tragedies. From the death of a loved one to the
loss of a job, health issues or the loss of critical monetary items
like the family home through fire or a natural disaster, plus
many other tragic events, we will all have to deal with them
at some stage. Interestingly, several studies have shown that
the impact of tragedies might be much less severe and less

lasting than we would expect. For example, Frank Infurna and Suniya Luthar from Arizona State University studied longitudinal data from 50,000 people in Germany to determine the effects that tragic life events have.[58] They looked at the life satisfaction ratings from people who had experienced events such as divorce, unemployment and death of a spouse. Their findings indicate that most people will experience a decline in well-being and happiness after such an event, but that they will recover from the experience over time and return to the same, or at least similar, level of happiness they had before the event.

Another study looked at the impact of major accidents that left the victims paralysed. Not surprisingly, paralysed people rated their overall life satisfaction lower than people who were not paralysed. However, they still rated their happiness as higher than the mid-point of the scale (2.96 on a scale from 1 to 5). What's maybe even more surprising, they reported getting more happiness from mundane everyday tasks than they did before the accident.[59] However, research also suggests that there are some tragic life events, for example, the loss of a child or the death of a spouse in a car crash, that we never fully recover from and that have a lasting negative impact on our happiness.[60]

Nevertheless, it seems as though we have the ability to get through most major crises in life without it necessarily impacting our happiness, at least not in the long-term. Remember Sergeant Travis Mills and Ashley Sullenger from the first chapter? Both overcame significant tragedies and managed to find happiness again. Something that is interesting, though, is that some people seem to deal with such tragedies better and faster than others. Anthony Ong, one of the leading researchers in this field, believes that our ability to cultivate positive emotions has a significant impact on how well we cope with tragic events. His research shows that daily positive emotions help us deal better with stressful situations and enable us to recover faster from stress.[61] Furthermore, his study of people who have lost a spouse shows that positive emotions help us deal more effectively with tragedies.[62] Therefore, it might be worth exploring some techniques and methods for fostering positive thinking and emotions as part of your Happiness Blueprint to help you overcome tragedies — or build up resilience for ones that might come your way in the future. We will talk more about positive thinking when we discuss the impact voluntary activities have on our happiness.

Education

Does better education lead to higher life satisfaction? Is knowledge the key to happiness or is ignorance bliss? Let's find out.

One could argue that education should be under voluntary activities since we do have control over how much we learn. However, there are significant external factors that determine the kind of education we have access to, especially in our early life (which is the most critical time in our lives from an education and learning perspective). The region and family we are born into has a significant impact on our education, as well as the schools we go to, teachers we engage with and the resources that are available to us. Nevertheless, as we get older, education becomes more and more our own responsibility and a factor that is fully within our control for most of us, so that's something to keep in mind.

As far as the scientific evidence goes, there seems to be support for both sides of the argument. Some studies have shown significant support for the hypothesis that people who are more educated are happier. David Blanchflower and Andrew Oswald, for example, have studied well-being and happiness in the United States and Great Britain and have found that education is a key factor that influences happiness.[63] Their findings also show that this correlation is not just a result of better education leading to higher income and higher social status. Education had a positive impact on happiness, independent of income. Philip Oreopoulos and Kjell Salvanes have come to a similar conclusion. They analysed data from the US General Social Surveys to compare self-reported happiness among people with different education levels, including high school graduates without college education, high school graduates with some college education but less than a bachelor's degree and those with a bachelor's degree. Their findings show that the group with the bachelor's degree rate their happiness as higher than the other two groups and those without any college education report the lowest level of happiness. This correlation remains even after adjusting for differences in income that are likely to be a result of higher education.[64] These findings have also been backed up by other studies.[65] [66]

However, not everyone believes that higher education leads to higher happiness. Most researchers agree that a very low level of education is linked to an overall lower well-being level and an increased risk of mental illness. However, a recent study from the University of Warwick suggests that higher education does not automatically lead to higher levels of happiness.[67] In an analysis of data from 13,983 participants of the 2010 and 2011 Health Surveys in England, the researchers found that all levels of education had similar odds of high mental well-being.

One thing that needs to be considered regarding all of the studies mentioned above is that they measure education based on the number of years spent at school and university (or other educational institutions) and degrees obtained. This is a somewhat narrow view of education and it is possible that the lower happiness levels of those who left the education system early are related to other life circumstances that caused them to leave school prematurely, such as their family's values and priorities, the environment they grew up in, their social circle, or hardship that required them to grow up quickly and contribute to the family income or look after younger siblings. All of these aspects can have a significant impact on both overall happiness and the education level they achieved. Therefore, it's possible that it's not lower education that causes people to be less happy but the factors that caused them to leave school early.

Education is generally defined as "the act or process of imparting or acquiring general knowledge, developing the powers of reasoning and judgment, and generally of preparing oneself or others intellectually for mature life".

It's worth noting that nowhere in that definition does it mention degrees or time spent at educational institutions. There are many ways in which we can acquire knowledge and develop reasoning skills. Traditional education is just one of them. Many well-educated people did not finish high school and never visited a university, but acquired their knowledge and skills through experience, reading, conversations and other strategies. We all know the stories about start-up founders who didn't finish high school but are now extremely capable and successful business people. Ted Turner, founder of CNN, never finished college (he got kicked out from Brown University for having a woman in his dorm room), billionaire and Oracle founder, Larry Ellison, doesn't have a university degree either and extremely successful serial entrepreneur Sir Richard Branson left school at 16 without any degree. Hardly anyone would argue that these three, and many other successful people, are not knowledgeable and well-educated. They just did not get their knowledge and education in the traditional way. If we consider education as the act and process of learning and acquiring knowledge, then research that compares happiness levels to degrees people have obtained does not actually answer the question of whether education can make us happier. We might then have to rely on more anecdotal evidence to answer this question.

It is my personal belief and experience that gaining knowledge can have a huge impact on your happiness. I consider this one of the key things I did to turn my life around and find happiness. I began soaking in knowledge, mainly through books, that helped me get a better understanding of myself, the world I live in and how I can bring more meaning and purpose into my life. Many other successful and happy people often mention continuous learning and reading as one of the key factors contributing to their achievements and overall well-being. Richard Branson considers his love for learning one of the key ingredients to his success and talks specifically about learning people skills — something that is not usually taught at school — as something that has helped him tremendously in his career. Oprah Winfrey refers to reading as her "personal path to freedom" and regularly introduces non-fiction books to her fans to encourage them to learn more about the world. Mark Zuckerberg set out to read a book a fortnight in 2015, explaining in a Facebook post that he is doing it "with an emphasis on learning about different cultures, beliefs, histories and technologies". Other famous advocates of lifelong learning include Bill Gates, Warren Buffet (who is said to read five to six hours every day), Mark Cuban, Steve Jobs and many more.

I highly recommend you consider all of this in the context of your own happiness and the blueprint for a happier life you will design later in this book. I realise that learning, and especially reading, are not for everyone and this book is about creating a plan based on your personality and strengths. However, there are many different ways in which one can learn and acquire knowledge; from audiobook to podcasts, courses, social gatherings, conversations, through to learning by trying new things and experimenting. I believe the benefits of continuous learning are enormous, no matter what personality type you are and what strengths and weaknesses you have — you just need to identify the right way of learning for you.

Health

Similar to education, health is also a factor that is partly out of our control and partly related to voluntary actions. Certain illnesses are genetic or random, and we have no (or very little) control over getting them or not. Getting injured in an accident is also mostly external — unless you crash your car while driving under the influence, in which case, it was entirely within your control to prevent it. However, other aspects that can significantly impact our health are internal. How well we eat, whether we smoke or drink excessively, how fit we are, how much sleep we get and many more, are all aspects fully within our control. And research suggests it's well worth investing in your health. A study based on the US Census data gives reason to believe that your health is a much more significant indicator for your happiness than your income and other factors like marital status and age. This finding was by no means surprising. The positive relationship between happiness and health is well established and may be one of the least disputed research insights around happiness — no one argues that you are more likely to be happier if you're of poor health. Most would agree that healthy people are more likely to be happy than unhealthy ones — which does not mean you can't be happy if you have some health issues (we'll come back to this). We seem to have a lot to gain from improving our health. In their analysis of the US Census data, Teng Guo and Lingyi Hu found that "improving health has the most impact on individual happiness. People of excellent health are predicted to be approximately

20% happier than those with fair health, and people with poor health are 8.25% unhappier than the base group".[68]

It makes sense that health and happiness are closely linked. It's easy to see that being healthy makes it easier for us to live happier, more fulfilling lives. We're able to do more activities, are more independent and have less to worry about. It might be slightly less obvious that happiness impacts health to an equal level. However, the positive impact of happiness on health has been confirmed by several studies. A review of existing literature concludes that happy people are more likely to have greater self-control, are better at dealing with adversity, have better immune systems and live longer.[69] The positive effect of happiness on health is especially clear and compelling when looking at studies where researchers follow a group of people over a longer period of time. According to Ed Diener, one of the leading researchers in this field, the level of happiness at the beginning of these studies — before any serious illnesses or injuries that might impact the subject's level of happiness — can predict the person's health many years later, as well as how long they live.[70] In short, being healthy makes it easier to be happy and being happy seems to make it easier to be healthy.

However, all of this does not mean that people who struggle with health issues or injuries are doomed to live unhappy lives. First of all, as with any research findings, there are always exceptions. In most studies that find that healthy people are happier, there are usually unhealthy study participants that report high levels of happiness just like there are healthy ones that report low levels of happiness. Secondly, there is also scientific evidence that health issues do not necessarily lead to unhappiness. One study of 383 people, 50 years of age and over, shows that many of the patients that consider themselves unhealthy still report being happy.[71]

According to the authors, adaptation might be one of the reasons for this, in that the patients have become used to their condition over time. Another possibility is that they have found ways of getting more enjoyment in other areas of their lives which compensates for the shortcomings in health. However, it is important to note that these findings were applicable only to patients with moderate illness and injuries and did not apply to patients who suffered from constant health issues like debilitating pain and urinary incontinence. It's likely that it is much harder for us to adapt to those types of conditions due to the constancy of the pain and symptoms.

It is without question that our health is partly out of our control. There are certain illnesses and injuries we cannot predict or prevent. However, it seems that we do have the ability to adapt to most of these conditions over time. Moreover, even when suffering from severe and constant pain and symptoms, we might be able to regain some of our happiness by finding more pleasure, meaning and joy in other areas of our life. The most important thing to consider, though, is the fact that there are large parts of our health that we can control. We can take measures to prevent illnesses and injuries, like regular exercise, getting enough sleep, reducing stress and a healthy diet, through to getting regular health checks and treating symptoms early. I think regardless of how healthy you are at the moment, all of us should consider maintaining or improving our health as a goal for our Happiness Blueprints.

I know from personal experience that being healthy and fit makes it a whole lot easier to be happy. However, just how important health is to your happiness comes down to your values, and how you best achieve any possible health improvements has much to do with your personality and your strengths and weaknesses.

Summary and Exercise

Now that we have reviewed the research and science around several key life circumstances, let's summarise what we've learned:

- **Money and materialistic goods:** Wealth and the things that money can buy on their own are unlikely to bring us any further happiness once we have enough to be comfortable. However, money may enable us to live more aligned with our values. The important aspect is not how much money we have, but whether our spending aligns with our personality and values.

- **Work:** Happiness at work seems to be all about finding meaning. If you want to increase your happiness by improving your satisfaction at work, looking for purpose instead of promotions and achievements seems to be the way to go.

- **Relationships:** Quality, meaningful relationships do seem to make us happier. Consider investing more time into your most important relationships and maybe even consider being open to new ones. However, remember, it's the quality that matters, not the quantity.

- **Major tragic events:** Major tragedies seem to have less of a long-term impact on our happiness then we might think. Being resilient and having a positive attitude can help us cope better with negative events.

- **Education:** There are mixed findings regarding the impact education, in the traditional sense, has on our happiness. However, if we look at education as ongoing lifelong learning, there is anecdotal evidence that suggests it can contribute significantly to our happiness.

- **Health:** Our health seems to have a significant impact on our happiness, and our happiness seems to impact our health. Investing in your health seem a pretty good bet if you want to improve your long-term happiness.

It is important to remember that not all of this is equally valid and important for everyone. Depending on your personality, values and beliefs, your strengths and weaknesses, as well as your general preferences, some of these factors might be especially important to your happiness while others will be less so, or maybe not at all. For all of this information to be valuable and for you to be able to design a blueprint that will help YOU be happier, it's important that you relate all of this back to what you've learned in the previous chapter. The exercise below will help you do this.

EXERCISE: WHAT AREAS DO
YOU WANT TO WORK ON

1. Review the key things you learned about yourself in the previous chapter. Review your notes and re-read your personal profile.
2. With all of that in mind, rate how important each of the external factors we discussed is to your long-term happiness. Rate each factor on a scale from 1 to 10 with 10 being 'very important' and 1 being 'not important at all'.
3. Now think about how well you feel you're doing in each of these areas. Rate your satisfaction and happiness with each area on a scale from 1 to 10 (10 = very happy, 1 = very unhappy).
4. Next, consider to what extent improvements in this area could impact your overall happiness. Rate each factor on a scale from 1 to 10 (10 = very much, 1 = not at all). For example, if you rated a factor as a 6 in the previous question, how much impact would it have on your overall happiness if you could lift your score in this area to an 8 or a 9?

5. Based on the ratings you've given, highlight the 2-3 factors you want to work on. These should be ones that you consider important to your happiness, that show some room for improvement (you haven't rated them as a 10 in step 3) and where you think improvements will have a significant impact on your overall happiness.

6. For each of the 2-3 factors you've highlighted (and the others if you want to), think about at least two or three things you could do to improve in this area. Don't worry too much about how realistic it might be, just write down any ideas you can come up with.

Factor	How important is this area to your happiness? (1-10)	How well are you currently doing in this area? (1-10)	How much could improvements in this area impact your overall happiness? (1-10)	How could you improve in this area?
Money / Materialistic Goods				
Work				
Relationships				
Education				
Tragic Events				
Health				

Great, now you have an idea of some of the things you might want to work on to improve your happiness. We will come back to this a bit later, so make sure you keep your notes handy. However, for now, let's look at some of the voluntary activities that may impact our happiness.

Voluntary Activities

As we have seen, there are several environmental factors that could potentially help us be happier. However, an increasing number of researchers and practitioners alike believe that internal factors and voluntary actions have an even more significant impact on how happy we are. They argue that our happiness is mostly determined by how we interpret and respond to what happens in the world around us, rather than what actually happens, and that voluntary activities can help us respond in ways that are beneficial to our well-being and happiness.

Voluntary activities can be just about anything that we can initiate and carry out without needing external support or luck (which doesn't mean that either can't be helpful at times). In his book Authentic Happiness, Martin Seligman argues that those voluntary activities that help us achieve three key goals are most likely to positively impact our happiness in the long-term. These three goals are: satisfaction about the past, optimism about the future and happiness in the present. Any activities you can incorporate into your life that help you achieve at least one of these three goals are likely to have a positive impact on your overall satisfaction with life. Seligman further argues that truly and lastingly achieving these goals requires a change in attitude, approach and mindset more so than a change in life circumstances. Other researchers have been more specific and have investigated the impact individual activities and practices, such as forgiveness, kindness, exercise, gratitude and self-reflection have on our happiness. So let's take a look at what they have found.

Gratitude

Gratitude is often seen as synonymous with the simple act of saying "thank you". However, the concept of gratitude is actually about much more than two little words. It's a positive emotion and a state of mind where we feel appreciation, not just towards a specific person or for a specific situation, but also for life on the whole. To get a better understanding of what gratitude is, the definition from Harvard Medical School is helpful. According to them, gratitude is "a thankful appreciation for what an individual receives, whether tangible or intangible. With gratitude, people acknowledge the goodness in their lives ... As a result, gratitude also helps people connect to something larger than themselves as individuals — whether to other people, nature, or a higher power".

Research findings suggest that gratitude impacts happiness both directly and indirectly. For example, Robert Emmons and Michael McCullough conducted a total of three studies to determine the relationship between gratitude and happiness.[72] One of these studies divided participants into three groups. All participants were asked to write either daily or weekly, but they were given different topics to write about. The first group was asked to write about negative events or hassles, the second group was asked to write about the things they felt grateful for and the third group wrote about neutral life events. Across various study conditions, the participants that wrote about gratitude consistently reported higher levels of well-being than the two other groups. Given this finding, as well as the results from their other studies, the researchers concluded that experiencing feelings of gratitude often leads to increased well-being and life satisfaction. Interestingly, they also found that gratitude might have a positive impact on sleep which, in turn, is likely to improve overall health and well-being. In another example, a total of four studies suggest that feelings of gratitude improve mood and that gratitude is a trait important to subjective well-being.[73] An in-depth review of the existing literature and research by Robert Emmons also concluded that gratitude positively impacts happiness.[74] However, most researchers who found a positive correlation between gratitude and happiness also point out that the cause and effect relationship is not sufficiently proven. It is possible that happy people are more likely to experience gratitude instead of gratitude causing happiness. However, one does not need to be a scientist to see how experiencing more gratitude can have an immense impact on our happiness.

For starters, gratitude is a positive feeling, so experiencing more of it is bound to make us feel good. People who regularly show gratitude for and towards others are also likely to be well-liked and have good relationships – which, as we've learned before, often has a positive impact on our happiness. We also know that comparing ourselves to others is a source of unhappiness for many. Feeling truly grateful for what we have and taking the time to recognise and appreciate all the good things in our lives is likely to make us less prone to envy others. Furthermore, since gratitude is essentially about being able to recognise and appreciate all the good in our life, it can help us deal better with negative emotions and stressful situations because we are able to focus on the good parts and the opportunities within the challenges.

And there is more. Remember the concept of hedonic adaptation that is often listed as the reason why many achievements and materialistic goods don't bring lasting happiness (because we get used to them after a while)? Gratitude can help us make the joy and happiness these positive events bring into our lives last much longer. Imagine this: you have just bought a new apartment. You absolutely love it, and you're so happy that you'll be living there. Chances are, after a few weeks this effect will wear off and the apartment will feel normal — you got used to it, and it's not as exciting and new any more. The initial spike in happiness you experienced is wearing off, and before you know it, you're back to feeling the same way you did in your old apartment. However, now imagine you have started a daily gratitude ritual. Each day, when you come home, you take a minute to stand in your apartment and appreciate it. For a minute you remind yourself how much you love this apartment, how much you enjoy living in it and how grateful you are that you were able to buy it and make it your home. Can you see how the feeling of happiness that you experienced when you first moved in is much more likely to stick around long-term if you go through this gratitude ritual every day?

We are all guilty of taking good things in our lives for granted sometimes. Whether it's our partner, friends or colleagues, our house and car, that we can take the whole family on a holiday every year, or the simple fact that we have a roof over our heads and food on the table — there are a lot of people in the world that don't have that. Most of us experience feelings of gratitude when we think about this, when we sit down for a moment to appreciate all the great things in our lives. However, most of us don't take time to do that anywhere near as often as we should, which is a real shame given that experiencing more gratitude is one of the easiest ways to feel happier. So here are some ideas on how you can bring more gratitude into your life.

- **Write a gratitude journal:** Once a day, sit down and write at least three things you're grateful for into your journal. You can write as many as you want.

- **Start a gratitude ritual:** Basically, this is just about taking a few minutes each day to think about all the things you're grateful for. You can do this any way you like, but for it to be a ritual it needs to be connected to a specific time or location (you do it every day first thing in the morning/ last thing in the evening, or every time you walk into your apartment or get into your car).

- **Go on a gratitude walk:** Fresh air and nature are always good for us, so combine them with gratitude for an extra happiness boost. Go for a walk and look for things to be grateful for — either in your surroundings (the trees, the sun, the fresh air) or within you (the fact that you can walk, that you can experience this, that you can take the time to go for a walk).

- **Write a gratitude letter:** This is a great way to express your gratitude to a specific person. Write them a letter or a short note to let them know how grateful you are to have them in your life.

- **Tell people:** Probably the most powerful way to show gratitude is to tell people. Maybe set yourself a goal of wanting to tell at least one person per week how grateful you are to have them in your life. It can be just a little comment here and there or a big emotional talk over a cup of coffee or a glass of wine. However, make sure it's more than just saying thank you, use words like "I'm really grateful to have you in my life because…"

Experiencing more gratitude can help all of us — no matter where on the happiness scale we are at the moment. However, it's important to understand that small, occasional acts of gratitude probably won't make a big difference. To really lift our happiness, we need to experience gratitude regularly and make it a part of who we are on a daily basis. We will experience the most significant positive impact when we get to the point where gratitude is our natural response and way of thinking, and not just something we experience when we make the effort.

As with pretty much everything we discuss in this book, gratitude will come easier to some than others. And it will have a more significant impact on some people's happiness than it will for others. You will also discover that some people find it much easier and more valuable to experience gratitude internally, on their own, while others find it much more valuable when they can share gratitude with others. To what extent more gratitude will increase your happiness depends on how much you already experience it, as well as your personality and values. If your natural preference is for a more negative or critical outlook on life (for example, if you scored high in neuroticism in the big five exercise) or you generally think you would benefit from being more positive, then gratitude is something you should consider for your Happiness Blueprint. Making an effort to feel gratitude regularly can be a great way to train our mind to focus on all the positive things we have in our life.

If you decide that gratitude is one of the things you want to work on and experience more of, have a play with the different ideas presented above. Start with the one that feels most comfortable to you and then work your way up to others. Think about what you learned about your personality and strengths and weaknesses to help you identify which techniques are most likely to work best for you. If you're an extrovert you're more likely to enjoy and value gratitude exercises that involve other people; if you love nature, the gratitude walk might be best for you; and if you're a creative person, you might prefer writing or even drawing or singing about the things you're grateful for. No matter how you go about getting it, experiencing more gratitude can be a real happiness booster.

Goals

Goals are an essential part of life. Most of us have some goals or ideals we're working towards, and most of us believe that achieving our goals will make us happier. Eighteenth-century philosopher Immanuel Kant even went as far as defining happiness as "the satisfaction of all our desires" which implies that happiness is a state where we do not have any further goals or desires — we're fully content with what we have and the status quo. Other thinkers and researchers disagree with this notion and argue that having and actively pursuing goals is a vital part of happiness — as long as we're pursuing the right goals for the right reasons. So which one is it? Does achieving all our goals make us happy or is it the pursuit that brings happiness? Or is it neither? Or both?

When it comes to analysing the effect of goals on our happiness, it is helpful to break it down into three components: goal setting, the pursuit of goals and the achievement of goals. Goal setting on its own seems to have a very limited impact on happiness. Setting goals and not achieving them can even have a negative impact. Several researchers have conducted studies with university students where they asked them to set goals at the beginning of the term and then measured both progress towards the goals and subjective well-being at several points throughout the term. Findings clearly show that increases in well-being are correlated with achieving progress towards the goal, while not making any progress has been shown to be related to a decrease in well-being.[75] [76] All the students in these studies set goals, but only those who achieved progress experienced an increase in happiness. This suggests that setting goals on its own does not contribute to our happiness. It's the pursuit and achievement of goals that matters. However, it's interesting to note that research also suggests that people who set clear, challenging but achievable and measurable goals are more likely to perform better and achieve more.[77] Therefore, even though simply setting goals does not seem to increase our happiness, it is an essential first step towards performance and achievements that can make us happier.

It's easy to see how achieving our goals will make us happy and not achieving them might have a negative impact on our happiness. However, as it turns out, those achievement-related effects are short-lived in most cases due to the concept of hedonic adaptation we've already discussed. In the studies mentioned above, the researchers found that the improvements in well-being only lasted for as long as the students achieved goals. Once students stopped making progress, their happiness levels were quickly back to where they were before the experiment started. That was the case even though none of what they had already achieved was taken away from them, they just didn't make any further progress. In line with those findings, several researchers and thinkers argue that lasting happiness is more likely to come from the ongoing pursuit of meaningful goals rather than from having achieved our goals. That means, it is important for our goals to evolve and grow as we make progress towards them and to find new goals once we've achieved others. As David Watson, one of the world's leading authorities on positive and negative moods, argues: "Contemporary researchers emphasise that it is the process of striving after goals — rather than goal attainment per se — that is crucial for happiness and positive affectivity".[78] David Myers and Ed Diener come to a very similar conclusion, stating that "happiness grows less from the passive experience of desirable circumstances than from involvement in valued activities and progress toward one's goals".[79] One very important word in this statement is 'valued'. Research has shown that selecting the right goals for us personally is key to achieving happiness. Kennon Sheldon is a leading researcher in this field and his studies have shown that increases in happiness and life satisfaction are more likely if the goals set align closely with a person's values, beliefs, personality and strengths. Sheldon refers to these as 'self-concordant goals' — goals that are a person's authentic and independent choice rather than those goals that are controlled or motivated by external factors. In other words, self-concordant goals are those we pursue completely for ourselves and not to impress or keep up with the world around us. To achieve or increase happiness, Sheldon and his colleagues suggest focusing on the pursuit of goals that involve growth, connection and contribution rather than money, beauty and popularity and goals that are interesting and personally important rather than goals we feel forced or pressured to pursue.[80] [81]

It seems that goals can be a valuable tool for our pursuit of happiness. Though it also appears as if Immanuel Kant, renowned and influential as he might have been, was not entirely right with his view that happiness comes from the achievement of our goals. As we have seen, it's the setting and pursuit of meaningful and personally valued goals that seems to have the most positive and lasting impact on our happiness.

The pursuit of goals has the potential to be a crucial aspect of finding and increasing happiness for all of us, regardless of our personality and values. However, personality, and even more so our values, will determine what goals are most valuable and meaningful to us and, as we've learned, pursuing the right goals is the most important part. Furthermore, our personality and strengths significantly impact how we can best pursue our goals and ensure we make progress towards them. Goal setting will be a significant aspect of designing your Happiness Blueprint later in this book, and the framework and process provided will make it easier for you to identify and set the right kind of goals for yourself. Towards the end of this book, I will also offer some tips for putting your plan into action and proactively pursuing your goals — since that is ultimately the key to happiness.

Mindfulness

Mindfulness is often associated with spiritual concepts and activities like meditation, yoga and Buddhism. However, at its core, mindfulness is merely about awareness and being in the moment. It doesn't necessarily require any specific practices or rituals. Mindfulness is simply about being fully present and aware of what is happening in the moment. Have you ever read a book and suddenly realised that you can't remember what you just read even though you've been turning the pages? Or have you ever been in your car, driving along, and suddenly realised that you don't really remember getting to where you are? Did you ever suspiciously look around the room wondering who ate all the cookies, only to realise you're the only one there, but you can't remember eating them all? Those are all examples of the opposite of mindfulness. When we're on autopilot and are lacking mindfulness, we're active, we're doing things and our body is present — but our mind isn't fully there. Mindlessness is especially common when we're doing repetitive and well-known activities, when we're stressed, when we are trying to multitask, or when our mind is caught up with a specific problem or situation. Most of us experience mindlessness every day, without even trying. Mindfulness, on the other hand, is a less common element of our everyday lives.

Most of us live in an extremely busy world where people, information, sounds, colours and smells are constantly competing for our attention. We often feel like we don't have the luxury to do just one thing at a time because our to-do lists are endless, and every minute of the day must be used to its fullest potential. Unfortunately, this mindless way of living might be getting in the way of our happiness.

Harvard researcher Matt Killingsworth conducted a study with more than 15,000 individuals to investigate what makes us happy. It's worth noting that the sample was very diverse, including people from more than 80 countries at different ages, from different socio-economic backgrounds and with varying levels of education and income, as well as different occupations and marital statuses. The data collection for the study was fairly simple. The participants were contacted via a mobile app on their phone at random times throughout the day. Participants then provided information about their level of happiness at that moment, what they were doing when they were contacted and whether they were focused on the activity or if their mind was wandering. What Killingsworth found when he analysed this data was that people who reported to be fully in the moment and focused on their current activity (those participants that were mindful), reported significantly higher levels of happiness than those people whose minds were wandering.

Interestingly, this is still true even when people are doing unpleasant activities like being stuck in traffic. Furthermore, thanks to the large sample size and having several data points from each participant, Killingsworth can prove with a high level of confidence that it is, in fact, a lack of mindfulness that causes lower levels of happiness, rather than unhappy people being less likely to be mindful. Matt Killingsworth did a very interesting TED talk about this study and his findings which I recommend watching.[82]

Mindfulness has also been shown to be extremely beneficial in a number of other ways that are likely to have a positive impact on our happiness. One study finds that people who score high on mindfulness measures are 83% more likely to have excellent cardiovascular health, suggesting that mindfulness significantly benefits heart health.[83] The same study also suggests that mindfulness increases self-awareness and reduces unhealthy cravings.

Mindfulness also might have a positive impact on our glucose levels, a major health predictor, suggesting that mindful people are less at risk of obesity and less likely to have type 2 diabetes.[84] Another study shows that mindfulness can help turn a mundane chore, like washing the dishes, into a stress reliever[85] and a group of Swedish researchers has found evidence suggesting mindfulness is a very effective method for treating depression and anxiety.[86] Furthermore, mindfulness meditations have been shown to improve quality of sleep to a similar extent that prescription drugs do.[87] Today, mindfulness is a treatment option that's well adopted across hospitals and other healthcare facilities around the world. A mindfulness-based stress reduction (MBSR) programme developed by Jon Kabat-Zinn in 1979 is now being used in more than 250 hospitals around the world to help people with stress, anxiety, depression, chronic pain, alleviating stress related to medical conditions and much more.

Given all those, and many more, benefits of mindfulness, it's easy to see how it has a positive impact on our overall life satisfaction and happiness. So why does mindfulness have such a significant impact on our well-being? It's likely that it all comes back to the earlier argument that happiness is mainly about how we interpret and respond to what happens in the world around us (rather than what actually happens). With everything that happens to us or around us, there is a brief moment of choice, a short moment where we can decide how to respond. The problem is, more often than not, we're not aware of this moment of choice. Instead, we react out of habit and instinct. Think about a challenging situation you've been in recently. Maybe your boss gave you some negative feedback or you found out your partner lied to you about something important. Perhaps you have been in an accident or your car broke down when you were already running late to a really important meeting. Do you remember choosing how you wanted to respond and feel about the situation? Most of you probably don't. However, consciously or unconsciously, you made a choice — and for most of us, that choice probably ended up having a negative impact on our mood and well-being. Mindfulness is so powerful because it helps us recognise that moment of choice.

Practising mindfulness regularly makes us more aware and alert to these situations and enables us to make a conscious decision as to how we want to respond. That is why mindfulness is especially valuable to people who suffer from overly negative thinking, anxiety and depression. Practising mindfulness helps them to recognise the moment of choice and enables them to choose a more positive response that causes fewer feelings of stress and anxiety. Let me give you an example. Imagine you are running late to an important meeting and then your car won't start. You immediately feel stressed, frustrated and maybe even angry ("Why do these things always happen to me…?"). You worry about what being late for the meeting will do for your career. The more you worry, the angrier you get and the more you become stuck in the situation.

Now imagine you would have had the mindfulness to stop yourself before diving into all these negative thoughts and realise you have a choice as to how you respond. Yes, your car not starting is bad news, especially when it's right before an important meeting. However, these things happen. There is nothing you can do about the car right now that will get you to your meeting in time so you might as well leave it for now and focus on the urgent problem; getting to the meeting. You could simply take the bus or call a taxi. Alternatively, maybe a friend, neighbour or family member close by can either drive you or lend you their car. Once the important meeting is done, you can get back to solving the car problem without feeling as stressed and frustrated about the whole situation. Can you see how being aware and mindful of the decision-making moment can help you deal with challenging situations much more efficiently and avoid a whole lot of negative feelings?

Of course, responding differently in one situation does not result in lasting happiness. As we learned in the first chapter, negative emotions are a part of life and don't automatically result in unhappiness, just like positive emotions don't automatically make us happy. However, mindfulness is not about one individual situation. It's about a general mindset and how we approach and deal with life on the whole every day. Feeling frustrated and stressed because your car broke down before an important meeting does not make you unhappy in a lasting sense (it's just a momentary negative experience). Responding negatively to most challenging situations in your life, however, likely will have a negative and lasting impact on your happiness. Mindfulness helps us be more aware and present in every moment of our life to make sure we respond to situations in a way that is beneficial and productive. However, getting to that level of mindfulness requires commitment and regular practice.

Mindfulness is about awareness of the present and being in the moment. As such, there is an endless number of ways one can experience and practise it. A few examples of tactics that can help you learn to be more mindful are offered on the next few pages. If you're interested in experiencing how mindfulness can help you increase your happiness, I would suggest doing some more research into the concept to discover other ways of practising mindfulness.

MINDFULNESS MEDITATION

Mindfulness meditation is a very popular and effective practice that has been proven to have tremendous health and well-being benefits. Mindfulness meditation is a specific type of meditation where distracting feelings and thoughts are not being ignored but simply acknowledged and observed in a non-judgmental way as they come up. The goal is to detach from these thoughts and feelings to gain insights and awareness. Sounds mystical? Don't worry; there are plenty of easy ways to learn how to do mindfulness meditations. There are great mobile apps like Calm and Headspace that guide you through the meditations. You can also download recorded meditations from the internet and, in many cities, you can find mindfulness and meditation courses and classes where a qualified practitioner will guide you through the process.

However, meditation is not for everyone. I have to admit, I have always struggled with the concept. Understanding the benefits well, I have tried to get into a regular practice on several occasions. While I've often experienced short-term benefits, I have struggled to stick with it. Luckily, there are many other ways in which we can experience and practice mindfulness.

A MINDFUL CUP OF TEA

Experiencing mindfulness can be as simple as drinking a cup of tea. However, not any cup of tea is a mindfulness practice. It's only when we really focus on the experience and take in every step of it in great detail that it becomes mindfulness. Start at the very beginning. Clear your head and make sure you have time and won't be interrupted. Prepare your tea. Take in the smell of the tea and the sound of the boiling water. Then put it in your cup. Experience the warmth of the cup in your hand, the smell of the hot tea and acknowledge its colour. Take your first sip, carefully taking note of the taste and the warmth in your mouth. Continue drinking your tea, fully recognising and experiencing every aspect of it. Focus on nothing else. If you find your mind wandering, simply let the thought go and return your attention back to your tea. For 10 or 15 minutes (or however long it takes) try to do nothing other than enjoying your cup of tea. Be fully present in the moment and let all other thoughts and feelings pass by. That's mindfulness. It sounds easy, doesn't it? But, give it a go, you might find it harder than you think. We're so used to multitasking and planning our next steps that doing something as simple as just drinking tea for 10 minutes can feel weird and challenging.

Of course, you could do the same thing with a cup of coffee, a hot chocolate, or even a glass of wine (now I've got your attention, haven't I?).

MINDFUL EATING

Similar to the mindful cup of tea (or glass of wine), you can turn a meal into a mindfulness practice. Pick a meal that you are most likely to be able to enjoy in silence and without distractions and then purely focus on the experience of eating for the duration of the meal. Acknowledge each bit, take in all the different smells and tastes, notice if the first bite tastes different from the second or third. Pay attention to the temperature and texture of each individual bite. If you find yourself getting distracted by other thoughts and feelings, simply let them go and bring your focus back to the meal and the experience of eating it.

Some research has suggested that mindful eating could help people lose weight and overcome obesity[88] so this practice might be especially relevant for those people who want to address weight concerns or generally want healthier eating habits.

A MINDFUL WALK

For those who like to be active and out and about, a mindful walk might be the way to get more mindfulness into your life. Fresh air is always good for clearing the mind, and a walk offers lots of things to be aware and mindful of. Whether you walk in nature or through the city, I would recommend finding a relatively quiet area with few distractions. While on your walk, be fully present. Take in all the smells and sounds, appreciate the sun and the wind or the rain. Take note of how the sun feels on your skin and how the soles of your feet feel when they touch the ground. Notice how you warm up and maybe even sweat a little as you continue to walk. For the duration of your walk, focus on nothing else but the present and how it makes you feel. Let all other thoughts and feelings go and simply focus on your walk.

There are many other ways to experience mindfulness. As you will have realised by now, it's all about being fully present in the moment, and you can combine that with almost any activity: from eating and drinking, through to a conversation, listening to music, admiring a piece of art, necessary household chores like doing the dishes or ironing or other activities and exercises. I've also recently discovered a very useful mindfulness mobile app developed by the US Department of Veteran Affairs. The app is called Mindfulness Coach and was designed for veterans and service members to help them improve their health and well-being. You don't have to be a veteran to benefit from it. It is just as valuable for ordinary people. If you like smartphone apps, this might be the way to go for you. If you find the app useful, maybe consider donating to the Department of Veteran Affairs, volunteer some time, or consider supporting veterans in another way — there's a good chance it will make you even happier, as we will learn soon.

Mindfulness is beneficial for all of us, but it is likely to have a particularly positive impact for people who feel stressed a lot, find they are too impulsive in their decision-making and response to events, as well as people who have to work through challenging situations or want to change or adjust parts of their behaviour. Mindfulness is also a valuable tool when dealing with teams and interpersonal differences. For example, if you're part of a team at work, chances are you're working with people with different personalities, values and strengths. This can, at times, cause challenges and conflict. Being mindful of individual preferences and how you respond to them can make you much better at working with others and can make otherwise stressful situations more enjoyable and productive. As we learned above, mindfulness can also be a valuable tool in improving health and managing weight. If any of this applies to you, it might be worth considering adding mindfulness to your Happiness Blueprint — make a note of it now, so you don't forget later.

Altruism and Kindness

Can helping others make us happier? You might find it hard to believe looking at the world around us today — the wars, poverty and violence — but as we will soon learn, there is substantial evidence that it might, in fact, be true.

Initially, the idea that helping others might help us lead happier, more fulfilling lives might seem foreign. After all, if kindness was the key to happiness, then why do we live in a world where so many people suffer and are in urgent need of kindness, while others have so much more than they need? If helping others is the way to achieve the most sought-after state and emotion, then why do those of us who seemingly have it all not spend more of our time and money helping those that struggle? Why do we spend our money on fancy new cars — something that has been shown to only lift our happiness temporarily — instead of spending that money helping to feed starving kids? That is, indeed, an excellent question because research convincingly shows that it would most likely make us happier in the long run to focus more on helping others and less on buying things we think we need.

Scientific research into the effects of kindness and altruism started as far back as the 1950s — partly through coincidence. In 1956 a group of researchers from Cornell University of Medicine began a longitudinal study following 427 married women with children to investigate whether women with more children would experience higher levels of stress and die earlier than those with fewer children. While they did not find anything to support this hypothesis, following these women for 30 years showed that there might be health benefits from volunteer activities. The researchers found that more than half of those women who did not belong to a volunteer organisation had experienced a significant illness while only 36% of the women who belonged to a volunteer organisation did.[89] This may have been one of the first studies that showed a correlation between kindness and health, but it certainly wasn't the last. Since then, countless other studies have looked at the possible health and well-being benefits of altruism and kindness — from research showing that seniors who volunteer time report higher levels of life satisfaction and fewer symptoms of depression and anxiety,[90] to studies showing that giving help has more mental health benefits than receiving help,[91] and those showing that doing simple acts of kindness increases our overall well-being and happiness.[92]

Highly regarded 'happiness' researcher Sonya Lyubomirsky and her colleagues argue that kindness and altruism increase our happiness in several ways.[93] For starters, kindness can help us feel closer to people around us and can make us feel like a more valuable and more highly appreciated member of our community. Altruistic behaviour is also likely to make us more aware of our own life circumstances in comparison to less fortunate people, making us appreciate and value our good fortune. Furthermore, Lyubomirsky argues that performing acts of kindness will make us feel better about ourselves, more confident and more in control, as well as more liked and appreciated by others. However, Lyubomirsky's research has also shown that real happiness increases do not come from sporadic, small acts of kindness but only from consistent and significant acts. In a 2004 paper, together with Chris Tkach and Kennon Sheldon, she outlines the findings of a study carried out among students.[94] The students participating in the study were told to perform five acts of kindness per week over a six-week period. Some of the participants were asked to carry out all five acts of kindness on the same day while others were asked to spread them out over the week. All participants, including a control group which was not asked to perform any acts of kindness, completed well-being questionnaires right at the beginning and right at the end of the six-week period.

Their findings showed that carrying out acts of kindness could significantly increase happiness — but only when all five acts of kindness were committed on the same day. Those participants whose acts of kindness were spread out throughout the week did not report significantly higher happiness than the control group. The researchers argue that it's likely that the small acts of kindness spread out over the week were not a significant enough change in behaviour compared to their normal lives to have a measurable impact over the relatively short timeframe of the study. It's likely that the participants simply forgot about the acts of kindness they did and that the experience as such was not memorable enough to make a difference. These findings suggest that it's not just about committing acts of kindness but that our awareness of them and appreciation for them is equally important for finding lasting happiness.

Another group of researchers around Kristin Layous looked at the effect kindness can have on happiness among young students aged nine to 11.[95] Their longitudinal study in 19 classrooms in Vancouver asked students to perform three acts of kindness per week over a four-week period. The control group was asked to visit three places each week. Both groups of students experienced an improvement in overall well-being, further suggesting that being kind has a positive impact on happiness. Furthermore, the research findings show that the students in the kindness group experienced significantly bigger increases in peer acceptance. Since peer acceptance is a critical aspect of long-term well-being, especially at such a young age, and is directly related to other important outcomes such as confidence and a reduced likelihood of being bullied, performing acts of kindness is likely to have a long-term impact on the overall life satisfaction of young people.

Don't just believe the research. Luckily, finding out if performing acts of kindness will make you happier is easy. Simply start your own kindness experiment. Set yourself a goal to perform at least five acts of kindness each week for the next four weeks. Make sure you record your acts of kindness (as we've learned above, awareness of your kindness might be vital to lifting your happiness). Notice if being kind to others makes you feel better about yourself and overall more satisfied with your life. Remember that there are many ways to show kindness. You can volunteer for a charity, donate money, help people in need, simply say a few nice words to someone who looks like they need it, or just hold the door open for others more often. As you design your own kindness experience, try to incorporate different types to see if any have an especially strong impact on your happiness. For example, while I donate money occasionally, I don't get much of a happiness boost from it. On the other hand, I volunteer my time to help run an annual charity event that raises money for the local children's hospital which brings me lots of happiness and positive feelings. It might be the other way around for you, or you might find that other forms of kindness give you the biggest happiness boost. Make sure you try a few different ones and see what works for you.

Exercise

It's nothing new that regular exercise is incredibly important for our physical health and well-being, but what about our mental health, well-being and happiness? Can exercise help us be happier?

As we've learned in the previous section, health has a potentially significant impact on our overall happiness and life satisfaction. Since exercise has long been proven to be an essential aspect of achieving and maintaining good health, it stands to reason that exercise impacts happiness indirectly, at the very minimum. However, research suggests the effect might be much more direct. Teymor Ahmadi Gatab and Sara Pirhayti conducted a study on the effect of exercise on the happiness and mental health of male students.[96] For their study, 80 male students were divided into two groups. One group then went through an eight-week exercise programme while the control group did not go through any specific programme. After the eight-week programme, the students in the exercise group reported significantly higher levels of happiness as well as improvements in physical symptoms, depression and impaired social functioning and general health indexes. The students in the control group, on the other hand, did not report any significant improvements.

A group of researchers from Penn State University conducted a study with similar conclusions. Amanda Hyde and her colleagues analysed data from 190 undergraduate students to investigate the feel-good effect of physical activity.[97] The students were asked to keep a daily diary of their life experiences and mental states. They were asked to record all physical activity that lasted 15 minutes or more and note the level of effort (mild, moderate or vigorous). The researchers then analysed this data. Their findings showed that people who exercised more experienced higher levels of excitement and enthusiasm than people who were less physically active. Furthermore, individual people seemed to be able to increase the amount of positive feelings they experienced on any given day by being more physically active on that day. In other words, their findings suggest that if you want an immediate burst of happiness, do some moderate to vigorous exercise.

Furthermore, there is evidence to suggest that exercise can not only boost our happiness but can actually help prevent depression. An extensive literature review conducted by a team of researchers from the University of Toronto found a total of 25 studies that suggested regular exercise could prevent episodes of depression in the long-term.[98] This is also supported by the findings of a study from Kings College in London where a team of researchers followed 33,908 healthy adults for 11 years. None of these participants showed any symptoms of depression at the beginning of the data collection. Their data analysis shows that regular physical activity provides protection against future depression — and it doesn't need to be high-intensity activity, low and moderate intensity exercise was just as beneficial. The researchers go as far as suggesting that 12% of future cases of depression could have been prevented if everyone who participated in the study had been physically active for at least one hour per week.[99] Other research goes even further and suggests that exercise is not just a way to lift our mood and **prevent** depression but could be a way to **treat** depressive symptoms and anxiety in some patients.[100] [101]

Exercise is highly beneficial to us. It's hard to argue with that statement. Of course, there are examples of people who overdid it and exercised to the point that it was harmful. There are stories of fit and healthy marathon runners who had heart attacks before they turned 40 or of professional athletes who collapsed on the sports field. However, those are exceptions and often a result of extreme physical activity. For most of us, regular exercise is hugely beneficial both concerning our health as well as our happiness. And you don't need to be a marathon runner to experience the benefits. Even moderate regular exercise like walking 30 minutes every day can make a huge difference. If you want to increase your happiness and you're currently not exercising regularly, this should be something you consider when you design your Happiness Blueprint.

If exercise makes us happy and is so beneficial for us, then why do so many of us find it so hard to stick to our exercise routines and goals? I believe it's because most of us don't really think about what type of exercise works for us. We follow advice from personal trainers and exercise experts as to what is the most effective kind of activity, without really considering if the suggested programme is right for us. At most, we consider our body type, physical strengths and weaknesses and our fitness goals, but hardly any of us consider our personality, values and mental strengths and weaknesses. As you would have read in my personal story earlier in the book, I struggled with health and fitness for many years. For more than 23 years I was overweight and unfit. It's not like I didn't try to change. I tried many different exercise programmes. I joined gyms, I started running, I cycled, I tried home videos and much more. While several of them were effective initially, I never stuck with any of them in the long run, and none of them helped me achieve my long-term fitness goals. Today, I'm fit and active, and it comes naturally to me. I'm physically active several times a week, and I no longer need to force or even remind myself to do it a lot of the time. It's become part of my life. What's changed? It's that I stopped following generic advice and instead developed exercise routines that work for me based on my personality and preferences. I love to be outdoors, so I quit the gym and instead go for a walk or bike ride in the fresh air, even when it's raining. I accepted the fact that I'm not an athletic type and I'm not overly competitive or ambitious, so I gave up on the idea of wanting to be a marathon runner and now go for long walks instead. I realised I like routines so when I do strength training, I have one set programme that I just work through again and again. Most people would get bored with that, but it works for me. I considered that I like efficiency and that time is one of my most scarce resources, so I looked at building activities into my life by, for example, taking the bike to work or walking to meet a friend instead of taking the car. Most importantly, I realised I generally don't enjoy exercise, so now I focus on activities instead. I got into hobbies that are active like kitesurfing, paddle boarding and surfing and made friends with the same interests. As a result, my life is active now. Being active is just what I do for fun and to spend time with my friends. I still 'exercise' occasionally but most of the time, I just live my active life.

The kind of exercise programme and activities that work for you might be very different from mine. You might be an outgoing person who loves spending time with people so a team sport would be best for you. Maybe you're competitive and ambitious, so something that involves regular competitions and comparison with others is the most fun for you. Maybe you love animals and getting a dog is the best way to get you out of the house to go for walks regularly. Maybe you're the kind of person that needs a big audacious goal to be motivated, so sign up for a marathon or some other significant event and make sure you tell everyone about it, so you really are motivated to go through with it. Whatever you do, don't just follow the one-size-fits-all advice from the experts. Remember, the most effective exercise programme for you is the one you stick with, and if it's not at least a little fun and enjoyable you probably won't. Think about who you are, what kind of environment and activities you enjoy and design your exercise programme based on that. If you find you have to force yourself to do your exercise most of the time, to the point where you regularly skip workouts, there is a good chance that you haven't chosen the right activities or programme for you.

Positive Thinking

It's not hard to imagine that people who think more positively and generally see the world in a more positive way, experience higher levels of overall life satisfaction. As we've discussed earlier in this book, lasting happiness is largely a matter of having the right mindset. It's about how we experience and interpret what happens in the world around us and less about what actually happens. With that in mind, it probably doesn't come as a surprise that research suggests positivity is a key element of long-term happiness.

Several studies have shown that happy people tend to have an overall more positive and optimistic outlook on life, while less happy people tend to view things in a more negative and pessimistic light.[102] Of course, you could argue that happier people have more reasons to be optimistic and that more positive things happen in their lives. However, this seems unlikely given there are several studies in which independent judges rate the experiences of both the positive and the negative people equally, as well as the fact that optimistic and more pessimistic people respond differently to the same hypothetical situations.[103] Bad things happen in the world. We all probably feel like our lives are especially hard or unfair sometimes. However, regardless of what happens, we always have a choice as to how we respond, and we can always choose to focus on the positive aspects and stay optimistic. We all know stories about people who have overcome incredible hardship — and other people who weren't able to deal with the same situation. Just think of the example of a young, active person who suffers a severe accident and ends up paralysed for the rest of his or her life. I think we can all see how hard it would be to stay positive in that situation. No one would blame them for feeling sorry for themselves and negative about the future.

However, there are plenty of examples of people who made it through such difficult times and ended up living very happy and fulfilling lives; just as there are examples of people who weren't able to get through it and ended up struggling for the rest of their lives. One of the main differences between those two types of people often is their attitude, their ability to see the good and to stay optimistic. Some people seem to be able to make the most out of very challenging situations while other people can find something negative even when everything seems to be going great. To some extent, our tendency towards being positive or negative is genetic. However, all that means is that some people need to work harder to have a positive mindset than others. It does not mean some of us are doomed to be pessimists. And it might be worth putting in the hard work.

A positive attitude and mindset are incredibly valuable for both immediate and lasting happiness. It's easy to see how being positive will make us feel happier in the moment, but more and more research is also pointing out the numerous benefits of positivity for long-term life satisfaction. One researcher who has done a lot of work in the area is Barbara Fredrickson from the University of North Carolina.[104] Her research has shown that people who are in a positive mindset are more productive and able to identify more possible responses and solutions than people in a neutral or negative state of mind. Furthermore, her research shows that people in a positive state of mind have an enhanced ability to build skills and develop resources that will still be useful later in life, long after the momentary positive emotion has passed. Fredrickson refers to this as the 'broaden and build' theory because a positive mindset enables us to identify more possibilities and opens our mind, which then allows us to develop new skills and resources that are of value in other areas of our life.

Furthermore, those of you who are career-focused and who are striving for financial goals might be interested to know that research also suggests that a positive attitude has a direct effect on wage. As a result of his research into the effects of positive attitude on happiness and wage, Madhu Mohanty from California State University suggests that in order to raise our earning potential we should not only focus on the development of skills but also the development of a positive attitude.[105]

Finally, in case you need another reason to be more positive, consider this: positivity has also been linked to higher life expectancy and might help protect us from onsets of dementia. As part of a famous nun study, Deborah Danner and her colleagues analysed personal essays written by 180 Catholic nuns in the 1930s.[106] They found that the nuns whose essays were worded positively and optimistically ended up living about 10 years longer than those whose essays included fewer positive and optimistic emotions. Furthermore, the more positive nuns also seemed to show fewer signs of early dementia. The findings of this study are particularly relevant because all the participants were nuns, which means they had very similar lifestyles and lived in similar environments. As a result, it's less likely that other environmental factors influenced the findings, and we can be more confident that there really is a link between positivity and the outcomes.

However, valuable as it might be, learning to be more positive can be challenging and takes time. It requires us to change the way we think, feel and respond to challenges, and even with the best intentions, it is often difficult to remember doing so in the moment. The best way to coach yourself to be more positive is by starting with deliberate practices and exercises that teach your brain how to think positively. Over time, your brain gets more and more used to focusing on positive thoughts instead of negative ones and you will find your intuitive responses and thoughts become more optimistic. Here are a few examples of such deliberate practices and exercises to help you get started.

START SMALL

First of all, don't start off with the goal of being positive all the time — especially if you're rating yourself quite low in positivity right now. Start with a smaller goal. Maybe you begin by focusing on one specific area, like your relationship or your job, or you pick a particular time of the day or week, or you focus on being more positive towards one specific person. Make a conscious decision to focus on the positive in this one specific area of your life for starters, and then expand over time.

POSITIVITY EXERCISES

Make time for positivity exercises. Take 15 or 20 minutes out of your day several times a week (ideally daily) to sit down and practice being positive. Think about a situation where you responded negatively and look at it with a positive and optimistic mindset. For example, you might have been hurt by something a friend or partner said to you. However, when you look at the same situation with a positive and optimistic mindset, you might find that the other person probably didn't mean it in the way you interpreted it, or that there was no way for them to know that what they said would hurt you. Or you might feel like things at work are not going your way and you're not achieving as much as you could, but when you specifically make yourself look for the positives, you find that you've accomplished a lot and that your boss complimented you for the great work you are doing just the other day.

Being optimistic and finding the positives will be challenging for some of you to begin with. If you're naturally more of a pessimistic person and you've been reinforcing that through your habits for years, you might often struggle to find anything positive about a problematic situation. However, most of the time there is something positive, even if it's just the things you've learned from the challenging experience that will help you deal better in the future. If you really struggle with this, ask a positive friend for help. Ask them to go through the situation with you and find the good parts. You might be surprised at what they can see. Over time, you get better and better at it yourself. However, you have to be open to it and really try to see and feel the positives about the situation.

While exercises like these are not the same as responding positively in the moment, they can help you slowly change your mindset and attitude. The more you practise, the sooner you will find yourself being optimistic and positive as things happen in the world around you.

REMINDERS
Thinking more positively is essentially a habit change. As such, it will take time and require persistence, and there will be setbacks. The hardest part is to remember in the moment, as something

happens, to be positive and not fall back into the old habit of negative thinking. Little reminders can be very helpful with this. Put post-it notes up in strategic places around your house, your workplace, or your car, add an inspirational quote as your phone and computer screen background, get a coffee or tea mug with a positivity message, or ask a friend, partner or colleague to remind you. Anything you can do to remind yourself as often as possible will help you get to a more positive mindset quicker.

Other Voluntary Activities That Might Make Us Happier

On the previous pages, we discussed a number of voluntary activities that might help us increase our happiness. There are many more factors that researchers have looked at, but to review them all in detail would be beyond the scope of this book. To give you an idea, here are a few other voluntary activities research has found to have a positive impact on happiness:

- **Finding Meaning:** Having meaning in our lives is a key to happiness. We will discuss this specific aspect of happiness in more detail in the next chapter.
- **Be Yourself:** For those of us in western societies, 'being yourself' has become a mantra and advice we hear all too frequently. While being yourself can be hard, especially when it means being different from everyone else, research suggests that it might be worth it. Studies have shown that being authentic and true to ourselves leads to higher levels of happiness and life satisfaction.[107]
- **Forgiveness:** Several researchers and authors have found that people who are more likely to forgive and people who forgive quicker are more likely to be happy.[108] [109]
- **Religion:** Several studies have investigated the correlation between religion and happiness — with mixed findings. While some have found that, on average, religious

people tend to be happier, other studies did not find any correlation.[110] Regardless of research findings, there are certainly many people who consider their religion key to their happiness. My grandparents were two such people. However, I think it is likely that this happiness is not merely a direct result of being religious but is mainly about the things that come with being religious: purpose and meaning, connection and community, kindness, gratitude and more — all of which have been argued to have a positive impact on our happiness.

- **Thoughtful Self-reflection:** Taking the time to reflect on one's thoughts, experiences and attitude has been argued to have a positive impact on overall well-being.[111]

Summary and Exercise

As we have seen, there are several voluntary activities that can potentially help us significantly increase our overall satisfaction with life and our happiness. Let's quickly summarise what we have learned:

- **Gratitude:** Several research projects have suggested that experiencing gratitude and taking the time to make ourselves aware of all the things we have to be grateful for can significantly lift our happiness.
- **Goals:** Goals can be a crucial factor towards achieving greater happiness. However, goals need to be meaningful and personally valued, and it's the pursuit of them more so than the setting or achievement of goals that makes us happy.
- **Mindfulness:** Mindfulness, or in other words, being fully present in the moment, has been shown to have many benefits — including being a tool that can help us achieve lasting happiness.

- **Altruism and Kindness:** Even though it might be hard to believe given the world we live in these days, there is substantial evidence that being kind to others and looking after those in need can make us feel happier and more satisfied with our life.
- **Exercise:** It's nothing new that physical activity is really important for our health and physical well-being, but research suggests that it is equally important for our mental health and well-being. An important aspect is to find the right exercise for us, based on our preferences and values.
- **Positive Thinking:** While it might be hard to achieve at times for some of us, it's even harder to argue with or ignore the research that has highlighted the benefits of positive thinking — not just for our immediate happiness but also for long-term gains.
- **And more:** Several other voluntary activities have the potential to increase our happiness such as religion, finding meaning and being true to yourself.

When it comes to embracing voluntary activities to try to enhance our happiness and well-being, we're spoiled for choice. Numerous activities have been shown to be beneficial for our pursuit of happiness. Which ones will ultimately work best for you, is up to you to discover. I strongly recommend giving a few of them a go. Regardless of which activities you choose to incorporate into your life, it is important to understand that the most significant and most lasting benefit of any of these voluntary activities comes from making them part of who we are. It's when we get to the point where we don't need to keep daily journals to be grateful, no longer need reminders to be positive and don't need to schedule kindness, that we will genuinely experience lasting happiness. Keep this in mind as you work on incorporating some of these activities into your life. The reminders and exercises are to help you get started, change habits and get an idea of what it should and could be like, but the ultimate goal is to change how you respond in the moment. The goal is that you are kind and grateful and positive not because of reminders or because it's that time of the day, but because you have changed your mindset to feel and think that way naturally.

With that in mind, time for another exercise. Just as we did with the life circumstances before, think about which of the voluntary activities you believe can be most beneficial for you and help you be happier.

EXERCISE: WHAT AREAS DO YOU WANT TO WORK ON?

1. Review the key things you learned about yourself in the previous chapter. Review your notes and re-read your personal profile.
2. With all of that in mind, rate how beneficial each of the voluntary activities we discussed could be to your long-term happiness. Rate each factor on a scale from 1 to 10, with 10 being 'very beneficial' and 1 being 'not beneficial at all'. If any of the other ones that were briefly mentioned at the end resonated with you, add them at the bottom of the table and include them in this exercise.
3. Now think about how well you feel you're currently doing in each of these areas. Rate your satisfaction and happiness with each area on a scale from 1 to 10 (10 = very happy, 1 = very unhappy).
4. Next, consider to what extent improvements in this area could impact your overall happiness. Rate each factor on a scale from 1 to 10 (10 = very much, 1 = not at all)

5. Based on the ratings you've given, highlight the 2-3 activities you want to work on. These should be ones that you consider beneficial to your happiness, which show some room for improvement (i.e. you haven't rated them as a 10 in step 3) and where you think improvements will have a significant impact on your overall happiness.

6. For each of the 2-3 activities you've highlighted (and the others if you want to), think about at least two or three things you could do to improve in this area. Don't worry too much about how realistic it might be, just write down any ideas you can come up with. You're not committing to anything yet, it's just about collecting ideas while they are still fresh in your mind.

Factor	How beneficial could this activity be to your happiness? (1-10)	How well are you currently doing in this area? (1-10)	How much could improvements in this area impact your overall happiness? (1-10)	How could you improve in this area?
Experiencing gratitude				
Setting meaningful goals				
Experiencing mindfulness				
Showing altruism and kindness				
Exercise regularly				
Have a more positive mindset				

Life Circumstances vs.

Voluntary Activities

In this chapter, we have learned about a number of life circumstances and voluntary factors that might have an impact on our happiness. We've reviewed scientific evidence to understand if and how different factors affect our overall life satisfaction and, in some cases, we have discussed how we might be able to improve in certain areas to lift our happiness. It is up to you, based on the knowledge you have gained about yourself in the previous chapter, to assess the information provided and decide which are likely to have the biggest positive impact on your life. However, there is one more piece of research I would like you to consider. As part of their research into happiness, highly regarded researchers Kennon Sheldon and Sonja Lyubomirsky conducted several studies to investigate how changes in life circumstances and changes in voluntary activities impact our overall well-being and life satisfaction.[112] They measured participants' well-being before any positive changes in life circumstances or positive changes in activities occurred. Well-being was then measured again directly after the positive change occurred and once more after some time had passed. Their findings suggested that both positive changes in life circumstances and in voluntary activities led to an immediate lift in happiness. However, only those people that made positive activity changes still reported high levels of happiness after some time had passed. Those people who changed life circumstances were back to their old levels of happiness. Sheldon and Lyubomirsky were able to confirm these findings in another study two years later,[113] giving us reason to believe they might be on to something when they argue that voluntary activities have a more lasting positive impact on our happiness than change in life circumstances. It makes sense when you think about it, thanks to the concept of hedonic adaptation. Hedonic adaptation means we experience spikes or drops in happiness following positive or negative events, but that we tend to adapt relatively quickly and, before long, find ourselves back at our old happiness level. It shouldn't come as a surprise, then, that voluntary activities have longer-lasting effects than changes in life circumstances do, simply because they are more repeatable and scalable. You can experience gratitude every day, you can take a positive view on everything that happens, all the time, you can exercise as often as you want (or your body lets you) and you can be kind to someone every day. On the other hand, getting a promotion or buying a nice new car every day is probably a lot less realistic, and even great relationships, good health and excellent education can quickly be taken for granted — unless we are mindful of them and experience gratitude for them.

Another factor to consider is that life circumstances are at least partly out of our control, while voluntary activities are, by definition, fully within our control. Even though we obviously have some control over how much money we earn, what kind of relationships we have, how we spend our money, how healthy we are and how much we educate ourselves, our overall life circumstances are, at least partly, dependent on other people's actions as well as luck. No matter how good you are at your job and how hard you work, you still rely on your boss to give you that promotion. No matter how well you look after your health, you can still get cancer or be injured in an accident. No matter how much you invest in a friendship, you still rely on the other person to care as well to have a meaningful relationship. Voluntary activities, on the other hand, are internal factors that are entirely within our control. It is completely up to us to embrace them and to make them part of our lives. We do not rely on anyone or anything else to experience gratitude or mindfulness, to be kind to others or to view things in a positive way. We all can choose whether or not we make those activities part of our life. That doesn't mean that it's always easy. Changing your attitude, mindset and habits is incredibly difficult and takes a lot of practice and effort. But it can be done, and it's completely up to us to choose whether we want to make the effort or not. This fact is another reason why voluntary activities are more likely to have a lasting, positive effect on our happiness. We're in control. We have the power to embrace them at any given time in our lives for as long and as much as we want to and need to, to find happiness. Changes in life circumstances, on the other hand, are almost always a lot less in our control. They rely on other people to do things a certain way or on luck and good fortune. No matter how much effort we put in, we might never really get what we want and what would make us happy. Wouldn't you rather place your bets for finding happiness on activities you control, than on circumstances that are up to others and luck?

Finally, we need to consider the influence that voluntary activities can have on environmental factors. This is something I know very well from my own experience. For an outsider looking at my life over the past 10 years, it might appear as though a lot of external factors have changed, and it would be easy to assume that is the reason why I am so much happier today. I've lost a lot of weight, I'm healthier and fitter, I have an amazing group of friends, I've done really well career-wise and I have much higher income and better financial security — all positive changes in external factors. However, what is less visible from the outside is that all these positive external changes were only possible because of significant internal mindset changes and voluntary activities. I didn't find happiness because I lost weight, I lost weight because I was happier. I didn't find happiness because I had more friends, I found amazing friends because I was happier, had a more positive outlook on life and was open to new experiences. I did well at work because I believed in myself and approached it with a positive mindset and because I learned to be more mindful. Voluntary factors are so incredibly powerful and important not only because they can directly make you feel happier but also because they can help you achieve the external changes that will then make you even happier. Twelve years ago, I decided to take control of my life and focus on changing the things I can change (voluntary factors). The more work I did in this area, the happier I became and the more it felt as if all those external factors I always thought were what would bring me happiness, just fell into place. Everyone is different, and everyone has a different path to happiness. However, from my own experience and everything I have learned through that and since, I would highly recommend starting your journey to a happier life by focusing on your mindset and voluntary activities.

That brings us to the end of this chapter. Hopefully it has given you a few ideas of what may or may not make you happy and how you might be able to start implementing some of it into your life. Given everything you've learned so far, you are almost ready to design your own Happiness Blueprint. However, there is one more thing to go through first: The Four Pillars of Happiness.

PART IV:

The Four Pillars of Happiness

"It isn't what you have or who you are or where you are or what you are doing that makes you happy or unhappy. It is what you think about it."

DALE CARNEGIE, HOW TO WIN FRIENDS AND INFLUENCE PEOPLE

THIS BOOK is all about looking at happiness through the lens of your individual personality, values and strengths and weaknesses to help you design your individual plan for a happier life. Therefore, I am trying to avoid any generic statements along the lines of 'you must do this' or 'you cannot do that'. I want you to analyse the information and insight provided and decide for yourself, based on who you truly are, what applies to you and what doesn't. However, I also strongly believe that there are certain things about happiness that do apply to everyone — to varying degrees. Based on my own experience and what I have learned through reading books, reviewing research findings and talking to a lot of people, I have become convinced that there are four pillars that play an important part in finding and maintaining happiness for all of us. Without them, achieving happiness will be incredibly hard — maybe even impossible. If you think back to our earlier example of comparing happiness to building a dream home, these pillars would be your foundation. Everyone's dream home looks different, but they all need a strong, solid foundation. That is not to say that these are set in stone and exactly the same for everyone. I do believe that each pillar can matter more to some than others. However, we all need a certain minimum level of each pillar to be able to find and retain happiness. This chapter will discuss these four pillars and will outline why they are so important to finding happiness.

Self-Love and Respect

Your mindset and attitude play a huge role in how happy you are. How you perceive the world, how you interpret events and how you respond emotionally can make all the difference between being happy or unhappy. With happiness being such an internal concept, how can you hope to find it, if you don't love and respect yourself? How can you expect to view the world in a positive light, if you cannot see yourself in a positive way?

Loving and respecting yourself does not mean you have to love everything about yourself and never doubt or question anything you do or feel. Loving yourself always and all the time is called arrogance, and that's not the goal. Doubt, and a feeling that we're lacking in some way, are enablers for change and growth and help us become better people in the future. If we were always 100% happy with ourselves, we wouldn't be looking for ways to improve or progress — and we probably wouldn't be very popular either. Self-love and respect are not about overconfidence or the total absence of doubts. It's about being able to look inside ourselves and feeling mostly positive about what we find. It's about being able to feel proud of who we are and having confidence in our ability to deal with the challenges life throws at us. It's about truly believing that we deserve to be happy.

Self-love and respect have been shown to be instrumental to finding happiness. An in-depth review of the research around self-esteem, carried out by Roy Baumeister and his colleagues, finds that self-love and respect have a surprisingly insignificant impact on performance indicators such as grades at school, job performance or general task performance. Similarly, there is little support for the idea that self-esteem results in higher likeability or attractiveness (even though people with high self-esteem might think it does). However, they do conclude that self-esteem has a strong relation to happiness.[114] While the exact reasons for this are not clear from existing research, the authors are convinced that high levels of self-love and respect lead to greater happiness. Furthermore, their findings also show that people with low self-esteem seem to be more likely to suffer from depression.

Independent of whether you believe the scientific research, consider these arguments for why self-love and respect are so important for finding happiness.

YOU'RE MORE LIKELY TO HAVE A POSITIVE OUTLOOK ON LIFE

Most importantly, self-love and respect are highly likely to lead to an overall more positive outlook on life. If you are happy and comfortable with who you are, it is a lot easier to feel comfortable and positive about the world around you. You are more likely to interpret events positively and to want to see the good in things and people. On the other hand, if you are constantly doubting and questioning yourself, you are more likely to feel the same way about life in general.

YOU'RE MORE LIKELY TO DEAL WELL WITH CHALLENGES LIFE THROWS AT YOU

Self-love and respect make you resilient and enable you to overcome setbacks and cope with challenges in life. Feeling positive about yourself means you are more likely to have confidence in your ability to deal with challenges. Moreover, if things go wrong, your inner strength and self-love will make it easier to get up and try again. If you do not love and respect yourself, it will be tough to find the inner strengths and resources to cope well with challenges or recover from setbacks.

YOU ARE MORE LIKELY TO LIVE LIFE YOUR WAY

As we have discussed several times in this book, happiness is a highly individual and subjective concept. There is no one-size-fits-all approach. It's up to each one of us to figure out what does and doesn't make us happy. If you love and respect yourself, you're more likely to have the confidence to go through with your idea of happiness. People with low self-esteem, on the other hand, are more likely to be influenced by the opinions of people around them and society in general and will be more likely to chase someone else's definition of happiness instead of their own.

Finding ways to love and respect myself has been an incredibly important aspect of my journey to a happier life. One of the main differences between now and 12 years ago is that I genuinely love and respect myself today. That was never the case before I started working on myself and actively searching for the path to a happier life. While I always had a certain level of self-love, it was very low, and I lacked self-respect almost completely. I didn't think of myself as someone I could be proud of, someone I would like to be friends with, or someone who makes a valuable contribution to society and people's lives. Learning about myself and starting to understand my strengths helped me slowly build self-respect. That increased self-esteem resulted in more achievements and success, which then helped me to lift my self-esteem further. Today, I don't always like myself, I doubt myself regularly and I still struggle to love myself occasionally, but I always respect myself and I have the inner confidence to do life my way.

How do you know if you lack self-love and respect? While it mainly comes down to how you feel internally about yourself, there are a few warning signs that might indicate you're not as strong in this area as you would like to be. One very common warning sign is frequent self-doubt. While occasional self-doubt and insecurities are perfectly normal, if you find you are struggling to believe in yourself more often than not and you generally don't have much confidence in your own ability, that is probably a sign that you lack self-love and respect. Another warning sign is a constant fear of being judged by others. We all want to please others, but when you find yourself constantly worried about how others think about you and your actions — rather than focused on what you think and feel — it's likely that you're low in self-esteem. Other warning signs are chronic indecisiveness, being overly sensitive to emotions caused by other people's actions, being too invested in relationships, taking every bit of remotely critical feedback personally and a tendency to give up quickly when things don't go your way. If you notice any of these warning signs in yourself, it's worth considering that you need to work on building up self-love and respect.

How much do you love and respect yourself? If you feel you can tick this one off, that's great. However, if you feel like there is room for improvement, this is something you want to keep in mind for your Happiness Blueprint. If you don't love and respect yourself enough, that is probably the first goal you should work towards in your blueprint.

How do you build up self-esteem? As with so many things in life, there is no simple one-size-fits-all answer. If this is an area you want to work on, I would suggest spending some more time reading and learning about it to fully understand self-love and respect, what it is, where it stems from and how you can build yours. Brené Brown's book Daring Greatly is a great resource on this topic and so is Love Yourself Like Your Life Depends On It by Kamal Ravikant. Furthermore, many of the other concepts and ideas we've discussed in this book can help you build self-esteem. Knowing yourself and your strengths and then building upon them is an excellent first step. Bringing things like mindfulness, positive thinking, exercise, forgiveness and altruism into your life can also do wonders for improving your self-love and respect. A key question to ask yourself is why you're lacking self-esteem. Once you know the answer to that question, you know where to start your journey to loving yourself more.

Purpose and Meaning

It is my strong belief and experience that a key to lasting happiness is having something in your life that provides purpose and meaning, something that excites you and that energises and motivates you. In fact, meaning and purpose are so important that many have included it in their definitions of happiness. For example, positive psychology researcher Sonja Lyubomirsky defines happiness as "the experience of joy, contentment, or positive well-being, combined with a sense that one's life is good, **meaningful**, and worthwhile",[115] and ancient Greek philosopher and scientist Aristotle has described happiness as "the **meaning and the purpose of life**, the whole aim and end of human existence." Meaning and purpose are also key aspects of positive psychology, the research field that looks at ways to increase happiness. In the book Authentic Happiness, Martin Seligman states "[Positive Psychology] takes you through the countryside of pleasure and gratification, up into the high country of strength and virtue, and finally to the peaks of lasting fulfilment: **meaning and purpose**", making it clear that meaning and purpose are the ultimate drivers of lasting happiness and life satisfaction.

Having purpose and meaning in your life is about being deeply invested in and passionate about something. It's caring greatly for a cause, feeling a sense of responsibility for making it the best it can be, as well as feeling proud to be part of it. It's being passionate about something that is bigger than just us, something we do because we believe in the greater meaning and impact of it. It's having something in our life that makes us feel like we're important and that what we do matters and is meaningful to us independently of society's expectations and standards. Meaning and purpose are usually found in goals and causes that help us express ourself — rather than ones that help us impress others. People find purpose and meaning in many areas; family, work, religion, friendships, charities, art, hobbies, causes and much more. The important thing is not what you do, but how it makes you feel. Being a mom doesn't automatically mean that it gives you meaning and purpose, just like being good at your job or going to church once a week doesn't mean work or religion bring you purpose and meaning. It's only those things that result in real, lasting fulfilment, pride and a deep sense of satisfaction that truly add meaning into your life.

It's important to understand that over time, you can get meaning and purpose from different things. Some might only be a part of your life for a relatively short period while others will become long-term sources of meaning and purpose. For example, several years ago, when I had just started my journey to a happier life, I got a lot of purpose and meaning from being part of a voluntary student organisation. For several years after I graduated, I got a sense of purpose and belonging from the work I was doing and I still do so today, though maybe to a slightly lesser extent because other things have become more important to me. In recent years, being part of a team that organises an annual charity event has given me a lot of meaning, as does my writing and sharing my stories and insights with people. Other things have been more constant, like reading and learning, which have been bringing meaning into my life for well over a decade now, and my amazing group of friends gives me a strong sense of belonging on an ongoing basis.

So why is a sense of meaning and purpose so important to finding happiness?

IT GIVES YOU DIRECTION

Having things in your life that bring purpose and meaning is like having an internal compass that points the way to happiness. By understanding what brings you purpose and acting accordingly, you are a lot more likely to spend your time with activities that ultimately contribute to your happiness. You're also a lot more likely to enjoy those activities while you're doing them. Knowing your purpose and meaning enables you to design your life around things that bring you fulfilment and lasting happiness.

IT CAN HELP MAKE UNDESIRABLE ACTIVITIES MORE ENJOYABLE

Looking for the underlying meaning and purpose can make tasks and events you generally don't like a lot more enjoyable. For example, you might struggle to motivate yourself to go to work every day because you don't enjoy your job. While you might want to consider looking for a different position, that is not always possible. Sometimes life circumstances require us to just stick it out. However, as we have learned when we discussed the impact work can have on our happiness, looking for ways to connect our work to something that is meaningful to us can make a boring job a lot more enjoyable. You can look for ways to change how you go about your job to make it more meaningful to you or you can connect your work to other things that bring you purpose outside of your job. For example, you might get a lot of meaning and purpose out of providing for your family and making sure your children can grow up in a safe, loving and secure environment. You could look at your job as something that enables you to do that better. The money you earn provides for your family and by going to work every day with a positive attitude and a desire to be the best you can be, you set a great role model for your children. While this might not make your job any more fun, it can change your attitude towards it and, through that, make it more enjoyable.

IT GIVES YOU STRENGTH IN TOUGH TIMES

Having things in your life that bring you meaning and purpose can give you strength in difficult times and will enable you to keep going and try again after failure. If you work towards a higher purpose in life, individual tasks and goals are just part of a bigger puzzle. Struggling or failing at one step is not a failure on the whole, but just a setback. Your underlying desire to pursue your life's purpose will enable you to find another way. Furthermore, people often get meaning from things that make them feel part of something bigger than themselves. In difficult times, that can offer a great support system as well as the motivation to put one's personal challenges aside and focus on the greater good for the group or the cause.

IT GENERATES SELF-LOVE AND RESPECT

We've already talked about the importance of self-love and respect for finding happiness. Having purpose and meaning can have a significant impact on self-love and respect. Purpose and meaning stems from having things in our life that we feel passionate about and feel proud to be a part of. It's also about a sense of belonging, feeling important and making a difference. These are all emotions that make us feel good about ourselves and can significantly lift our self-worth.

If all of that is not enough to convince you, a recent study has shown that a sense of purpose in life may play an essential role in maintaining physical function and independence as we age.[116] With all of this in mind, it should be easy to see why purpose and meaning are such critical aspects of lasting happiness. So how do you know if you have purpose and meaning? Unfortunately, there is no test for this. In many ways, it's a lot like asking how you know if you're in love. You just know. Some signs that might indicate that you don't have things in your life that bring you purpose and meaning include feeling lethargic and unmotivated a lot of the time, not having anything in your life that really excites you, struggling to generate interest in or passion for anything, being bored a lot and having no idea how to spend your free time.

If you feel like you would benefit from having more things in your life that bring you true meaning and purpose, keep this in mind when you develop your Happiness Blueprint. Finding something that will bring you a sense of purpose is relatively simple in theory, though it might require a bit of trial and error. In essence, it's about bringing something into your life that you really believe in, feel very passionate about and that gives you a sense of belonging and being part of something bigger.

Taking Responsibility

I read a lot, especially about happiness, the meaning of life and how to be the best version of myself. Despite the fact that I love reading and learning about these topics, it's rare for me to remember individual statements or sentences from a book for long after I read it. If one does stick, it's usually because it had a significant impact on me, like this one that Mark Mason makes in his bestselling book The Subtle Art of Not Giving a F**k:

"There is a simple realisation from which all personal improvement and growth emerges. This is the realisation that we, individually, are responsible for everything in our lives, no matter the external circumstances. We don't always control what happens to us. But we always control how we interpret what happens to us, as well as how we respond. Whether we consciously recognise it or not, we are always responsible for our experiences."

Mark Mason is not alone with this belief. Many other authors, researchers and thinkers have made the same argument: we're responsible for our lives! As an extension of that, we are also accountable for our own happiness. That doesn't mean that everything in our life is in our control, but what is in our control is how we respond. In happiness terms, it means we might not be able to prevent bad and negative things from happening to us, but we can control how we react to them — and that can make a huge difference as to how much they will impact our long-term happiness. For example, you can't control if your spouse forgets your birthday, but you can choose to forgive, let go and focus on all the positive things he or she has done for you. Or, you can dwell on it forever, feel sad and take it as a sign that he or she doesn't really love you. Likewise, a colleague might get the promotion you have worked for really hard and consider yourself to be much more qualified for. You can get upset, doubt yourself and your skills, start feeling very negative about your work and ultimately hate your job and be unhappy with it. Or, you can let it go, focus on all the great things you have achieved in your position and the parts you enjoy most about it. Or you can start looking for a new job because you believe in yourself and that you can do better. Of course, there are times when choosing the 'happy path' is much harder. When a loved one dies unexpectedly, for example, it is hard to focus on the positive. However, even then you have a choice about how much time of mourning you give yourself before you start to look ahead again and find it in yourself to be grateful for the good things you still have in your life.

This kind of thinking might feel controversial and a bit uncomfortable for some people. The idea that, while we might not always be at fault or in control of what happens in our lives, we are fully responsible for how we respond to it, feel about it, what we do with the cards we've been dealt and, ultimately, how happy we are, can seem foreign at first. However, when you think about it, it's actually a good thing. Imagine if our happiness was completely out of our control. Imagine we had to rely on luck and on other people to do things a certain way to be able to find happiness. Isn't it better to be in control ourselves? It is incredibly hard to change other people unless they are motivated to change themselves — everyone who has ever tried can attest to that. We can't control other people's behaviour, and even in situations where we can, it is exhausting and the results are often short-term. On the other hand, we do control our own actions and reactions. Changing ourselves is a lot easier than changing other people. So why would you want to put your happiness in the hands of others, and trust to luck, if you can control it yourself?

Researchers have also long identified the vast benefits that come from taking control of our own lives. Several studies have shown that people who feel in control of their lives tend to perform better, are better at dealing with stress and adversity and overall, live happier lives.[117]

Taking responsibility for our happiness and our life is one of the four pillars of happiness because it gives us the motivation to work on ourselves. If we don't believe that happiness is in our control, then what's the point in investing time and effort into it? If we don't believe we can change ourselves and our lives, then why spend time figuring out what we would have to change to be happier? Taking full responsibility for our life and believing we have the ability and power to make our life what we want it to be, is key to finding and retaining happiness. Being happier requires a mindset change. Believing that everything in our life is our responsibility enables that mindset change. Next time something negative happens in your life, or you find yourself doubting yourself, remember this. Remember that you choose how you respond and it's your responsibility to make the most out of every situation and see the positive. You will probably find that this way of thinking, while challenging at first, will enable you to deal much better with negative emotions and events.

Realising the importance of taking responsibility and, even more importantly, fully accepting and internalising it, is what I still consider the turning point in my life. This was long before I read Mark Mason's book and I don't think I was fully aware of precisely what I was doing at the time. However, looking back now, I realise that it was the day that I started to take responsibility for my life — all aspects of it — that was the starting point for finding happiness. I stopped blaming the world for everything that was wrong in my life. I stopped blaming my genes for being overweight, I stopped blaming my teachers for not being inspiring, I stopped blaming my friends for not being supportive and I stopped blaming my family for not being that warm and emotional ideal of a family I had in my head. Instead, I accepted responsibility for my own life and the fact that not everything that happens is my fault, but all of it is my responsibility. If it hadn't been for that realisation and mindset change, I don't think everything I learned afterwards would have had the kind of impact on me that it did. Taking responsibility, in many ways, was the first step I took on my journey to a happier life and what enabled me to fully leverage everything else I have learned since.

How do you know you're not taking full responsibility for your life? First and foremost, you probably don't wholeheartedly agree with the argument that everything in your life is your responsibility and how you interpret and respond to things that happen in your life is a choice. Other signs to look out for are frequently blaming others for how you feel, often making excuses for yourself (especially excuses for why you can't live the life you want), feeling like other people dominate and control your life and generally not feeling in control of your own life.

This book is all about taking responsibility. I'm not providing you with an easy 'five steps to a happier life' plan or any kind of ultimate advice for finding happiness. Throughout the whole book, you are challenged to take responsibility, to analyse the information provided in the context of who you are and to identify the areas that matter most to your happiness. As we progress further, it will be your responsibility to design your blueprint for a happier life and, most importantly, it will be up to you to put it into action. Therefore, if you find you can't currently buy into the idea that happiness is fully within your control and that you are responsible for making it happen, I strongly suggest you spend some more time reading up on this and warming yourself up to the idea. I highly recommend Mark Mason's book. Likewise, if you find yourself believing in the concept in general, but having a hard time putting it into practice in the real world (you frequently find yourself playing the blame game again or making excuses), you might want to consider including some strategies in your blueprint to help with that. Regular affirmations or reminders can be very helpful with this, as can asking those people closest to you to keep an eye out for this type of behaviour and to let you know if they feel like you're at risk of not taking responsibility.

As with almost everything we discuss in this book, taking control will come easier to some than others. However, it's important to point out that some serious mental health issues like depression can make taking control particularly challenging. Many people who suffer from depression report that they understand, in theory, that they have control over their life but there is some sort of internal block that stops them from putting it into action. If you find yourself regularly demobilised and unable to take control of your life even though you want to and believe it would be a significant step towards feeling happier, I strongly recommend consulting with a mental health professional to explore this further as it might be a sign of a more significant mental health issue.

Open-Mindedness

The fourth and final pillar of happiness is open-mindedness. This pillar is about the importance of being open to new ideas, concepts and methods and being willing to truly and whole-heartedly give them a go. Throughout this entire book, I have repeatedly challenged you to get to know yourself and interpret and analyse the information provided in the context of your personality, values and strengths. This book is about helping you design a blueprint for a happier life based on who you are — not based on what generic research and general wisdom suggests. However, don't use that as an excuse to not be open-minded. Knowing yourself is really important for finding happiness, but you also need to be willing to challenge what you think you know and to experiment. Just because something doesn't feel right initially, doesn't mean that it's not for you. Just because something feels weird or uncomfortable doesn't mean it can't be valuable to you. If you have seriously tried something, with commitment and a positive attitude, and you learned that it didn't work for you, you can absolutely disregard those tactics going forward. However, until you have really given something a go, you should be open-minded to any ideas presented. And giving something a go does not mean doing it half-heartedly for a couple of days. Being open-minded and willing to explore new ideas and concepts means ignoring, or at least tuning down, your scepticism and doubts and being positive towards, and curious about, the new opportunities and ideas life is presenting you with.

Open-mindedness is one of the pillars of happiness because, as many people will tell you, sometimes happiness comes from the most unexpected places. Sometimes, it's the things we are most wary about at first that end up having the biggest positive impact on our life. Therefore, part of finding ways to be happier is a willingness to try new things and to experiment to find out what does and doesn't work for us. However, this pillar is about more than just trying new things. There is a reason it is called open-mindedness and not 'willingness to try new things'. It's easy to try something new that aligns with our existing values and experiences. It's a lot harder to commit to something new that does not align with our current beliefs. We're often quick to disregard things that are outside of our known world and comfort zone. For example, a rational, scientifically minded person might be very willing to try techniques like lists and calendar reminders even if they have never used them before, but they find it very hard to consider spirituality, affirmations and meditation as valid methods to increase happiness. Similarly, a creative, visionary person is likely to be open to trying things like vision boards and writing gratitude letters but might struggle to buy into things like lists, schedules and structured goal-setting activities. However, sometimes the most valuable insights and experiences come from places we least expect them to. Open-mindedness is about being truly open to all new things, not just the ones that feel comfortable.

I'm someone who values routine and constancy in my life and for a long time, that extended to my work. I used to be very set in the belief that a stable full-time job with a fixed desk in an office, somewhat regular hours and a regular pay cheque are what would make me happy. A few years ago, I had the opportunity to find out what the much less regular freelancing lifestyle would be like. Even though it felt unnatural and a bit scary at the time, I managed to be open-minded about it. And it turns out that I love it. Even though I value routine in many aspects of my life, I've learned that, when it comes to work, I actually value diversity, flexibility and freedom. Today, my work situation is one of the reasons why I'm so happy with my life, because I enjoy the work I do but also because it gives me the time and flexibility to do other things that are important to me (like writing a book). I would have not figured all of that out if I had not been open to trying the freelancing lifestyle when the opportunity presented itself. Chances are, there is something out there that could significantly lift your happiness but you have never even considered it simply because it doesn't align with your current lifestyle, values and beliefs.

At this point, it is essential to make one clear distinction. I am not arguing that you need to score high in openness in the Big Five Model to be happy. While there is some research that suggests that openness to experience, as a personality trait, has an association with overall happiness,[118] there is nothing to suggest that you cannot be happy even if you score relatively low in openness. However, those who strive to increase their happiness need to be open to new ideas and experiences. While this might come more naturally to some than others, I strongly believe all of us can be open-minded if we set our minds to it. Some of us just need to work on it a bit more.

What you learned about yourself earlier in this book will give you an idea as to whether openness comes relatively easily to you or not. If you scored low, that is an indication that you should pay particular attention to this and remind yourself regularly to be open-minded towards new ideas. However, even if your personality type suggests that openness comes naturally to you, it is worth checking in and reminding yourself regularly, as it is easy to get caught up in the known and familiar, even if you're generally an open person.

So to summarise, these are the Four Pillars of Happiness:

1. Loving and respecting yourself (at least most of the time)
2. Having things in your life that bring you purpose and meaning
3. Taking responsibility for your life and your happiness
4. Being open-minded to new ideas and concepts

EXERCISE: IDENTIFY THE PILLARS YOU SHOULD WORK ON

Now that you've learned about the four pillars and why they are so important to your happiness, it's worth spending a few minutes thinking about which of the pillars you might want to work on to lift your overall happiness.

1. Start by simply listening to your gut feeling. How do you think you're currently doing regarding the four pillars? Give each a rating between 1 and 10, with one meaning you feel like you don't have the pillar at all and 10 meaning you feel like you excel in this area and it's one of your biggest strengths.
2. Next, think about each pillar in a bit more detail. Think about what you have or are doing well regarding each pillar. For example, you might rate your overall self-love and respect fairly low, but you do feel very proud of your ability to

connect with people or you feel proud about your work or something else you do.

3. Think about the opposite. What are areas for improvement regarding each pillar? Why did you give this area a low rating? Or, if you gave it a relatively high rating, are there smaller things that could be better even though, overall, you're pretty happy with this pillar?

4. Next, try to come up with some specific ideas for how you could improve in each area. Focus specifically on those you've rated the lowest, but it's always worth thinking about those you feel good about as well. Sometimes the biggest happiness boosts come from leveraging our strengths and taking things from good to great.

Pillar	Overall rating (1 = doing really poorly, 10 = doing extremely well)	What do you have or are doing well?	What are areas for improvement?	How could you improve in this area?
Self-Love and Respect				
Meaning and Purpose				
Taking Responsibility				
Open-Mindedness				

5. Look through all your answers and highlight the things that feel most important to you with regard to lifting your happiness. Highlight those parts you think are worth working on as part of your plan for a happier life.

These last two chapters should have given you a much better idea of what the ingredients to happiness are and how you can create a happier life. Now it's time to pull all of that together and start developing your personal blueprint for a happier life.

PART V

Design YOUR Happiness Blueprint

"By recording your dreams and goals on paper, you set in motion the process of becoming the person you most want to be. Put your future in good hands — your own."

MARK VICTOR HANSEN

L ADIES AND gentlemen, this is the moment you've all been waiting for. It's time to start designing your personal Happiness Blueprint. This is where you bring everything you've learned up until now together to develop a plan that will lead you towards a happier life, taking into account your individual personality, values and strengths. The goal of this chapter is for you to develop and commit to goals and actions that will help you be happier and live your best possible life.

So what is this thing I'm calling a Happiness Blueprint? I used to call it my happiness formula, but then I learned about Martin Seligman's happiness formula and to avoid any confusion, I decided to come up with a different name. Blueprint seemed very fitting, maybe even more so than formula, because it is more action-oriented. The Oxford Dictionary defines a blueprint as "a plan which shows what can be achieved and how it can be achieved". A blueprint is a plan that outlines how you can achieve the desired outcome by following specific steps and instructions. It's not just about setting goals, but it's also about describing how, specifically, we will achieve those goals. In our case, the desired outcome is a happier life. Your blueprint will break that down into more tangible sub-goals and will outline how you will achieve those. However, it is important to note that a blueprint, or plan, as such is not doing anything. A blueprint for the most beautiful house or for an amazing product doesn't give you a house to live in or a product to use. It's when you put the plan into action, when you follow through with the plan, that you will achieve the desired outcome. That is one of the reasons why the chapter following this one will specifically focus on putting your plan into action.

This chapter is about helping you develop your highly personal blueprint for a happier life. It's not about providing you with a generic plan or designing your plan for you. Only you know what makes you happy and what will help you achieve the fulfilling, meaningful and happy life you're striving for. What you've learned in the previous chapters should have given you the knowledge and insights into happiness and yourself to provide you with everything you need to design your personal blueprint. And you might be surprised how simple that plan can be. When I say blueprint, some people think of those big sheets of paper with complicated drawings, symbols and processes. Yes, some blue-prints are certainly fairly complex and some of you, those who like having lots of detail and want to document the specifics, might end up with complex blueprints at the end of this chapter. However, if you do, then that's because it's who you are and how you like it. For most of you, it will probably be much less complex.

Simply put, your Happiness Blueprint is a plan of action, outlining what you will do to achieve your goal of a happier life. However, it's not as simple as sitting down and coming up with a few things you will do to be happier. Of course, that might work for some, but most of you have probably done that at least once in your life and then either didn't go through with it, or did, but nothing changed. There is a reason why this chapter is several pages long and not just one page that says, "write a list of what will make you happy". We will work through a process that will help you design a blueprint that aligns very closely with your values and personality. You will develop a plan that specifies your goals and the individual steps you will take to get there. The process will encourage you to think about your core values and real desires, to make sure your goals will bring you lasting happiness and not just temporary joy and pleasure.

Before we dive into it, we need to discuss some basic rules for designing your blueprint. There are five golden rules. The purpose of these rules is to make sure your blueprint is powerful, inspiring, impactful and achievable.

The Five Blueprint Rules

1. Make sure it is within your control

A key goal of this book is to make you realise that your happiness is within your control. As we have learned in several sections in this book, voluntary activities, those factors that we control, tend to have the most significant and lasting impact on our happiness. If you make your happiness dependent on something other people need to do, or something that needs to happen in your environment, you're not in control of putting your plan into action. Your best chance of living a happier life is to make your happiness 100% dependent on things that are fully within your power! That is why it is so important for your blueprint to only include things you control. However, that doesn't mean certain goals are excluded. It's more about framing your goals in a way that puts them within your control. For example, if you think getting married is key to your happiness, you might be tempted to include "Find my perfect match and get married" in your blueprint. However, that means the success of your plan will be dependent on being lucky enough to, firstly, meet someone you fall in love with and want to spend the rest of your life with. They then need to feel the same way about you and have the same goal (wanting to get married). "Getting married" is not a good goal to include in your blueprint because there is so much involved that you can't control. A better way to approach this is to focus on meeting new people and being open to a relationship. For example, you could include "Meet new people" as your goal and actions such as "Go to places and events where I meet new people at least once a week" or "Be proactive and approach a stranger at least once a week." Do you see the difference? By framing it this way, you are in control, but you also significantly increase your chances of meeting the person you want to marry.

Another example might be that your goal is to get a promotion because, even after reading about the studies that suggest otherwise, you believe getting that promotion will significantly and lastingly improve your happiness (maybe because it would enable you to live more by your values). That is absolutely okay. However, the problem with having this specific goal in your blueprint is that, while you might be able to control how hard you work, how committed you are or what new job-related skills you learn, at the end of the day your boss is in control of giving you that promotion. Therefore, a better way to frame it for your blueprint is to think about the goals and activities you can control. For example, your goal could be to "Be the best I can be at my job" and your actions could then be "Master a new important skill (name the skill) in the next three months" or "Show initiative and commitment by taking on work outside my direct job description, at least once a fortnight." A slightly different way to look at it might be "Always do my work in a way that I can be proud of." Regardless of how you frame it, make sure you are 100% in control of making it happen.

2. Design it for long-term happiness

At the beginning of this book, we talked about the difference between happiness and positive emotions. Happiness is a state of inner fulfilment and positivity, a love for life on the whole. Positive emotions, on the other hand, are mostly in-the-moment, temporary emotional responses to something that has happened or is happening. The goal of your Happiness Blueprint is to help you find lasting happiness. However, positive emotions like joy and pleasure can play a role in helping you achieve happiness. Experiencing greater happiness requires a change in mindset, but for many of us, that is not easy to achieve. More tangible goals and achievements that bring immediate pleasure and joy can help us along the way. Small mindset changes lead to more joy and pleasure which then leads to more confidence and makes mindset changes easier, which then enables us to achieve that lasting happiness state of mind. For example, one of your goals might be to improve your relationship with your father. Maybe you've had a difficult past and spending time with him often feels like hard work. Think about ways that you can make your time together more enjoyable. For example, you could suggest doing activities you really enjoy or meeting for a nice dinner, both things that are enjoyable and generate positive emotions. That way, you will feel more positive about spending time together, which is likely to have a direct impact on how you engage, making the overall experience more enjoyable. Over time, if you continue to work on it, your relationship improves and you start enjoying spending time with your father without needing any extra incentives. Using little things that bring you immediate positive emotions can help you make a difficult situation more enjoyable, which means you are more likely to go through with it and have a more positive mindset.

What does that mean for your blueprint? First of all, all your goals should always be about achieving lasting happiness (not temporary positive emotions). However, you can absolutely include tangible short-term actions that will help you achieve these goals AND bring you joy and pleasure. But make sure they are actions that will ultimately lead to a change in mindset and lasting happiness. A key aspect of making sure your blueprint will lead to lasting happiness is taking the time to really understand the underlying motivation behind your goals and actions. For example, if your goal is to eat healthy food or exercise more, ask yourself why. Maybe it's because you want to lose weight. While seeing the numbers on the scale drop will make you feel great in the moment, that in itself is not going to make you happier in the long-term. Make sure you fully understand why you want to lose weight and how that will help you achieve lasting happiness (you will be more comfortable with who you are, you will be more confident, you will be able to do activities and live life to the fullest, you will be healthier and live longer, etc.). With all the actions and goals you include in your blueprint, make sure you have thought it through and understand how it will lead to lasting happiness and a change in mindset — rather than just an abundance of temporary positive emotions.

3. Take your specific personality, situation and values into account

The whole point of this book is to help you design a tailored and personal action plan for a happier life, based on who you are and what matters most to you. You have put a lot of effort into getting to know yourself better, so make sure you use and apply that knowledge. Make sure you don't include things in your plan because you think you should. Only include actions and goals that align with your personality and values. We live in a world where it can sometimes be hard to ignore the constant onslaught of information and people that try to tell us what happiness looks like, how we should live our life, all the things we should buy to be happier and the things we need to do and be in order to be valuable members of our society. If you want to find lasting happiness, you need to figure out how to block all that noise out and listen to yourself, to that inner voice that tells you what will make you happy. Do you want to be successful in your job to be able to afford that fancy car because it will really make you happy, or is it because all those commercials have you believe it will? Do you really want to get fit and healthy or do you just think you should because everyone else does? Do you want to find a partner to start a family with because that is really what will make you happy or is it more about wanting to live up to society's expectations and making your mom happy, as she keeps asking for grandchildren?

Make sure you also think about how you will achieve your goals, given who you are and what you value. If you want to get fit and healthy and you know you get bored quickly, make sure you have a diverse exercise routine that keeps things interesting and keeps you engaged. On the other hand, if you're a creature of habit who prefers routines over anything new, a set programme you do several times a week will probably give you a better chance at success. If one of your actions is to keep a gratitude journal, think about when and how is the best way for you to do so. If you're a morning person maybe that's the best time, but if you know you are always running late then maybe evenings or during lunch-time works better. If you love to be creative and visual, perhaps a drawing or some other kind of artistic interpretation works better for you than a written journal. If you don't like writing or drawing, maybe you voice-record it on your smartphone. If you love technology, perhaps you can use an app to keep your journal. Whatever you do, make sure you really tailor it to who you are.

4. Be specific

Imagine a blueprint for a new building that says a wall should be close to 10 metres long, the drains for the kitchen should be roughly in location x and the glass for the windows is between 5-7 square metres. Do you think that's the kind of plan that will result in a successful outcome? Probably not. Blueprints need to be specific to work. Unless you specify exactly how long each wall is, where the drains need to go and precisely what dimensions the windows will be, you probably won't end up with your dream home (or any home for that matter). The same applies to your Happiness Blueprint. For it to give you the best chances of success, you need to be specific. Say exactly what you will do, when and how often. For example, don't say "Exercise more" but specify what that means (x times a week or month). Don't say "Spend more time with my kids" but say "Spend at least every second Saturday doing a fun activity with my kids." Don't just aim to "Be more positive" but specify that you will spend at least 15 minutes before bedtime every day to review any negative events that happened that day and find something positive about it. Your blueprint should be worded in a way that enables you, or anyone, to go through regularly and say, with absolute certainty, whether you have done what you committed to doing.

5. Make sure it's realistic and achievable (but challenging)

You don't want to set yourself up for failure. If you design the blueprint for a massive mansion but you only have the budget for a small bungalow, or you create a plan for a very complex high-tech building, but your contractors don't have the experience and skills needed to build it, you will struggle to achieve your goal. Your blueprint has to be realistic and achievable in the context of who you are and your life circumstances. For example, you might want to set an action to practice mindfulness five times a week, but you have three young kids and getting even just five minutes to yourself to take a shower is a challenge. Making time for mindfulness exercises five times a week is probably unrealistic for you. Maybe start with two or three sessions a week or consider combining your five minutes in the shower with a mindfulness exercise. Similarly, if you want to read more, but you're not used to reading much, you're a slow reader and don't have a lot of time on your hands, then setting an action of "reading a book a week" is probably too ambitious and one per month might be more realistic.

However, you do want to challenge yourself, and you do need to be realistic about the fact that finding happiness takes work and commitment. You will have to make some sacrifices, and you will have to make time for putting your plan into action. There should be at least one or two things in your blueprint that push you outside of your comfort zone. Be realistic, but don't be too comfortable.

In summary, these are the five rules you should follow when designing your Happiness Blueprint:

1. Everything you include (goals and actions) needs to be fully within your control
2. It needs to be designed for long-term happiness, not short-term joy or pleasure
3. It needs to take your specific personality, situation and values into account
4. You have to be specific about what you will do and when
5. It has to be realistic and achievable (but challenging)

Let's Look at Some Examples

As I was writing this book, I dug out an old journal and looked up one of the first Happiness Blueprints I ever wrote down for myself. This was at a time when I was deeply engaged in my self-improvement and happiness journey. I already had some great successes like doing a half marathon (something I never thought I could do) and maybe for the first time in my life, I felt like I had a solid, supportive group of friends around me that gave me a sense of belonging. But I also felt like I had a lot more work ahead of me. I still had a lot of self-doubts and often didn't love and respect myself as much as I wanted to. I still often felt sorry for myself and occasionally still blamed others when things didn't go my way. I didn't feel like I was living life to the fullest yet, and I noticed I was often using my busy work schedule as an excuse for not being open to new experiences because I lacked the confidence to give them a go. Here is what my blueprint at the time looked like:

Goals	Actions
Get fit and healthy	• Exercise at least four times a week for at least 45min — two of those have to be fun (bush walks, mini golf, etc.) • Track your food every day (especially on 'bad' days)
Strengthen my friendships	• Reach out to at least two friends per week, even if it makes you uncomfortable (be proactive)
Be more open to new opportunities	• Don't work weekends more than once a month
Continue to learn	• Read at least one 'growth' book per month • Read for 30 minutes every morning at least five days per week
Be positive	• Write down at least one thing you're grateful for every night • When experiencing negative emotions, self-doubt and stress, stop and try to see the positive. Do a check before going to bed every night if any situations during that day need 'review'.

It looks simple, but you'd be surprised how much thought went into it. I think it will help you with the design of yours if I take a minute to explain the individual goals and actions in a bit more detail and outline how they relate specifically to who I am.

GET FIT AND HEALTHY

Being fit and healthy was a critical step towards finding happiness at the time (and still is). I knew I wouldn't be able to live the life that I wanted, where I had the right mindset and attitude, was open to new experiences and felt proud of who I am, if I wasn't fit and healthy. At the time, that meant I had to overcome my biggest lifelong challenge and lose weight — and keep it off. I knew to achieve that goal I needed to exercise. However, I also knew myself well enough to understand that I would struggle with it and possibly give up if I forced it, like I had done so many times before. Therefore, my action was to commit to exercising four times a week, but at least two of those had to be fun activities like a bush walk, going for a swim in the ocean or playing mini golf. You might argue that's not exercise, but it's much better than sitting on the couch. I also knew I am a creature of habit and I like routines. Therefore, I chose a gym programme that was basically the same every time, and I could just come in and get it done, without thinking much about it. While most people would get bored with that, it was exactly what I needed to make it work.

Of course, food is the other big (and more important) part of losing weight and keeping it off. I've always had a complicated relationship with food, so this part was much harder for me than exercising — and it still is. However, I had figured out that tracking works really well for me as it keeps me accountable and honest. I didn't set myself a calorie limit or a weight loss goal, nor did I forbid myself from eating certain foods. I simply realised that, as long as I track, I'm likely to stay on track (note that at this point I had already lost a lot of weight and was less strict. There was definitely a bunch of 'forbidden' foods and calorie limits in the earlier days).

STRENGTHEN MY FRIENDSHIPS

As an introvert, I am very good at spending time on my own. I have this vibrant inner world and can spend hours just thinking and daydreaming without ever getting bored. I love the independence and control over my own life that gives me. However, I also realised it often makes me a bit lazy when it comes to friendships and, even though I don't need many friends, a few close, loyal friends are crucial to my happiness. I also learned that I enjoy smaller groups or one-on-one meetings with friends the most, so I tried to initiate those whenever I could, instead of trying to talk myself into going to big parties. Today, I have a fantastic group of friends, and I don't feel I have to make an effort to be in touch any more, it just comes naturally. But back then, I had to actively remind and push myself to get in touch and make an effort to make sure I developed my friendships and spent valuable time with them.

BE MORE OPEN TO NEW OPPORTUNITIES

This was a time in my life where I still struggled a lot with lack of confidence. I was good at my job, so it gave me confidence and made me feel good. However, I realised that I often used work as an excuse and something to hide behind. I would tell myself I couldn't do things on the weekends because I had to work and would decline people's invitations with the excuse of being too busy at work. I wanted to change that and create space in my life for new things and no longer make excuses, so I set a limit of only allowing myself to hide behind my work once a month. Other people might have addressed this by setting goals like "Say yes to everything" or "Only say no to invitations a maximum of twice a month." But I wasn't quite ready for goals like that at the time. I was just starting to be more open to new experiences and my lack of confidence still often got the better of me. Moreover, as an introvert, new people and experiences take a lot of energy, which I didn't always have. I wasn't ready for the pressure of having to say yes, so I decided to start with merely creating space. I didn't commit to accepting all invitations, I just removed the main excuse I had to say no.

CONTINUE TO LEARN

This one is simple. I had come to realise that for me, knowledge is the foundation of a happy life, and the best way to soak up knowledge was to read. The things I learned have often been incredibly valuable on my path to happiness, and I continue to read to learn every day.

BE POSITIVE

This was still at a time where I wasn't always so good at positive thinking and often fell back into having a rather negative outlook on life and lots of self-doubts. By making myself sit down and think about the great stuff that was going on in my life every night, I slowly became more conscious and appreciative of how much I had to be grateful for. I love writing and keeping journals, so a gratitude journal was the natural thing for me to do. I also set myself a challenge to look for the positive whenever I felt negative, stressed or was doubting myself. Whenever possible, I tried to do it right in the moment, but I also made sure I checked in with myself every night before going to sleep in case I had missed any negative moments during the day. I didn't always find something positive. Some situations just sucked and sometimes I just had to admit that I had failed or disappointed myself. However, simply looking for the positive gave me a better outlook on life and most of the time, I did find something positive.

Are you getting an idea of how it works? You can see that my blueprint was fully within my control, everything was specific and clear and it felt challenging but realistic to me at the time. Do you also notice how most of it is very specific to who I am and how I tailored my blueprint to what works specifically for my personality and values? And even though they were all relatively short-term goals, and some of them led to immediate joy and pleasure (like mini-golf), they were all very clearly leading towards overall happiness and life satisfaction by ultimately changing my mindset and attitude and enabling me to live life to the fullest.

I followed this plan with only a few minor modifications for well over a year, and it helped me get from medium happy to pretty happy. Today, happiness is more about maintenance for me than achieving specific goals. I am very happy with my life and have reached a point where I believe I will be happy no matter what life might throw at me. I'm not working towards specific goals at the moment (other than finishing this book, of course), but that might change again in the future. The main purpose of my current Happiness Blueprint is to help me realise early when I might be at risk of getting off track or when I'm not living life to my fullest potential, being as happy as I could be.

Here is my blueprint at the time of writing this book:

Every week:
Spend time at/in the ocean
Nurture my friendships
Eat well

At least once a fortnight:
Do something creative
Write to inspire people

You can see that some things are still on there (friendships and food) while others are new. Overall, it's a little less specific, and I'm no longer as strict with checking that I live by it all the time. Remember that this is my maintenance blueprint, not one that is designed to make me happier. I don't tick things off as I complete them any more, but the blueprint still guides me and is extremely valuable to me. Often, if I'm feeling a bit down or like I'm not as happy as I could be, I just need to look back at this blueprint and can see right away what's missing — most of the time it's that I haven't been eating well (damn, food!!). Other times I realise I haven't done anything creative or written anything to inspire in too long, so I focus on doing that and feel energised and back to my old self right away. A lot of the time, simply spending a day at the ocean reminds me of all the great things I have in my life, how far I've come and how great my life is. However, something important to understand as well is that not following through with one of the five actions in my blueprint doesn't mean I'm completely unhappy. I'm just not as happy as I could be.

I hope these examples have illustrated what a Happiness Blueprint is: your action plan towards a happier life based on who you are, what your values and goals are and designed around your strengths and weaknesses. The following pages will provide you with a framework for figuring out exactly what should be in your blueprint. The first step will be taking a quick look at your life circumstances to make sure your blueprint aligns with the key building blocks of your life. You will then be challenged to identify and document what makes you happy and what gets in the way of your happiness and to identify the areas you want and need to work on. Finally, you will combine all of that into your first Happiness Blueprint. Remember that the templates for all exercises are in the workbook that you can download at www.lisa-jansen.com/workbook.

1. The Building Blocks of Your Life

If you want to design a plan for a better life, you first have to figure out what you have to work with. You need to take a good look at your life and take note of what the critical elements of your life are, how you spend your time, how happy you are with each area, where you see the biggest room for improvements, how much time you can make available to put your plan into action and when the best time is. As we discussed above, one of the five rules for your blueprint is that it has to be realistic and achievable. That means it needs to fit into your life or you need to be able and willing to change your life to make room for it. The following exercise will help you identify the key elements of your life, their importance to you and your happiness and the threats and opportunities each area presents.

EXERCISE: AREAS OF YOUR LIFE

1. Identify the key areas of your life. These are the people and activities that take up most of your time. The table below gives you some ideas. Cross out those that are not relevant to you and add any that are missing. Just think about how you spend

your time and thoughts and make sure everything that takes
up significant amounts of your time or thoughts is included.

2. Think about what you love most about each area. Think about
a time when you were particularly happy in this area. What
was going on? What made you happy? What were you doing
that made you feel good?

3. Now think about the opposite. How can this area be better?
Think about a time when you were particularly unhappy with
this area of your life. What was going on? What made you
unhappy? What could you do to make it better? Make sure
you focus on things you can control.

4. In the fourth column, rate how important each area is to you
and your happiness on a scale of 1 to 10 (with 10 being super
important, and 1 being not important at all). Make sure you're
honest and try to focus on how you really feel about each area,
not how you think you should feel. Remember, no one else
will see your answers unless you decide to show them. Note
that this is not about how happy you are with this area right
now (that's what the next step is about). This step is about
how important, for example, family or friends are to your
happiness. How much of a difference would it make in your
life if you did not have an area?

5. Next, rate how satisfied you are with each area of your life
(10 = super happy, 1 = very unhappy). Try to take a big picture
view as much as you can and think about how you feel about
this area in general or on average over the past six months, not
just today.

6. In column six, rate how much you think improvements in
this specific area would improve your overall happiness and
life satisfaction (1 = not at all, 10 = very much). For example, if
you've rated your happiness with an area as a 6 in the previous
step, how much of a difference would it make to your overall
satisfaction with life if you could lift it to an 8?

Area of your Life	What do you love about this area of your life? When are you the happiest with it?	How could this area be better? When are you the least happy with it?	How important is this area to you (1-10)	Overall, how satisfied are you with this area? (1-10)	To what extent could improvements in this area improve your overall happiness? (1-10)
Family					
Friends					
Work					
Hobbies					
Health, Wellness & Fitness					
Free Time (time when you have nothing scheduled)					
Spirituality (incl. religion)					
Thoughts / Mindset					

Now that you have filled in the table, you should have a better idea of what the building blocks of your life are, which areas are most important to you and where you might have room for improvements. We're not quite done yet; there are a couple more steps left in this exercise.

7. Read through column two (what you love about each area) and highlight any trends and commonalities you notice across different areas.
8. Now do the same for column three (how could this area be better). Highlight any trends and commonalities you notice.
9. Finally, have a look at your table as a whole and highlight anything that stands out to you that you think will be relevant for your blueprint. Any areas you might want to work on, opportunities for improvement, anything that contributes to your happiness, anything you feel is important enough to be considered when you write up your blueprint.

2. What Will Make You Happy?

Most of us feel happy about some aspects of our life, so we already have an idea of what will make us happy. You've also learned a lot about happiness and yourself throughout this book, so at this point, you should already have a pretty good idea of what will make you happy. The exercise above should have given you some ideas as well and referring back to your personal profile might also be useful. With all of that combined insight and knowledge, it shouldn't be too hard for you to complete the exercises below. The goal here is to put together a list of goals and activities that you believe will make you happier. Don't worry too much at this point about how realistic they are. Try to be as open-minded as possible. This is the brainstorming and ideas phase of designing your blueprint, which means you're not committing to anything yet. You're just throwing around ideas.

EXERCISE: WHAT WILL MAKE YOU HAPPY

1. As a first step, write down everything you can think of that either already does contribute to your happiness, or you believe would if you did it or had it in your life.
2. Make sure you are clear about how it does or would contribute to your lasting happiness (as opposed to just bringing you joy and pleasure in the moment).
3. Next, think about what you can do, that is fully in your control, to get this, get more of it, or simply ensure you keep it in your life. Don't worry if you can't think of anything yet or if you feel the ideas you come up with are unrealistic. Remember, we're brainstorming.

What does or would contribute to you finding lasting happiness and life satisfaction?	How does or would it contribute? (i.e. help you change your mindset)	What can you do that is fully in your control to get this or get more of it?

3. What Brings You Joy and Pleasure?

In this book, we make a very clear distinction between happiness and positive emotions such as joy and pleasure. Our goal is to design a blueprint for a fulfilling life you love, not a plan for experiencing as many positive emotions as possible. However, joy and pleasure can make life a whole lot more fun, and I think it would be hard to find true happiness without them. Furthermore, lasting happiness requires a mindset change and, as we've already discussed, this can be hard to achieve for many of us. More immediate positive emotions can be a crucial guide and motivator along the way. The important thing is to focus on the right kinds of joy and pleasure — those that will ultimately contribute to lasting happiness and a more positive mindset.

Including joy and pleasure, and other positive emotions, in your blueprint is not mandatory, but I highly recommend it as it makes the execution more fun. For example, you might remember in my original blueprint, I specified that at least two of my four weekly exercises need to be fun in the sense that they bring me immediate joy (even if they might not be the kind of exercise that has the most significant impact towards my weight-loss goal — like mini golf). However, even though it was mostly about joy in the moment, it still contributed to my goal of becoming fit and healthy and, through that, having a better mindset. In my current blueprint, I'm specifying that I will do something creative at least once a fortnight. The main reason I put it in there is that I love it and it makes me feel good. At first glance, there isn't much long-term impact, especially since most of my creative projects tend to fall apart in the execution phase (think of those expectations vs. reality memes you see on the internet). However, a closer look shows that it does help towards a mindset change because it's an outlet for my creativity and it shows me that I can be creative (at least at the idea stage) even though I spend most of my life believing I'm rational, logical and uncreative. So in that sense, those little projects do contribute to having a more positive attitude and mindset.

For this next exercise, think about anything that brings you joy and pleasure that you feel is worth considering for your blueprint. Make sure you focus on those things where the momentary joy and pleasure will ultimately lead to lasting happiness in some way. Write down how it will contribute. Finally, think about what you can do, that is fully under your control, to get this joy or pleasure or get more of it.

EXERCISE: WHAT BRINGS YOU
VALUABLE JOY OR PLEASURE

1. Write down everything you can think of that brings you joy and pleasure (or similar positive emotions). Remember we're still at the brainstorming phase, so just get it all out. But also remember to focus on those things where the momentary joy and pleasure will ultimately lead to lasting happiness in some way.
2. Write down how it will contribute to your lasting happiness.
3. Think about what you can do, that is fully within your control, to get this positive emotion or get more of it.

What brings you momentary joy or pleasure (or other positive emotions) that will contribute to your overall happiness in some way?	How will it contribute to your lasting happiness? (i.e. help you change your mindset)	What can you do that is fully in your control to get this or get more of it?

4. What Gets in the Way of Your Happiness?

Now it's time for our inner nay-sayer to shine (briefly). In the above exercises, I asked you to be as open-minded as possible and just write down any ideas you can come up with. I'm sure a few of you found that hard, constantly thinking: "Yeah, but that's never going to happen." I used to be like that. I knew what I needed to do, but I didn't believe I could do it. I was holding myself back with excuses like I don't have time, I'm not strong enough, I'm not smart enough, I can't afford it and so on. We all have things that get in the way of us doing what we know we should do to be happier. Some of them are perfectly valid and just a reality of life, but many others are mostly just in our heads, and we could probably overcome them if we really tried. This next exercise is about identifying everything you feel is getting in the way of you doing what you need to do to be happier.

EXERCISE: WHAT GETS IN THE WAY OF FINDING HAPPINESS

1. Write down everything you can think of that might get in the way of your happiness — absolutely everything! Don't worry about whether it's justified or not. If it's in your head, it's worth looking at. I highly recommend using words like 'feel' or 'think' whenever applicable. For example, don't write "I don't have time," instead write "I feel I don't have time." Or instead of "I'm not strong enough" say "I think I'm not strong enough." This will help put things into context — they are not necessarily facts, most of them are just beliefs.

2. Once you've got your list, however long or short it may be, describe how each item you listed gets in the way. Be specific!

3. Now it's time to take control. Some of your items might be perfectly valid, but I think for most of them you can come up with at least one or two things you could do that are entirely in your control that would help you overcome this. Keep in mind that coming up with ideas on how you could overcome them doesn't mean that you have decided you WILL do them — that part comes later. Right now, you're not committing to anything. Take some time to think about it. Maybe come back to it the next day.

What gets in the way of finding lasting happiness and life satisfaction?	How does it get in the way?	What can you do that is fully in your control to overcome this or at least lessen its impact?

5. Identifying Goals

The above exercises were all about brainstorming and coming up with ideas. Now it's time to narrow things down a bit more and to make some commitments. The first step is for you to identify your happiness goals. The good news is, if you've completed the exercises throughout this book, you should already have a reasonably good idea of what your goals should be. So let's get right into it.

EXERCISE: IDENTIFYING GOALS

1. Write down all possible happiness goals you can think of. At this point, we're still brainstorming so don't overthink it. Just write down every goal that comes to mind.

2. Dig up the definition of happiness you wrote at the end of chapter 1. What happiness goals are implied?

3. Refer back to your core values that you identified in chapter 2. Do they suggest any specific happiness goals? Also think about what else you learned about yourself in chapter 2. Maybe re-read your personal profile to see if that brings up any goals.

4. Refer back to the exercises in chapter 3 that identified environmental factors and voluntary activities you want to focus on. What possible goals are highlighted there?

5. Refer back to the exercise at the end of chapter 4 that asked you to rate how you're currently doing regarding the Four Pillars of Happiness. If you don't feel confident you are doing at least all right in all of those four areas, you should consider setting goals to work on this.

6. Read through your responses to the exercises above about the building blocks of your life, what makes you happy, what brings you joy and pleasure and what gets in the way of your happiness. What happiness goals can you identify in your responses?

Your Possible Happiness Goals

Now you have a list of possible happiness goals for your blueprint. Some of you might only have a few while others could have lots. Regardless of how many you have, it's important to consider a few more things before you decide which ones your actual blueprint goals should be.

7. First of all, review your possible goals with the blueprint rules in mind. Cross out any goals that don't align with them:

   A. Are all possible goals within your control? Remember, it might just be a matter of wording it differently. If you really think there is no way to make it something that is fully within your control (for example, winning the lottery) then cross it out.

   B. Are your goals designed for long-term happiness, not short-term joy or pleasure? We will also come back to this in the next step so don't worry if you're unsure about it right now. Just cross out those goals you know for sure are not about long-term happiness.

   C. Do the goals take your specific personality, situation and values into account? Are they truly your goals and not goals you think you should have?

   D. Are all your goals clear and specific?

   E. Do the goals feel realistic and achievable (but challenging)?

8. Next, think carefully about which of your goals genuinely have a lasting impact on your overall happiness. All your goals are likely to fit into one of the four categories below. Cross out those that are in category A or B, keep the ones that are in category C and underline the ones that are in Category D.

   A. The goal provides no or little short-term pleasure and no or little perceived long-term happiness gains — Cross out

   B. The goal provides short-term pleasure but no or little perceived long-term happiness gains — Cross out

   C. The goal provides no or little short term-pleasure but lots of perceived long-term happiness gains — Keep

D. The goal provides short term-pleasure and lots of perceived long-term happiness gains — Underline (these are the best kind of goals)

9. By now you have probably narrowed down your list of possible goals quite a bit. For the remaining goals, spend some time thinking about exactly how they would contribute to your long-term lasting happiness. How would they help change your mindset? How would they provide ongoing purpose and meaning? How would they enable you to live life to the fullest?

Goal	How would the goal help you achieve lasting happiness?

10. Final step. Go through your responses above and decide which goals you want to include in your Happiness Blueprint. Underline or highlight them. Choose the ones you feel most excited about and the ones you think will have the biggest, lasting impact on your happiness. Make sure you have some that will challenge you but also some you're looking forward to (life should be fun, after all). How many you pick is really up to you. One important aspect to consider is how much work you think each goal will take. If you feel your goals are big and audacious, then it might be better to only have two or three for now. If you think at least some of your goals won't take too much time and effort, you might want to have five or six. Remember, you can always work on some goals for now and then shift focus to others once you've made progress and have spare time and energy. Just because you're not including something right now, doesn't mean you will never work towards it.

There you go, you've completed the first significant part of your Happiness Blueprint. Now that you know what goals you want to work towards, it's time to figure out how to get there.

6. Committing to Actions

Setting goals won't do much for our happiness. As we've learned when we reviewed the research findings around goals, happiness comes from pursuing goals and making progress, more so than setting them. That means to change how happy you are, you need to figure out how you can achieve your goals and then work towards them. Therefore, the next step in designing your Happiness Blueprint is deciding which actions will help you achieve your goals and then committing to them.

EXERCISE: COMMITTING TO ACTIONS

1. Let's start with some brainstorming. For each of the goals you want to work on as part of your Happiness Blueprint, think about what you could do to make it happen. Don't overthink it, just write down any possible actions that come to mind. You're not committing to anything yet.

Your Goal	Possible actions to achieve the goal

2. Go through your possible actions and identify those that are not fully within your control. See if you can reframe them in a way that puts them within your control. If not, cross them out.
3. For each possible action, think about whether it is really right for you (based on your personality, values and strengths). For any that are not, see if you can reframe them in a way that does suit you. If not, cross them out.
4. Check that each remaining action is realistic and achievable (but challenging). Modify or cross out those that are not.

This should leave you with a list of actions that are entirely within your control, tailored around who you are and realistic and achievable. If you still have more than three actions for any of your goals, I would suggest picking your top three and proceeding with those for now. If the above steps have resulted in there being no actions left for one or more goals, go back to the drawing board and come up with more possible actions. If you can't come up with anything, maybe do some research online or ask a friend. Once you have new possible actions, make sure you take them through steps 2 and 3 above. Repeat this until you have at least one action per goal that you feel comfortable committing to.

7. Bringing it All Together

You know what goals you want to work towards, and you know what actions will help you achieve your goals. Now it's time to bring it all together and design your Happiness Blueprint.

EXERCISE: BRINGING IT ALL TOGETHER

1. In the template below or in the workbook, add your goals and short descriptions of how each goal will help you find happiness (or be happier).
2. For each goal, write down 1—3 actions that you are confident will help you make progress towards your goals. This is the point in the process where you make commitments (we're no longer brainstorming). Make sure you take your time with this and think it through.
3. Specify when and how often you will do this action. Remember, your blueprint needs to be specific.
4. Sense-check yourself by adding a short summary of how each action will help you achieve your goal.

My Goals	How this will help me find lasting happiness	Actions			How this will help me achieve my goal
		What I will do to achieve my goal	When / how often		
		1.			
		2.			
		3.			
		4.			
		5.			
		6.			

		7.			10.			13.	
		8.			11.			14.	
		9.			12.			15.	

You're getting pretty close to completing your first Happiness Blueprint. There are only two more quick steps left to do.

5. Read through your blueprint and check how you feel. Do you feel good about it? Excited? Do you feel confident that it can help you be happier? If not, identify those parts that don't feel quite right yet and review them. It's important that you feel good and excited about your plan.

6. Do a quick check to make sure your plan follows the five rules of the Happiness Blueprint:

   1. Is everything in this plan fully within your control? Remember, it being in your control doesn't mean that it is easy and it doesn't mean that there are no external factors that get in the way occasionally. All it means is that you control whether you do it or not. At times other things, for example, sick children or a big deadline at work, might be more important. But you always have a choice.

   2. Are you confident your plan will help you find lasting happiness and life satisfaction, not just momentary joy and pleasure?

   3. Is the plan realistic and achievable (but challenging)?

   4. Is each action specific regarding what you will do and when/how often?

   5. Does each action take your personality, values and strengths into account?

If you answer 'no' to any of those questions, go back and review your plan and the individual elements. The five rules are designed to give you the best chances of success, so don't just ignore it if something doesn't feel right or doesn't add up. If you can respond with a confident 'YES' to all of the questions above then, congratulations, you have completed your first Happiness Blueprint and are ready to put it into action.

I really hope the process above and everything you've learned in this book have you feeling energised, motivated and positive. However, chances are, you're also feeling a bit uncomfortable and challenged. That's how it should be at this stage, so don't worry if you do. Remember, magic happens when you step outside your comfort zone. The most important thing now is for you to put your plan into action. How well you do that is up to you. It's your plan and your happiness — no one else can do it for you. However, there are a few tips and ideas that can help. That's what the next and final chapter of this book will focus on.

PART VI

Living your Blueprint

"Happiness is the consequence of personal effort. You fight for it, strive for it, insist upon it, and sometimes even travel around the world looking for it. You have to participate relentlessly in the manifestations of your own blessings. And once you have achieved a state of happiness, you must never become lax about maintaining it. You must make a mighty effort to keep swimming upward into that happiness forever, to stay afloat on top of it."

ELIZABETH GILBERT, EAT, PRAY, LOVE

I T'S EASY to think that the hard work is done, now that you have created your Happiness Blueprint. However, while your blueprint is an important first step, it is just that — a first step. The best plan on its own won't make you any happier, just like the blueprint for your dream home alone won't give you a house to live in. Everything you've learned in this book and the process you've worked through to design your blueprint have helped you create a plan that is robust, inspiring, realistic and highly actionable. However, for it to really lift your happiness and satisfaction with life, you need to put it into action. You need to live your plan and continuously put effort into making it happen. I can't stress enough how important this is. Right now, you may feel excited and positive about your plan. You may already experience a noticeable difference in how happy you are just because of what you've learned, smaller mindset changes that have already happened while reading this book and because of the excitement and confidence your blueprint gives you. That is great! However, there is a strong chance that this feeling won't last if you stop now. It's great that you're feeling positive and inspired but, as with so many other factors we discussed, the principle of hedonic adaptation means you will most likely get used to these new feelings, and they will wear off over time. The good news is, there is an easy way to make sure that doesn't happen and, instead, your happiness keeps expanding and becomes lasting. All you have to do is make sure you put your plan into action and continuously work towards your goals and then review and adjust your goals as you achieve them. This chapter will help you do just that. First, I will share some advice and tips that will help you successfully execute your plan. We will look at key mindsets and attitudes, as well as different tactics and little tips and tricks that can help you achieve your goals. The second part of this chapter will outline how you can review, revise and improve your blueprint over time to ensure you live your best possible life — for the rest of your life.

Putting Your Blueprint into Action

Hopefully, you are excited about your Happiness Blueprint and putting it into action. However, you might also be a bit unsure about how to make some things happen, or you might wonder how you can make it stick. Chances are, you've tried achieving some of your goals before and, for whatever reason, have not been able to get there or to make it last. A lot of what you've learned in this book about yourself — your personality, values and strengths and weaknesses — as well as the process you went through to design your blueprint, should give you a much better chance to achieve your goals and make it last. If you look at what scientific research suggests improves our odds of achieving our goals, you tend to find studies that show the importance of documenting your goals, breaking big goals down into smaller action-focused steps, understanding why a goal is important to you, having a specific plan that outlines what you will do to achieve your goals and when, and setting realistic and achievable goals. The good news is, the process you worked through in the previous chapter has already covered all of this. That means you're already in an excellent position to achieve your goals. However, there are a few other factors, tactics and concepts that give you an even better chance of achieving your happiness goals. We will discuss some of them here. Unfortunately, we will only be able to scratch the surface on most of these topics. Anything more than that would go beyond the scope of this book. However, there are many further resources about each topic including books, podcasts, articles and much more. I recommend spending a bit more time learning about those aspects that resonate with you.

As with almost everything we've discussed in this book, not all of it will be relevant to everyone equally. It will, once again, be up to you to consider and analyse the information provided in the context of what you've learned about yourself and the blueprint you've developed. However, don't use that as an excuse to dismiss ideas that might seem strange or uncomfortable at first. You might be surprised how valuable they can be. Remember, one of the pillars of happiness is open-mindedness.

Get in the Right Mindset

At this point in the book, it should come as no surprise when I say that the most important thing to enable you to achieve your happiness goals is the right mindset and attitude. We've already discussed the importance of our approach and attitude throughout this book. When it comes to putting your blueprint into action, three specific mindsets are particularly valuable: taking responsibility, changing your habits and dealing with setbacks.

TAKE RESPONSIBILITY
As I'm sure you remember, taking responsibility is one of the

four pillars of happiness. This is particularly important when it comes to putting your blueprint into action. It helps that one of the five rules of designing your Happiness Blueprint was that everything you commit to needs to be fully within your control, which makes it easier to take responsibility for the execution. However, just because something is theoretically within your control doesn't mean it always feels that way in the moment. Life happens, we get busy, other people demand our time and unexpected events ruin our carefully designed schedules. That is just the reality of life. Everyone deals with those challenges. Yet somehow, some people seem to still manage to achieve their goals while others get derailed and give up. I don't think it's as simple as arguing that people who achieve their goals have less busy lives or fewer distractions. In fact, often when you look at the lives of very successful people who achieve many of their goals, you find that they tend to have very busy lives and have to deal with many demands for their time. So why do some people achieve their goals and others don't? While there are probably numerous different reasons including differences in personality, approach and environment, one reason is that people who achieve their goals have a greater sense of responsibility to make it happen and feel more committed.

It's been my personal experience that the first, and maybe most important, step towards putting any plan into action and achieving goals is to take personal responsibility for making it happen. That doesn't mean that you always have to stick to the plan and schedule, no matter what. If you're a busy mum and your child is sick, then looking after them takes priority over everything else. If you're involved with a really important project at work, you might need to work late on a day where you had planned to work towards your happiness goals in the evenings. Taking responsibility doesn't mean ignoring those interruptions and stubbornly following your plans.

It means making things happen regardless. They might not happen exactly the way you had planned and according to the schedule you had set, but what's important is that you feel an underlying sense of responsibility for making them happen in the best way you can. It means that if something gets in the way of your plan, you don't just give up, telling yourself it's out of your control and that you'll get back into it next week. Instead, you focus on how to make it work. For example, if your plans for Tuesday get interrupted or derailed, people who take responsibility and feel committed would find a way to make time on Wednesday or Thursday instead. Taking responsibility is about being flexible and working around the challenges life throws at you. If your child is sick and you can't make it to the gym on that day, you might be able to modify your workout to something you can do from home. Alternatively, you could focus on another happiness goal on that day (like working on your positive mindset or reading a book) and then do your exercise on another day instead. If you really want to make changes and achieve goals, you will have to take responsibility, and you will have to make room for it in your life. A key aspect of this is making sure that your goals are realistic and achievable, which is why that was a focus of the process you worked through to design your blueprint. At this point in the book, I assume that your goals are achievable, so it is really up to you to make it happen — even if that means removing other things from your life or making sacrifices elsewhere.

FOCUS ON BREAKING BAD HABITS AND FORMING NEW ONES
It's likely that at least some of your happiness goals require you to change your habits. Our habits are the things that we do regularly without thinking much about them. For example, most of us have a habit of brushing our teeth before going to bed at night. We don't need reminders to do so, and we don't

need to consciously think about the individual steps involved. We just do it. We all have lots of little habits, and often we're not even really aware of them. From everyday things like how we tie our shoelaces, to how we pack the dishwasher and how we arrange our desk at work, to processes like what we do after we wake up in the morning or when we first arrive at the office, through to how we think and feel and how we talk and engage with people and much more — our lives are made up of countless little habits. Some of them we've picked up on purpose. For example, I have a habit of spending at least 30 minutes reading every morning, something I started doing a few years ago with the goal of making it a habit. However, most of our habits are probably more unconscious things that we've either picked up from our parents or environment, or that we've been taught by society from an early age (like the fact that you brush your teeth every night). Many of our habits make our lives easier because they enable us to do things on autopilot without much thought or effort. However, there are also many habits that can be harmful to us. These include obviously harmful habits like smoking, excessive drinking or unhealthy eating but also less obvious ones like having a habit of focusing too much on the negative, treating others poorly, giving up too quickly or spending too much time in front of the TV or our smartphones. Additionally, there are habits that we currently don't have that could significantly increase our quality of life. For example, regular exercise, spending time in nature or reading more. In short, most of us can significantly lift our happiness by changing some of our habits.

Breaking old habits or creating new ones is a massive opportunity to achieve lasting change and, in our case, lasting happiness. Without habit changes, most changes we make will be short-term and, consequently, the benefits we experience won't last. For example, you might have a goal to be kinder to others.

You can schedule time for kindness and set reminders. Through being kind to others, you feel good about yourself and overall happier. However, unless kindness becomes a habit and just the way you act without thinking much about it, these benefits will wear off as soon as you stop scheduling time for it or setting reminders. For any change to be lasting, we need to change the habits around it. Otherwise, you're always at risk of falling back into old behaviours. This is one of the reasons why many people find it relatively easy to get started with plans to improve their lives but struggle to see it through and often don't manage to make it last — they haven't changed their underlying habits.

How do we change habits or create new ones? The answer is as simple as it might be frustrating. We form habits through repeating behaviours. In other words, if you want to develop a new habit you need to make yourself do the same thing over and over again until it becomes a habit. Just like parents need to force little kids to brush their teeth (often with not insignificant objections) while we adults just do it without much thought. Or, like kids need to concentrate when they learn to tie their shoelaces while we can do it with our eyes closed. Changing habits or creating new ones takes effort and is an uphill battle at times, but there is no trick or secret to forming new habits overnight. It takes effort and persistence. I never used to be a morning person and would usually only get up just in time to not be late for work. That's how it's always been. I remember when I was still in high school, I would usually ride to school with my older brother. I would wake up, get dressed, make coffee, get in the car — all within about 15-20 minutes. However, at some point, I decided I didn't like those rushed mornings. Therefore, a few years ago I decided I wanted to get up earlier and make more of my mornings. I created a morning routine which, at the time, involved reading, writing and meditation, and then I set my alarm an hour earlier. It was hard in the beginning. I often had to resist hitting the snooze button five times, and for a few weeks, I did feel tired throughout the day. However, I got used to it. Over time, getting up earlier became a new habit. It took several months, but then I started to love my early mornings. Today, I wake up early even when I don't set the alarm, and I just get up and start my morning routine without much thought or struggle.

How long it takes to change a habit varies significantly based on the person, the environment and the habit. Phillippa Lally, a health psychology researcher at University College London, conducted a study to understand how long habit changes take. Lally and her colleagues observed 96 people over a 12-week period as they set out to change a habit. Each day, the participants reported on whether or not they completed the new behaviour and how automatic it felt. What they found was that, on average, it takes 66 days for the new behaviour to become automatic. However, the findings also show that the actual range is much wider. In the case of the participants in this study, it took anywhere from 18 to 254 days for people to form a new habit.[119] The takeaway from this is that even if you are someone who picks up new habits fairly quickly, chances are, it will still take at least about three weeks, and for most of us, it will take longer. Changing habits requires persistence and commitment. However, it's likely to be worth the effort. As with so many things in life, you get out what you put in. Simple changes might be easier in the short-term and lead to some momentary lifts in happiness, but they are unlikely to last. Habit changes, on the other hand, are much harder to achieve but they are what will lead to long-term, lasting changes and a happier, better life.

If you're interested in learning more about habits, how they impact our lives and how to change them, I can strongly recommend reading Charles Duhigg's book The Power of Habit: Why we do what we do and how to change.

DON'T LET SETBACKS DERAIL YOU

As you work through your Happiness Blueprint, you're likely to experience setbacks at some stage. Whether or not you will achieve your goals is less about how many setbacks you have, but mostly about how you respond to them. As we've discussed a few times throughout this book, happiness is mostly about how we respond to what happens in the world around us and much less about what actually happens. This is just another example of that. Setbacks will happen, it's how you respond to them that will determine whether or not you achieve your happiness goals.

You will struggle to find anyone who has found great success and happiness without having had to overcome some setbacks and failures along the way. In fact, there are countless stories of people who achieved greatness after failing (or maybe because of failing first). You've probably heard the famous quote from Thomas Edison, who invented the light bulb — but not until after failing thousands of times. He said: "I have not failed. I've just found 10,000 ways that won't work." It was this attitude that kept him going long after many others would have given up and, eventually, enabled him to achieve his goal. Similarly, Stephen King's first novel Carrie was rejected by publishers 30 times before it was eventually published and became a massive bestseller, putting King on the path to becoming one of the most successful authors of our time. Before Harry Potter, J K Rowling was a divorced mother living on welfare. World famous singer, Katy Perry, was dropped from three record labels before she eventually became successful. Bill Gates' first business failed. Both Steven Spielberg and George Lucas released films that flopped before the big hits that they are now famous for. I could probably fill several more pages with examples of people who failed and who had to overcome setbacks before being successful. The difference between people who achieve their goals and those who don't, is not that the former don't experience challenges along the way; it's that they don't let those get in the way of achieving the overall goal. If they fail, they just try again.

This is also backed up by research findings. Psychologist Angela Duckworth is one researcher who has done extensive work in this field. She calls the ability to overcome setbacks and recover after failure 'grit'. Her numerous studies on the topic have shown time and again that 'grit' is one of the most common traits of people who achieve their goals.[120] Duckworth's book Grit: The Power of Passion and Perseverance provides further insights into what goes on in our heads when we fail and experience setbacks. She provides many examples and stories of people who have managed to succeed despite setbacks and outlines how it's this ability to recover from failure that will ultimately help people succeed.

Having said all that, I also think it is important to take failure seriously, especially when it happens repeatedly, and to consider that it might mean you need to change something. Persistence or 'grit' does not mean that you should do the same thing over and over again, no matter how often you fail. Yes, a lot of the time the best way to deal with failure is to try again, but sometimes trying differently or trying something else is the better way to overcome failure and setbacks. Thomas Edison did not invent the light bulb by doing the same thing 10,000 times. He iterated and tried something different after each failure. Stephen King did not succeed by sending the same book to the same publisher 30 times, but by trying different approaches with different publishers. And Bill Gates didn't become successful by stubbornly pursuing the same business but by giving up on his first failed business and starting a new one instead. A key to achieving your goals is to not give up too quickly. But stubbornly following a plan or trying again endless times can also be a path to unhappiness. If you find yourself failing once, try again. However, if you're failing at something repeatedly, it might be worth considering if you need to change your approach or if there is maybe a better goal for you to chase.

Another important aspect of dealing with setbacks is to remember to be kind and forgiving to yourself — but to always take responsibility. We all fail, and we all disappoint ourselves sometimes. Many of us have very high expectations of ourselves and tend to beat ourselves up when we don't manage to live up to those expectations. However, when it comes to achieving your happiness goals, this mindset is not helpful. Remember, this is all about finding happiness, not making yourself miserable. Be kind to yourself, allow yourself to fail occasionally. You don't always have to be perfect. Just make sure that after you fail, you get up and try again or try something else.

More Tips for Putting Your Blueprint into Action

Above, we have discussed three of the key mindsets and attitudes that will help you achieve your happiness goals. However, even when you have the right mindset and attitude, putting your Happiness Blueprint into action can still be a challenge. Luckily, there are a few other tips and ideas that can help you live your plan, make it fun and make sure you achieve your goals. Here are some of them:

SCHEDULE TIME IN YOUR CALENDAR
Book time to work on your happiness goals. This is a great way to make sure you have time to make it happen. Depending on

your goals, this might be short daily slots or more extended sessions two or three times per week. Adding it to your calendar is especially useful for those of you who tend to forget things, double book, or simply struggle to find the time. However, it will probably work best for those who already use their calendars to manage their days. If you don't see and use your calendar daily, it probably won't really help you remember. When you do schedule time in your calendar, make sure you set reminders as well. In some cases, it might be worth having a reminder go off a few hours beforehand and then again closer to the time, at least in the beginning until you're used to your new schedule and rhythm.

CREATE A PLAN OR PROGRESS POSTER
This is something that has really helped me achieve some of my goals. I had a big sheet of paper on the wall in my room where I listed all the actions I had committed to for a month (you could do it for a different timeframe), and then I ticked them off as I completed them. This worked really well for me for two reasons. Firstly, it served as a reminder of what I had committed to and, secondly, because ticking things off made me feel good and meant my progress was visible on the wall, which motivated me to keep going. If you like, you can get creative with this. Make your poster look fun and vibrant by using images and colours. You can use stickers or something similar instead of just 'ticking off' what you've completed. You don't have to get creative with it, but I found it made things a lot more fun.

TRACK PROGRESS
The poster above is one way to track progress. However, it's limited in that it only focuses on whether or not you've done something. It can often be useful to monitor progress at a

more detailed level. This is especially the case if you have goals where the progress is directly measurable, for example, fitness or weight loss goals, reading or learning goals, or goals around your attitude and mindset (for example, how often you manage to take a positive perspective when you usually would have been negative). However, if you track progress at such a detailed level, it's important not to get discouraged right away if the numbers are not moving in the right direction. Sometimes progress is happening internally and is not measurable right away, so be patient. On the other hand, when the numbers are moving in the right direction, it can be incredibly rewarding and motivating. You can track your progress in detail using a notebook, a simple spreadsheet, or a mobile app (there are many specialised tracker apps for different kinds of goals, as well as some generic ones).

TELL PEOPLE

This is another tactic that has worked really well for me. A few years ago, improving my fitness and losing weight was a big part of my Happiness Blueprint. As one of my actions at the time, I committed to doing a half marathon. To make sure I would go through with it, I told everyone and wrote a public blog about it. While this might not work for everyone, I'm the kind of person who hardly ever backs out of something once I've said it out loud, so for me, this was an excellent tactic. I knew I would hate having to admit to people that I gave up much more than I hated getting up at 6am to do my training. You don't have to tell everyone. You could just share your goals with a few close friends whose opinions matter to you. It's also important to note that this strategy will likely work much better for goals that are specific and for which it is very obvious to outsiders if you have achieved them or not. For example, if your goal is to have a more positive mindset, you can tell everyone about it, but it's kind of hard for people to know whether you've accomplished it or not, or if you're even making progress. On the other hand, more tangible goals like a fitness goal, writing a book, or doing a course, are more visible to others and, therefore, telling people provides more accountability.

TEAM UP WITH A BUDDY

In addition to just telling people, you could go one step further and team up with a buddy. I mentioned in the very beginning of the book that it could be valuable to work through this book with a buddy (or even a book club) and the same applies when it comes to putting your plan into action. Doing it with a friend or family member gives you accountability and can make a lot of things more fun. You could team up with someone who has similar goals so you can actually work towards them together. It could also be someone who has very different goals, but you agree to get together regularly to give each other accountability and support.

VISUALISE YOUR BLUEPRINT

This is a great and fun tactic for those who are very visual and like to be creative. Think about ways to visualise your blueprint. You could create a big vision board that you put up on the wall or something you use as the screen background on your phone or computer. You can visualise your whole blueprint at once or focus on individual goals or actions that are most important right now and then move on to another one after a while. Visualising your goals this way is a great strategy because it's fun to create and then serves as a regular reminder and inspiration. Make sure you include your end-goal in your visualisation, as that's the ultimate inspiration.

REMINDERS

One of the main reasons why people don't achieve goals, especially ones that require mindset and habit changes, is because they simply forget. Putting your blueprint into action will likely require you to do new things and change your habits and the way you think. A lot of this needs to happen in the moment throughout your day, so booking it in your calendar at certain times won't work. If you need more regular reminders to achieve your goals, think about creative ways to do so. Here are some ideas to get you started, but you can probably come up with more and better ones; put post-it notes in key places, add messages to yourself on your phone screen or your coffee mug (you can get your own designs printed on coffee mugs pretty cheaply these days), put inspirational quotes up around you, ask people to remind you, set an alarm to remind you regularly, or get a ring or some other piece of jewellery to remind yourself. Just make sure it's something you see frequently — an earring or a tattoo on your back might not be the best reminder.

ENVISION THE END-GOAL

This strategy is particularly valuable when you find yourself at risk of getting off track or when you've had a few setbacks and are tempted to give up. It's also a strategy I still use a lot today to keep myself motivated. It's about reminding yourself of the end-goal. However, it's not as simple as thinking about what the goal is. Instead, focus on how you will feel. Imagine yourself once you've achieved your goals and focus on how it makes you feel. You might feel things like pride, a sense of accomplishment, confidence, self-love, or just an overall lighter, happier feeling. Also, remind yourself why this goal is so important to you and how achieving it will improve your life. I find it helps when you have a specific timeframe in mind. For example, you might have a big event coming up, a holiday or a birthday. Focus on how you will feel on that day when you've achieved your goal by then. This strategy works especially well for goals that require discipline and self-control. Envisioning the end-goal is the number one strategy that helps me keep my weight under control. As I've mentioned a few times throughout this book, eating healthily and maintaining a healthy weight is one of my ongoing challenges. Whenever I've been a bit slack and my jeans are getting a bit too tight, I need to reset and be stricter with what I eat. When I'm in one of those phases and I find myself tempted by delicious but unhealthy food (usually chocolate), I focus on how I will feel when I'm at my ideal weight again, how much fitter and more energised I will feel and how much more confident and healthier — 99% of the time that helps me resist the temptations.

EXERCISE: WHAT OTHER IDEAS
CAN YOU COME UP WITH?

All of the above should give you some ideas, but there are many other tactics and strategies that can help you achieve your goals. Take a few minutes to think about what else you could do to put your Happiness Blueprint into action. Think big, you're not committing to anything, you're just coming up with ideas. Once you have some ideas, you can decide which ones you want to implement.

Other ideas to put your blueprint into action

At this point, you should have a much better idea of how you can put your plan into action, and you hopefully feel confident that you can achieve your happiness goals. Before we wrap things up, there is one more important topic we need to cover: how to make sure your Happiness Blueprint stays relevant in the long run.

Review, Revise, Improve

We all change all the time. The world around us changes. Our values, goals and priorities change. To some extent, even our personality changes over time. What makes you happy today might not be the same thing that makes you happy next year. If the blueprint you developed does its job, you will be much happier in the future, but you will then need to set new goals and actions to continue living your best life. If you are rating yourself fairly low on the happiness scale at the moment, your first blueprint will probably not get you all the way to your end-goal. I have had a total of five or six different blueprints over the past eight years. In short, you can't count on your current blueprint being the path to happiness for the rest of your life. To achieve lasting happiness and life satisfaction, you need to review, revise and improve it regularly — or maybe even create a completely new one at times. This section will provide some tips around how to know when it's time to review your blueprint and will then outline a simple process to review and improve it over time.

WHEN TO REVIEW YOUR BLUEPRINT
There are a few signs that indicate it might be time to review your Happiness Blueprint. One thing to note before we discuss these indicators is that reviewing your blueprint doesn't always

mean you need to change it. Sometimes, simply reading it again and reminding yourself why you chose the goals and actions is enough to get you back on track.

YOU'RE JUST GETTING STARTED

I would recommend reviewing your blueprint regularly in the first few months as you start working towards your goals. This is simply because you will learn new things and your perspective might change, and also because you're still new to the whole concept and reviewing your plan regularly serves as a great reminder of what you want to achieve and why. Consider making it a regular 'event' in the first few months. For example, book time once a month to sit down, look at your blueprint and check in with yourself to make sure it's still valid. You could do this over a nice cup of coffee or a glass of wine and make it a bit of an experience and a chance to reflect on what you've achieved and where you're heading. As you progress, you might decide to keep this review ritual but do it only once a quarter or even just once a year.

YOU'VE ACHIEVED SEVERAL OF YOUR MAIN GOALS

This is the best reason for why it's time to review your blueprint. Just achieving one of your goals usually shouldn't require you to review your entire blueprint, you should just be able to shift focus to your other goals. However, if you get to a point where you've achieved several of your overarching goals, it might be time to review and maybe set some new goals.

YOU'RE FEELING STUCK OVER A LONGER PERIOD OF TIME

As we've discussed in the previous section, experiencing setbacks are part of living your blueprint. It's completely normal to feel a bit stuck at times to not be making any visible progress. However, if this state lasts for a longer period of time, like several weeks, it's probably worth taking a closer look at why. It might be a sign that you need to change your goals or your tactics.

YOU'VE LOST YOUR MOTIVATION

Right now, you probably feel pretty motivated to put your plan into action. It's normal for this to wear off a bit as you start working towards your goals and it's not as new and exciting any longer. However, you should still feel a certain level of motivation for making your plan happen. If you find yourself at a point where you really struggle to find the motivation to work on your goals, it's probably time for a review — even if it's just to remind yourself why your goals are so important to you.

YOUR GOALS NO LONGER EXCITE YOU

Your happiness goals are the things you want to accomplish more than anything else. That should be exciting. If you find that imagining what it will be like once you've reached your goals does not excite and energise you any more, it's time to look at whether you still have the right goals and why you chose those goals in the first place. Simply reminding yourself of why you chose them might bring back the excitement but it's also possible that you need to change your goals or tactics.

YOU FEEL MISERABLE

Happiness won't come easy. It will require effort and patience. However, while certainly challenging at times, living your blueprint should, overall, be an enjoyable and rewarding experience. It's normal to have bad days, but if you're having bad weeks and months during which you feel living your plan makes you miserable, then it's time for a review. Achieving your happiness goals should be hard at times, but it should not make you miserable.

IT JUST DOESN'T FEEL RIGHT

Sometimes there is no other reason than your gut feeling telling you that it's time to review your plan. If you look at your blueprint and it just doesn't feel right for you any more, it's time to find out why.

IT'S BEEN A WHILE SINCE YOU DESIGNED YOUR BLUEPRINT

Finally, another sign that it's time for a review is the simple fact that it's been a while since you developed your blueprint. Reviewing it doesn't mean you have to change anything, but I would recommend reviewing it every six months or so to make sure everything is still relevant, and you're on the right track.

How to Review Your Blueprint

Let's say you have, for whatever reason, decided it's time to review your blueprint. You essentially have two options for doing so. You can make a completely fresh start, or you can review and revise individual aspects of your existing blueprint. Which option is best for you, depends on your situation. The table below gives some guidance.

Option 1, the completely fresh start, is a good option when:	Option 2, a partial review and revision, is a good option when:
• You feel like your whole plan does not work any more • You've achieved (almost) all of your key goals • It's been more than 12 months since you've reviewed your plan • It's been more than two years since you've designed your blueprint • It's been a while since you've actively engaged with your plan • Something significant has changed in your life, your environment, or within yourself that is likely to have an impact on your values, priorities and overall goals.	• You've achieved one or several of your goals and want to add new ones • You think your goals are still right but specific actions you've committed to are not leading to results or don't work for other reasons. • Minor changes in your life require you to make some adjustment to how and when you complete your actions • You still feel confident and excited about your overall plan, but specific aspects don't really work for you any more (e.g. individual goals or actions). • You simply want to add something

OPTION 1: COMPLETELY FRESH START

The complete refresh is the right option when you feel like it's best to start over and design a new blueprint — either because you feel like the old one no longer fits or because it's been a while and you can't be sure that the goals are still the right ones for you.

This option means designing a completely new Happiness Blueprint. The way to do this is fairly simple: go back and work through the process outlined in this book, again. The best way to do so is to download a new version of the workbook and redo the exercises. For it to really be effective, make sure you redo all the exercises, including the ones about your personality, values and strengths and weaknesses in part 2. When unsure, re-read the relevant sections in the book to refresh your memory.

OPTION 2: PARTIAL REVIEW AND REVISION

In many cases, it might not be necessary to redo your entire blueprint. Often, it's particular aspects that need adjustment, while the rest of your plan is still perfectly valid. The most important step with this option is figuring out what needs to be reviewed and revised, keeping in mind that it might not always be the most obvious part. The process below will help you work through this option.

1. Re-read your personal profile. Does it still feel accurate? If not, this is where you want to start your review. Pay particular attention to your personal values. These are the backbone of your plan. If they are not right, chances are your blueprint won't be either. If you find your values or other details in your personal profile have changed significantly, it might be worth creating a completely new blueprint.

2. Once you're confident your values and personal profile are still accurate, review your entire blueprint and identify the parts that might need adjustment.
   a. Do you need to add a new goal because you've achieved others?
   b. Does a goal no longer feel right?
   c. Are actions you've committed to not delivering results or, for other reasons, no longer working for you?
   d. Do you feel like there is something important missing from your blueprint?

3. Challenge yourself to understand the 'why?'. Why do goals not feel right any more? Why are actions not effective? Why is something missing? Consider that the real reasons might be that your values or priorities have changed or that you've learned something new that has changed your perspective. It's also absolutely okay to admit that maybe you didn't get things completely right the first time around and that you

need to adjust.

4. Going through the three steps above should have helped you identify which aspects of your blueprint need to be updated. It might be as simple as tweaking a goal or an action or adding new ones. If you feel like there might be more fundamental gaps, I recommend redoing all the 'Designing your Blueprint' exercises from the previous chapter. If you really struggle with this, it might be a sign that option 1 (a completely new blueprint) is the better approach for you.

5. Once you have your new blueprint, make sure you test it.

    a. Read through your blueprint and check how you feel. Do you feel good about it? Excited? Do you feel confident that it can help you be happier? If not, identify those parts that don't feel quite right yet and review them. It's important that you feel good and excited about your plan.

    b. Do a quick check to make sure your plan follows the five rules of the Happiness Blueprint:

        a. Is everything in this plan fully within your control?

        b. Are you confident your plan will help you find lasting happiness and life satisfaction, not just momentary joy and pleasure?

        c. Is the plan realistic and achievable (but challenging)?

        d. Is each action specific regarding what you will do and when/how often?

        e. Does each action take your personality, values and strengths into account?

While this review and revise process might seem like a bit of effort right now, it will quickly become second nature once you've done it a few times. You'll instinctively know what's working and what isn't and will become much better at adjusting individual parts as needed.

Reviewing, revising and improving your Happiness Blueprint regularly is key to finding long-term happiness. Remember that happiness is not an end-goal but a journey. Even once we find it, we need to continuously put effort into keeping it. Also remember that the ongoing pursuit of valued goals can have a significant impact on our happiness. In other words, you can significantly increase your chances of enjoying lasting happiness if you continue to have goals that are valuable to you personally and by continuously pursuing these goals. So make sure you keep your Happiness Blueprint up to date and continue to work towards goals that really matter to you.

Epilogue

"Be grateful for what you already have while you pursue your goals. If you aren't grateful for what you already have, what makes you think you would be happy with more."

ROY T. BENNETT, THE LIGHT IN THE HEART

THAT BRINGS us to the end of this book. Now you have a personal plan for lifting your happiness, designed around your specific personality, values and strengths. You should also have a plan for how you will put your blueprint into action and an idea of which tactics and tricks will give you the best chances of success. I hope you have enjoyed the journey. Hopefully it was valuable, interesting and challenging, but also fun and inspiring to work through the different sections and exercises, to get to know yourself better and to learn more about this elusive thing called happiness. Let's quickly recapture the key things we've learned:

- Lasting happiness is a mindset that is mainly about how we respond to what happens, not about what actually happens. That means, finding happiness requires us to change our mindset (rather than change the world around us).
- Happiness is about more than being successful in the traditional sense or experiencing lots of positive emotions, but it's also not about the complete absence of negative emotions.
- Happiness is highly individual, and there is no one-size-fits-all approach to finding it. We all need to design our

individual plan for a happier life based on who we are and what matters most to us.

- We need to take care when considering research findings around happiness and remember that they often report on averages and generalisations. Therefore, not all research findings apply to all of us, and we should not blindly follow any generic advice. This is especially the case for research findings reported in mainstream media as they often focus only on the most impactful headlines and skip over details.
- Voluntary activities seem to have a much more significant impact on our happiness than environmental factors. This is mainly because they help us achieve a positive mindset, they are entirely within our control and there is no limit to how much we can have and leverage them.
- There are four pillars to happiness; self-love and respect, purpose and meaning, taking responsibility and open-mindedness. If we do not have at least the basic amount of each of these pillars, finding happiness will be very difficult.
- Designing our personal blueprint for a happier life is only the first step on our journey. True happiness will come from actively pursuing our goals, regularly checking in to make sure our blueprint is still relevant and continuously updating our plan to make sure we always have goals and actions that are highly valuable to us.

As you march ahead in the coming weeks and start implementing your blueprint, remember that finding happiness requires patience, determination and commitment. It will be challenging at times. You will experience setbacks. There will be times where you feel like you're not making any progress and you will, occasionally, be tempted to give up. Don't! Don't give up when things get hard. Push through it, try something else or try in a different way. I know from my own experience that chasing our happiness goals is hard and frustrating at times. But I can promise you wholeheartedly that it will be worth it. Every ounce of effort you put into living your blueprint will be worth it and the more effort you put in the happier you will be. As the famous saying goes: "The more you put in, the more you get out."

And there is more good news. What you learned about yourself and happiness in this book has helped you develop your personal Happiness Blueprint. Over the coming weeks and months you will probably realise that this new-found knowledge has changed your perspective and will continue to impact how you analyse information. You now have the knowledge and insights to better assess the value and fit of any information you hear or read in the future, whether it's about happiness or any other topic. Through having learned about yourself as well as getting a better understanding of how research works and what some of the limitations of scientific research are, you will be able to analyse information and decide, with confidence, whether it is relevant to you or not. You're no longer at risk of blindly following one-size-fits-all advice and insights. Instead, you can focus on what matters most to you and what will have the most positive impact on your life. I encourage you to leverage this in all areas of your life. Finding happiness is not the only thing that is highly individual and requires us to figure out what works best for us. In many other aspects of our life there are some ground rules that apply to everyone, like the Pillars of Happiness, but beyond that it is up to us to design strategies and plans based on who we are and what works best for us. Whether it's about the best form of exercise, eating well, how we learn, communication styles, relationships, our careers and much more — there is no one-size-fits-all path to success that will work equally for all of us. I hope what you have learned about individuality and happiness in this book will enable you to take a similar individual perspective in other areas of your life and figure out what works best for you, instead of just following generic advice. However, with all of this, always keep in mind how important open-mindedness is. You have to be open to trying new things and stepping out of your comfort zone if you want to achieve any kind of lasting success and achievement. Don't disregard insights and ideas just because they feel foreign and uncomfortable.

This whole book has been about change and progress. We've worked hard to figure out what we can do to be happier. What new goals can we set? How can we have a more beneficial mind-set? What should we remove from our lives? What will bring us happiness and how can we get there? It's important to look for ways to improve ourselves and our lives. Making progress towards goals that are meaningful to us is a key aspect of happiness and it's also a key driver of human evolution. We need to continue to grow and evolve. However, it is my experience that there is another key element to finding lasting happiness beyond setting and pursuing goals. And that is to simply decide to be happy with what you have. To decide that you will be happy and make the most of whatever life throws at you. At the end of the day, happiness is a choice. Progress towards our happiness goals makes it easier to make that choice, but the most important thing to finding and retaining happiness is to simply choose it.

With this in mind, I want to wrap up this book with one of my favourite quotes. Many of you will have heard the saying "Live the Life you Love". There is another version of this quote that is less well-known but, in my opinion, much more powerful, even though all it does is swap around two words, so that "Live the Life you Love" turns into:

Love the Life you Live!

Notes

1   Khoddam, R. (2015, June 16). What's Your Definition of Happiness? Retrieved from Psychology Today website: https://www.psychologytoday.com/us/blog/the-addiction-connection/201506/whats-your-definition-happiness

2   Lyubomirsky, S. (2008). The How of Happiness: A Scientific Approach to Getting the Life You Want. London, England: Penguin.

3   Ricard, M. (2015). Happiness: A Guide to Developing Life's Most Important Skill. London, England: Atlantic Books

4   Seligman, M. E. (2002). Authentic Happiness: Using the New Positive Psychology to Realize Your Potential for Lasting Fulfillment. New York, NY: Simon & Schuster.

5   Harris, R. (2008). The Happiness Trap: How to Stop Struggling and Start Living: A Guide to ACT. Boulder, CO: Shambhala Publications.

6   Bradburn, N. M., & Noll, C. E. (1969). The Structure of Psychological Well-being. Chicago: Aldine Publishing Company.

7   Watson, D., & Clark, L. A. (1992). Affects separable and inseparable: On the hierarchical arrangement of the negative affects. Journal of Personality and Social Psychology, 62(3), 489-505. doi:10.1037//0022-3514.62.3.489

8   Diener, E., & Seligman, M. E. (2002). Very Happy People. Psychological Science, 13(1), 81-84. doi:10.1111/1467-9280.00415

9   Larsen, J. T., McGraw, A. P., & Cacioppo, J. T. (2001). Can people feel happy and sad at the same time? Journal of Personality and Social Psychology, 81(4), 684-696. doi:10.1037/0022-3514.81.4.684

10 Wood, W., Rhodes, N., & Whelan, M. (1989). Sex differences in positive well-being: A consideration of emotional style and marital status. Psychological Bulletin, 106(2), 249-264. doi:10.1037//0033-2909.106.2.249

11 To learn more about Travis' story, visit www.travismills.org

12 To learn more about Ashley's story, visit her blog: www.sullengers.com

13 Lyubomirsky, S., Sheldon, K. M., & Schkade, D. (2005). Pursuing happiness: The architecture of sustainable change. Review of General Psychology, 9(2), 111-131. doi:10.1037/1089-2680.9.2.111

14 Staley, O. (2017, April 18). What is the evolutionary purpose of happiness? Retrieved from https://qz.com/930860/what-is-the-purpose-of-happiness/

15 Nettle, D. (2005). Happiness: The Science Behind Your Smile. Oxford, England: OUP Oxford.

16 Seligman, M. E. (2002). Authentic Happiness: Using the New Positive Psychology to Realize Your Potential for Lasting Fulfillment. New York, NY: Simon & Schuster.

17 Lykken, D., & Tellegen, A. (1996). Happiness Is a Stochastic Phenomenon. Psychological Science, 7(3), 186-189. doi:10.1111/j.1467-9280.1996.tb00355.x

18 Okbay, A., Baselmans, B. M., De Neve, J. E., & Turley, P. (2016). Genetic variants associated with subjective well-being, depressive symptoms, and neuroticism identified through genome-wide analyses. Nature Genetics, 48, 624 — 633. doi:10.1038/ng.3552

19 Lyubomirsky, S., Sheldon, K. M., & Schkade, D. (2005). Pursuing happiness: The architecture of sustainable change. Review of General Psychology, 9(2), 111-131. doi:10.1037/1089-2680.9.2.111

20 Lyubomirsky, S., Sheldon, K. M., & Schkade, D. (2005). Pursuing happiness: The architecture of sustainable change. Review of General Psychology, 9(2), 111-131. doi:10.1037/1089-2680.9.2.111

21 Brickman, P., Coates, D., & Janoff-Bulman, R. (1978). Lottery winners and accident victims: Is happiness relative? Journal of Personality and Social Psychology, 36(8), 917-927. doi:10.1037//0022-3514.36.8.917

22 Lyubomirsky, S., Sheldon, K. M., & Schkade, D. (2005). Pursuing happiness: The architecture of sustainable change. Review of General Psychology, 9(2), 111-131. doi:10.1037/1089-2680.9.2.111

23 Mengers, A. A. (2014). The Benefits of Being Yourself: An Examination of Authenticity, Uniqueness, and Well-Being (Master's thesis). Retrieved from https://repository.upenn.edu/mapp_capstone/63/

24 Seligman, M. E. (2002). Authentic Happiness: Using the New Positive Psychology to Realize Your Potential for Lasting Fulfillment. New York, NY: Simon & Schuster.

25 Lyubomirsky, S., Sheldon, K. M., & Schkade, D. (2005). Pursuing happiness: The architecture of sustainable change. Review of General Psychology, 9(2), 111-131. doi:10.1037/1089-2680.9.2.111

26 Furnham, A., & Cheng, H. (1999). Personality as predictor of mental health and happiness in the East and West. Personality and Individual Differences, 27(3), 395-403. doi:10.1016/s0191-8869(98)00250-5

27 Furnham, A., & Brewin, C. R. (1990). Personality and happiness. Personality and Individual Differences, 11(10), 1093-1096. doi:10.1016/0191-8869(90)90138-h

28 Grant, S., Langan-Fox, J., & Anglim, J. (2009). The Big Five Traits as Predictors of Subjective and Psychological Well-Being. Psychological Reports, 105(1), 205-231. doi:10.2466/pro.105.1.205-231

29 Furnham, A., & Cheng, H. (1999). Personality as predictor of mental health and happiness in the East and West. Personality and Individual Differences, 27(3), 395-403. doi:10.1016/s0191-8869(98)00250-5

30 Furnham, A., & Brewin, C. R. (1990). Personality and happiness. Personality and Individual Differences, 11(10), 1093-1096. doi:10.1016/0191-8869(90)90138-h

31 Grant, S., Langan-Fox, J., & Anglim, J. (2009). The Big Five Traits as Predictors of Subjective and Psychological Well-Being. Psychological Reports, 105(1), 205-231. doi:10.2466/pro.105.1.205-231

32 Lucas, R. E., & Donnellan, M. B. (2011). Personality Development Across the Life Span: Longitudinal Analyses With a National Sample From Germany. Journal of Personality and Social Psychology, 101(4), 847-861. doi:10.1037/a0024298.supp

33 Hudson, N. W., & Fraley, R. C. (2015). Volitional personality trait change: Can people choose to change their personality traits? Journal of Personality and Social Psychology, 109(3), 490-507. doi:10.1037/pspp0000021

34 Boyce, C. J., Wood, A. M., & Powdthavee, N. (2012). Is Personality Fixed? Personality Changes as Much as "Variable" Economic Factors and More Strongly Predicts Changes to Life Satisfaction. Social Indicators Research, 111(1), 287-305. doi:10.1007/s11205-012-0006-z

35 McCrae, R. R., & Costa, P. T. (1989). Reinterpreting the Myers-Briggs Type Indicator From the Perspective of the Five-Factor Model of Personality. Journal of Personality, 57(1), 17-40. doi:10.1111/j.1467-6494.1989.tb00759.x

36 Diener, E., & Suh, E. (1997). Measuring quality of life: Economic, social, and subjective indicators. Social Indicators, 40, 189-216. Retrieved from http://dx.doi.org/10.1023/A:1006859511756

37 Seligman, M. E. (2002). Authentic Happiness: Using the New Positive Psychology to Realize Your Potential for Lasting Fulfillment. New York, NY: Simon & Schuster.

38 Kahneman, D., & Deaton, A. (2010). High income improves evaluation of life but not emotional well-being. Proceedings of the National Academy of Sciences, 107(38), 16489-16493. doi:10.1073/pnas.1011492107

39 Diener, E., Horwitz, J., & Emmons, R. A. (1985). Happiness of the very wealthy. Social Indicators Research, 16(3), 263-274. doi:10.1007/bf00415126

40 Brickman, P., Coates, D., & Janoff-Bulman, R. (1978). Lottery winners and accident victims: Is happiness relative? Journal of Personality and Social Psychology, 36(8), 917-927. doi:10.1037//0022-3514.36.8.917

41 Gardner, J., & Oswald, A. J. (2007). Money and mental wellbeing: A longitudinal study

of medium-sized lottery wins. Journal of Health Economics, 26(1), 49-60. doi:10.1016/j.jhealeco.2006.08.004

42 Pchelin, P., & Howell, R. T. (2014). The hidden cost of value-seeking: People do not accurately forecast the economic benefits of experiential purchases. The Journal of Positive Psychology, 9(4), 322-334. doi:10.1080/17439760.2014.898316

43 Whillans, A. V., Dunn, E. W., Smeets, P., Bekkers, R., & Norton, M. I. (2017). Buying time promotes happiness. Proceedings of the National Academy of Sciences, 114(32), 8523-8527. Retrieved from https://doi.org/10.1073/pnas.1706541114

44 Matz, S. C., Gladstone, J. J., & Stillwell, D. (2016). Money Buys Happiness When Spending Fits Our Personality. Psychological Science, 27(5), 715-725. doi:10.1177/0956797616635200

45 Heller, D., Judge, T. A., & Watson, D. (2002). The confounding role of personality and trait affectivity in the relationship between job and life satisfaction. Journal of Organizational Behavior, 23(7), 815-835. doi:10.1002/job.168

46 Judge, T. A., & Watanabe, S. (1994). Individual differences in the nature of the relationship between job and life satisfaction. Journal of Occupational and Organizational Psychology, 67(2), 101-107. doi:10.1111/j.2044-8325.1994.tb00554.x

47 De Neve, J. E., & Ward, G. (2017, March 20). Does Work Make You Happy? Evidence from the World Happiness Report. Retrieved from https://hbr.org/2017/03/does-work-make-you-happy-evidence-from-the-world-happiness-report

48 Wrzesniewski, A., & Dutton, J. E. (2001). Crafting a Job: Revisioning Employees as Active Crafters of Their Work. The Academy of Management Review, 26(2), 179. doi:10.2307/259118

49 Dutton, J. E., Debebe, G., & Wrzesniewski, A. (2016). Being valued and devalued at work: A social valuing perspective. In B. A. Bechky & K. D. Elsbach (Eds.), Qualitative Organizational Research: Best Papers from the Davis Conference on Qualitative Research: 9-51. Charlotte, NC: Information Age Publishing.

50 NAB Business View. (2017, February 13). Rethink Success. Australia's view on success today. Retrieved from https://business.nab.com.au/rethink-success-australias-view-success-today-22468/

51 Walsh, L. C., Boehm, J. K., & Lyubomirsky, S. (2018). Does Happiness Promote Career Success? Revisiting the Evidence. Journal of Career Assessment, 26(2), 199-219. doi:10.1177/1069072717751441

52 Diener, E., & Seligman, M. E. (2002). Very Happy People. Psychological Science, 13(1), 81-84. doi:10.1111/1467-9280.00415

53 Hills, P., & Argyle, M. (2001). Happiness, introversion–extraversion and happy introverts. Personality and Individual Differences, 30(4), 595-608. doi:10.1016/s0191-8869(00)00058-1

54 North, R. J., Holahan, C. J., Moos, R. H., & Cronkite, R. C. (2008). Family support, family income, and happiness: A 10-year perspective. Journal of Family Psychology, 22(3), 475-483. doi:10.1037/0893-3200.22.3.475

55 Argyle, M. (1999). Causes and correlates of happiness. In Kahneman, D., Diener, E., & Schwarz, N. (1999). Well-Being: Foundations of Hedonic Psychology. New York, NY: Russell Sage Foundation.

56 Lucas, R. E., Clark, A. E., Georgellis, Y., & Diener, E. (2003). Reexamining adaptation and the set point model of happiness: Reactions to changes in marital status. Journal of Personality & Social Psychology, 84(3), 527-539. doi:10.1037//0022-3514.84.3.527

57 Camfield, L., Choudhury, K., & Devine, J. (2007). Well-being, Happiness and Why Relationships Matter: Evidence from Bangladesh. Journal of Happiness Studies, 10(1), 71-91. doi:10.1007/s10902-007-9062-5

58 Infurna, F. J., & Luthar, S. S. (2016). Resilience to Major Life Stressors Is Not as Common as Thought. Perspectives on Psychological Science, 11(2), 175-194. doi:10.1177/1745691615621271

59 Brickman, P., Coates, D., & Janoff-Bulman, R. (1978). Lottery winners and accident victims: Is happiness relative? Journal of Personality and Social Psychology, 36(8), 917-927. doi:10.1037//0022-3514.36.8.917

60 Lehman, D. R., Wortman, C. B., & Williams, A. F. (1987). Long-term effects of losing a spouse or child in a motor vehicle crash. Journal of Personality and Social Psychology, 52(1), 218-231. doi:10.1037//0022-3514.52.1.218

61 Ong, A. D., Bergeman, C. S., Bisconti, T. L., & Wallace, K. A. (2006). Psychological Resilience, Positive Emotions, and Successful Adaptation to Stress in Later Life. Journal of Personality and Social Psychology, 91(4), 730 — 749.

62 Ong, A. D., Fuller-Rowell, T. E., & Bonanno, G. A. (2010). Prospective predictors of positive emotions following spousal loss. Psychology and Aging, 25(3), 653-660. doi:10.1037/a0018870

63 Blanchflower, D., & Oswald, A. (2000). Well-Being Over Time in Britain and the USA. doi:10.3386/w7487

64 Oreopoulos, P., & Salvanes, K. G. (2011). Priceless: The Nonpecuniary Benefits of Schooling. Journal of Economic Perspectives, 25(1), 159-184. doi:10.1257/jep.25.1.159

65 Troste, P. (2015). It's Not Just The Money The Benefits Of College Education To Individuals And To Society. Available online at https://www.luminafoundation.org/files/resources/its-not-just-the-money.pdf

66 Becchetti, Leonardo & Castriota, Stefano & Londono-Bedoya, David. (2007). Climate, Happiness and the Kyoto Protocol: Someone Does Not Like it Hot.

67 Stewart-Brown, S., Samaraweera, P. C., Taggart, F., Kandala, N., & Stranges, S. (2015). Socioeconomic gradients and mental health: implications for public health. British Journal of Psychiatry, 206(06), 461-465. doi:10.1192/bjp.bp.114.147280.

68 Teng Guo , Lingyi Hu (2011): "Economic Determinants of Happiness: Evidence from the US General Social Survey Economic Determinants of Happiness". https://arxiv.org/abs

69 Lyubomirsky, S., Sheldon, K. M., & Schkade, D. (2005). Pursuing happiness: The architecture of sustainable change. Review of General Psychology, 9(2), 111-131. doi:10.1037/1089-2680.9.2.111

70 Science and Religion Today. (2011, March 4). Are Happy People Healthier or Are Healthy People Happier? Retrieved from http://www.scienceandreligiontoday.com/2011/03/04/are-happy-people-healthier-or-are-healthy-people-happier

71 Angner, E., Miller, M. J., Ray, M. N., Saag, K. G., & Allison, J. J. (2009). Health Literacy and Happiness: A Community-based Study. Social Indicators Research, 95(2), 325-338. doi:10.1007/s11205-009-9462-5

72 Emmons, R. A., & McCullough, M. E. (2003). Counting blessings versus burdens: An experimental investigation of gratitude and subjective well-being in daily life. Journal of Personality & Social Psychology, 84(2), 377-389. doi:10.1037//0022-3514.84.2.377

73 Watkins, P. C., Woodward, K., Stone, T., & Kolts, R. L. (2003). Gratitude and happiness: development of a measure of gratitude, and relationships with subjective well-being. Social Behavior and Personality: an international journal, 31(5), 431-451. doi:10.2224/sbp.2003.31.5.431

74 Emmons, R. A. (2004). The Psychology of Gratitude. The Psychology of Gratitude, 3-16. doi:10.1093/acprof:oso/9780195150100.003.0001

75 Brunstein, J. C. (1993). Personal goals and subjective well-being: A longitudinal study. Journal of Personality and Social Psychology, 65(5), 1061-1070. doi:10.1037//0022-3514.65.5.1061

76 Sheldon, K. M. (2002). The self-concordance model of healthy goal-striving: When personal goals correctly represent the person. In E. L. Deci & R. M. Ryan (Eds.), Handbook of self-determination research (pp. 65 — 86). Rochester, NY: University of Rochester Press

77 Locke, E. A., & Latham, G. P. (2002). Building a practically useful theory of goal setting and task motivation: A 35-year odyssey. American Psychologist, 57(9), 705-717. doi:10.1037//0003-066x.57.9.705

78 Watson, D. (2000). Mood and Temperament. New York, NY: Guilford Press.

79 Myers, D. G., & Diener, E. (1995). Who Is Happy? Psychological Science, 6(1), 10–19. https://doi.org/10.1111/j.1467-9280.1995.tb00298.x

80 Sheldon, K. M., & Houser-Marko, L. (2001). Self-concordance, goal attainment, and the pursuit of happiness: Can there be an upward spiral? Journal of Personality and Social Psychology, 80(1), 152-165. doi:10.1037//0022-3514.80.1.152

81 Sheldon, K. M., & Elliot, A. J. (1999). Goal striving, need satisfaction, and longitudinal well-being: The self-concordance model. Journal of Personality and Social Psychology, 76(3), 482-497. doi:10.1037//0022-3514.76.3.482

82 You can watch Matt's TED talk here: https://www.ted.com/talks/

matt_killingsworth_want_to_be_happier_stay_in_the_moment

83 Loucks, E. B., Britton, W. B., Howe, C. J., Eaton, C. B., & Buka, S. L. (2014). Positive Associations of Dispositional Mindfulness with Cardiovascular Health: the New England Family Study. International Journal of Behavioral Medicine, 22(4), 540-550. doi:10.1007/s12529-014-9448-9

84 Loucks, E. B., Gilman, S. E., Britton, W. B., Gutman, R., Eaton, C. B., & Buka, S. L. (2016). Associations of Mindfulness with Glucose Regulation and Diabetes. American Journal of Health Behavior, 40(2), 258-267. doi:10.5993/ajhb.40.2.11

85 Hanley, A. W., Warner, A. R., Dehili, V. M., Canto, A. I., & Garland, E. L. (2014). Washing Dishes to Wash the Dishes: Brief Instruction in an Informal Mindfulness Practice. Mindfulness, 6(5), 1095-1103. doi:10.1007/s12671-014-0360-9

86 Sundquist, J., Lilja, Å., Palmér, K., Memon, A. A., Wang, X., Johansson, L. M., & Sundquist, K. (2015). Mindfulness group therapy in primary care patients with depression, anxiety and stress and adjustment disorders: Randomised controlled trial. British Journal of Psychiatry, 206(02), 128-135. doi:10.1192/bjp.bp.114.150243

87 Black, D. S., O'Reilly, G. A., Olmstead, R., Breen, E. C., & Irwin, M. R. (2015). Mindfulness Meditation and Improvement in Sleep Quality and Daytime Impairment Among Older Adults With Sleep Disturbances. JAMA Internal Medicine, 175(4), 494. doi:10.1001/jamainternmed.2014.8081

88 Dalen, J., Smith, B. W., Shelley, B. M., Sloan, A. L., Leahigh, L., & Begay, D. (2010). Pilot study: Mindful Eating and Living (MEAL): Weight, eating behavior, and psychological outcomes associated with a mindfulness-based intervention for people with obesity. Complementary Therapies in Medicine, 18(6), 260-264. doi:10.1016/j.ctim.2010.09.008

89 Moen, P., Dempster-McClain, D., & Williams,, R. M. (1992). Successful Aging: A Life-Course Perspective on Women's Multiple Roles and Health. American Journal of Sociology, 97(6), 1612-1638. doi:10.1086/229941

90 Hunter, K., & Linn, M. W. (1981). Psychosocial Differences between Elderly Volunteers and Non-Volunteers. The International Journal of Aging and Human Development, 12(3), 205-213. doi:10.2190/oh6v-qppp-7jk4-lr38

91 Schwartz, C., Meisenhelder, J. B., Ma, Y., & Reed, G. (2003). Altruistic Social Interest Behaviors Are Associated With Better Mental Health. Psychosomatic Medicine, 65(5), 778-785. doi:10.1097/01.psy.0000079378.39062.d4

92 Buchanan, K. E., & Bardi, A. (2010). Acts of Kindness and Acts of Novelty Affect Life Satisfaction. The Journal of Social Psychology, 150(3), 235-237. doi:10.1080/00224540903365554

93 Lyubomirsky, S., Sheldon, K. M., & Schkade, D. (2005). Pursuing happiness: The architecture of sustainable change. Review of General Psychology, 9(2), 111-131. doi:10.1037/1089-2680.9.2.111

94 Lyubomirsky, S., Tkach, C., & Sheldon, K. M. (2004). Pursuing sustained happiness through random acts of kindness and counting one's blessings: Tests of two six-week interventions. Unpublished raw data. doi:10.1037/1089-2680.9.2.111

95 Layous, K., Nelson, S. K., Oberle, E., Schonert-Reichl, K. A., & Lyubomirsky, S. (2012). Kindness Counts: Prompting Prosocial Behavior in Preadolescents Boosts Peer Acceptance and Well-Being. PLoS ONE, 7(12), e51380. doi:10.1371/journal.pone.0051380

96 Gatab, T. A., & Pirhayti, S. (2012). The Effect of the Selected Exercise on Male Students' Happiness and Mental Health. Procedia – Social and Behavioral Sciences, 46, 2702-2705. doi:10.1016/j.sbspro.2012.05.550

97 Hyde, A. L., Conroy, D. E., Pincus, A. L., & Ram, N. (2011). Unpacking the Feel-Good Effect of Free-Time Physical Activity: Between- and Within-Person Associations with Pleasant–Activated Feeling States. Journal of Sport and Exercise Psychology, 33(6), 884-902. doi:10.1123/jsep.33.6.884

98 Mammen, G., & Faulkner, G. (2013). Physical activity and the prevention of depression: a systematic review of prospective studies. American Journal of Preventive Medicine, 45(5), 649-57. doi:10.1016/j.amepre.2013.08.001

99 Harvey, S. B., Øverland, S., Hatch, S. L., Wessely, S., Mykletun, A., & Hotopf, M. (2018). Exercise and the Prevention of Depression: Results of the HUNT Cohort Study. American Journal of

Psychiatry, 175(1), 28-36. doi:10.1176/appi.ajp.2017.16111223

100 Blumenthal, J. A., Smith, P. J., & Hoffman, B. M. (2012). Is Exercise a Viable Treatment for Depression? ACSM's Health & Fitness Journal, 16(4), 14-21. doi:10.1249/01.fit.0000416000.09526.eb

101 Peluso, M. A., & Andrade, L. H. (2005). Physical activity and mental health: the association between exercise and mood. Clinics, 60(1), 61-70. doi:10.1590/s1807-59322005000100012

102 Boehm, J. K., & Lyubomirsky, S. (2012). The Promise of Sustainable Happiness. Oxford Handbooks Online. doi:10.1093/oxfordhb/9780195187243.013.0063

103 Lyubomirsky, S., & Tucker, K. L. (1998). Implications of individual differences in subjective happiness for perceiving, interpreting, and thinking about life events. Motivation and Emotion, 22(2), 155-186. http://dx.doi.org/10.1023/A:1021396422190

104 Fredrickson B. L. (2004). The broaden-and-build theory of positive emotions. Philosophical transactions of the Royal Society of London. Series B, Biological sciences, 359(1449), 1367–1378. doi:10.1098/rstb.2004.1512

105 Mohanty, M. S. (2009). Effects of positive attitude on earnings: Evidence from the US longitudinal data. The Journal of Socio-Economics, 38(2), 357-371. doi:10.1016/j.socec.2008.07.012

106 Danner, D. D., Snowdon, D. A., & Friesen, W. V. (2001). Positive emotions in early life and longevity: Findings from the nun study. Journal of Personality and Social Psychology, 80(5), 804-813. doi:10.1037//0022-3514.80.5.804

107 Mengers, A. A. (2014). The Benefits of Being Yourself: An Examination of Authenticity, Uniqueness, and Well-Being. Master of Applied Positive Psychology (MAPP) Capstone Projects. 63. http://repository.upenn.edu/mapp_capstone/63

108 McCullough, M. E., Pargament, K. I., & Thoresen, C. E. (2001). Forgiveness: Theory, Research, and Practice. New York, NY: Guilford Press.

109 Seligman, M. E. (2002). Authentic Happiness: Using the New Positive Psychology to Realize Your Potential for Lasting Fulfillment. New York, NY: Simon & Schuster.

110 Lewis, C. A., & Cruise, S. M. (2006). Religion and happiness: Consensus, contradictions, comments and concerns. Mental Health, Religion & Culture, 9(3), 213-225. doi:10.1080/13694670600615276

111 King, L. A. (2001). The Health Benefits of Writing about Life Goals. Personality and Social Psychology Bulletin, 27(7), 798-807. doi:10.1177/0146167201277003

112 Sheldon, K. M., & Lyubomirsky, S. (2009). Change your Actions, Not Your Circumstances: An Experimental Test of the Sustainable Happiness Model. Happiness, Economics and Politics. doi:10.4337/9781849801973.00024

113 Sheldon, K. M., & Lyubomirsky, S. (2012). Achieving Sustainable New Happiness: Prospects, Practices, and Prescriptions. Positive Psychology in Practice, 127-145. doi:10.1002/9780470939338.ch8

114 Baumeister, R. F., Campbell, J. D., Krueger, J. I., & Vohs, K. D. (2003). Does High Self-Esteem Cause Better Performance, Interpersonal Success, Happiness, or Healthier Lifestyles? Psychological Science in the Public Interest, 4(1), 1-44. doi:10.1111/1529-1006.01431

115 Lyubomirsky, S. (2008). The How of Happiness: A Scientific Approach to Getting the Life You Want. London, England: Penguin.

116 Kim, E. S., Kawachi, I., Chen, Y., & Kubzansky, L. D. (2017). Association Between Purpose in Life and Objective Measures of Physical Function in Older Adults. JAMA Psychiatry, 74(10), 1039. doi:10.1001/jamapsychiatry.2017.2145

117 Myers, D. G., & Diener, E. (1995). Who Is Happy? Psychological Science, 6(1), 10–19. https://doi.org/10.1111/j.1467-9280.1995.tb00298.x

118 Steel, P., Schmidt, J., & Shultz, J. (2008). Refining the relationship between personality and subjective well-being. Psychological Bulletin, 134(1), 138-161. doi:10.1037/0033-2909.134.1.138

119 Lally, P., Van Jaarsveld, C. H., Potts, H. W., & Wardle, J. (2009). How are habits formed: Modelling habit formation in the real world. European Journal of Social Psychology, 40(6), 998-1009. doi:10.1002/ejsp.674

120 Duckworth, A. L., Peterson, C., Matthews, M. D., & Kelly, D. R. (2007). Grit: Perseverance and passion for long-term goals. Journal of Personality and Social Psychology, 92(6), 1087-1101. doi:10.1037/0022-3514.92.6.1087